Time
Passages

A M E R I C A N CULTURE

Edited by Stanley Aronowitz, Sandra M. Gilbert, and George Lipsitz

Alice Echols, *Daring to Be Bad: Radical Feminism in America, 1967–1975*

Henry Giroux, *Schooling and the Struggle for Public Life*

George Lipsitz, *Time Passages: Collective Memory and American Popular Culture*

Nancy Walker, *"A Very Serious Thing": Women's Humor and American Culture*

George Lipsitz

Time Passages

Collective Memory and American Popular Culture

University of Minnesota Press • Minneapolis

Part or all of the following articles have been reprinted in this book with
permission: "This Ain't No Sideshow: Historians and Media Studies," from *Critical
Studies in Mass Communication*, v. 5, n. 2 (June) 1988. Reprinted by permission of
the Speech Communication Association. "The Meaning of Memory: Family, Class,
and Ethnicity in Early Network Television Programs," reproduced by permission of
the American Anthropological Association from *Cultural Anthropology* 1:4, 1986.
"Against the Wind: The Class Composition of Rock and Roll Music," from
Knowledge and Society, v. 5 (1985), JAI Press Inc., Greenwich, Connecticut.
"Cruising Around the Historical Bloc: Postmodernism and Popular Music in East
Los Angeles," from *Cultural Critique*, n. 5 (1986). "Mardi Gras Indians: Carnival
and Counter-Narrative in Black New Orleans," from *Cultural Critique*, n. 10 (1988).
"Myth, History, and Counter-Memory," from Adam Sorkin, ed., *Politics and the
Muse: Studies in the Politics of Recent American Literature*. 1989, Bowling Green
State University Popular Press. "Land of a Thousand Dances: Youth, Minorities, and
the Rise of Rock and Roll," from Lary May, ed., *Recasting America*. University of
Chicago Press, 1989.

Cover photo of Mardi Gras Indians courtesy of Gayle Plummer.

Published by the University of Minnesota Press
2037 University Avenue Southeast, Minneapolis, MN 55414.
Printed in the United States of America.

Library of Congress Cataloging-in-Publication Data

Lipsitz, George.
    Time passages : collective memory and American popular culture /
    George Lipsitz.
        p.   cm. — (American culture)
    Includes bibliographical references.
    ISBN 0-8166-1805-4
    ISBN 0-8166-1806-2 (pbk.)
        1. United States—Popular culture—History—20th century.   2. Mass
    media—United States—Social aspects.   3. Memory—Social aspects—
    United States—History—20th century.   I. Title.   II. Series :
    American culture (Minneapolis, Minnesota)
    E169.12.L55   1990   89-5209
    973.9—dc20   CIP

The University of Minnesota is an equal-opportunity educator and employer.

Contents

Contents

Preface

This is a book about collective memory and popular culture in the United States since 1945. It does not survey or analyze the aesthetics of popular culture itself, nor does it chronicle direct references to "historical" issues within popular culture texts. Rather, I wish to explore the ways in which collective memory and popular culture are peculiarly linked—how the infinitely renewable present of electronic mass media creates a crisis for collective memory, and how collective memory decisively frames the production and reception of commercial culture. This is not an uncritical celebration of mass-mediated imagery. I believe that the ever expanding influence, reach, and scope of the mass media has worked insidiously to legitimate exploitative social hierarchies, to colonize the body as a site of capital accumulation, and to inculcate within us the idea that consumer desire is the logical center of human existence. But neither is this a jeremiad against popular culture and the individuals who create and receive it. People act in the arenas open to them; there is nothing intrinsically better or worse about the generation and circulation of ideas through electronic mass media than through the printed word. Our time has more than its share of barbarism, but that barbarism is more the product of very old patterns of social organization than it is the product of new communications technology. New technologies do lend themselves to new forms of exploitation and oppression, but they also have possible uses for fundamentally new forms of resistance and revolution.

In the first section of this book I present discussions of history and popular culture. My intention is to show how forms of popular culture emerging over the past two centuries have helped make a crisis of historical memory the constitutive problem of our time. Rather than signaling the death knell for historical inquiry, electronic mass media make collective memory a crucial constituent of individual and group identity in the modern world. In section two I examine the relationship between commercial network television and popular memory, first by examining the "meaning of memory" in a series of early network programs on American commercial television in the 1950s, and second by exploring the dynamics of remembering and forgetting surrounding one representative show of that era, *Mama*. In section three I turn my attention to popular music, starting with a general inquiry into the "dialogic" nature of rock-and-roll music, and then concluding with a detailed case study about the relationship between past and present in rock music made by Mexican-Americans in Los Angeles since World War II. Section four outlines an approach to motion pictures and collective memory, emphasizing the ways in which Hollywood films do more to reveal social contradictions than to provide political solutions to them. I conclude section four with a detailed examination of two Hollywood auteurs, Samuel Fuller and Edgar Ulmer, for whom questions of past, present, and future offered a guiding aesthetic and a recurrent source of dramatic tension. In section five I turn my inquiry to popular narrative, first examining the sense of "counter-memory" pervading novels by women and "minority" authors, and then exploring the "open closures" of a subcultural oppositional narrative, that of the Mardi Gras Indians in New Orleans. Finally in "Buscando America" (looking for America), I try to survey the cumulative effects of the struggle for collective memory within popular culture over the past five decades.

This ordered framework obscures the tortuous struggle that brought this book into existence. A conceptual revolution in the humanities and social sciences has given new vigor to inquiries about cultural studies in a variety of fields over the past twenty years, but that ongoing revolution leaves investigators with no stable ground on which to stand. A dizzying succession of new methods and theories has shattered traditional disciplinary paradigms, forcing scholars to engage in bold departures from their own training, to become "specialists" in fields with few acknowledged experts and few firm standards of evidence and argument. My own inquiries have often left me between fields — too historical for the sociologists, too sociological for the linguists, and too linguistic and too sociological for the historians. Under those circumstances, speaking to readers and audiences outside of academic circles becomes even more difficult, because one must explain or at least neutralize the special vocabularies and concerns of many disciplines, not just one. But this book is not a product of some abstract revolution in scholarly methods; rather, it is a manifestation of the more general social crisis that brought that scholarly revolution into being in the first place. That social crisis is not something I learned about solely in libraries and classrooms; it has been the determinant experience of my life, and I would not be telling the whole truth about this book if I failed to relate it to the personal life struggles of which it is a part.

Over the past ten years I have been teaching American history and culture courses in colleges under conditions that have demanded a series of detours. I went to school in the politically charged 1960s and 1970s, and made myself the kind of teacher I wished that I had encountered in those years. But when I started to teach, I faced students who came of age in more quiescent and apolitical environments. My graduate research focused on labor history at precisely the time when deindustrialization and political reaction devastated the constituencies most interested in that subject. My deepest personal and professional commitments connected me to scholarship and social change at a moment when anti-intellectualism and materialism dominated American culture and politics. In my teaching and writing, I too often seemed to be delivering the wrong message to the wrong audience at the wrong time.

My career and professional development took place in the context of extraordinary changes in American society. The painful aftershocks of the Vietnam War, the startling misuses of power revealed by the Watergate investigations, and the deindustrialization of the American economy added elements of uncertainty and instability to the lives of all Americans in the 1970s. I found myself facing some of the contrasts of that era directly. The economic crises engendered by deindustrialization wreaked havoc on American higher education in those years; I moved from St. Louis to Houston to Minneapolis in pursuit of secure employment. In St. Louis, I rode to work everyday on the City Limits bus through a devastated inner-city ghetto, and at the University of Missouri-St. Louis I taught working-class students who were afraid that for the first time in generations higher educa-

Preface

tion would not result in upward mobility. In Houston, I routinely saw homeless people scavenging food from garbage bins as I drove off to teach at a campus in the middle of one of the most affluent suburban areas in the country. In Minneapolis, my students directed my attention to the ways in which the concurrent demise of blue-collar manufacturing jobs and the family farm undercut the political, moral, and economic foundations of their lives. Through all of this turmoil, my students and I attempted to study "American culture" from books that, for the most part, treated America as a secure stable repository of timeless truths.

Popular culture texts provided me with one means of understanding and enduring the circumstances I found myself in. Popular music and films seemed to resonate with the tensions of the time in a way that more formal academic texts did not. Even older works of popular culture seemed to speak to my personal crises and anxieties in important ways. For example, in the 1958 film "Wind Across the Everglades," Burl Ives advises Christopher Plummer that "sometimes the long way around is the shortest way through." In the context of that motion picture, Ives's counsel concerns the best way to cross a swamp, but his phrase also encapsulates the devotion to detour characteristic of the film's director, Nicholas Ray. For Ray, film making itself was the long way around, an ostensibly escapist medium that afforded him an opportunity for serious social criticism. A one-time architecture student at the University of Chicago and a former director for John Houseman's Group Theatre, Ray made his mark on the world in Hollywood as the creative force behind such eminently commercial ventures as *They Live by Night* (1949), *Johnny Guitar* (1954), and *Rebel without a Cause* (1955). A disillusioned 1930s radical working in 1950s Hollywood, Ray found no easy venue for expressing the political and social views closest to his heart. But denied "the shortest way through," he took "the long way around," negotiating the swampy ground of commercial culture by injecting subtle critiques of capitalism, McCarthyism, and suburbanization into "escapist" films. I feel a deep affinity for Nicholas Ray's work, in part because I know what it is like to take the long way around. For me, too, popular culture has been a way of expressing indirectly values and beliefs about which I had no direct means of expression.

I have spent the better part of a decade struggling to remain in the profession and to keep my voice alive. I do not want this to sound

x

like whining. I know that I was better off than most: better off than my fellow graduate students who never got jobs, better off than my colleagues who got fired through no fault of their own when enrollments declined, and certainly better off than the urban underclass and dispossessed industrial workers who have suffered so brutally from the radical restructuring of American society in this age of neo-conservatism.

I know as well that my own choices had something to do with my difficult working conditions. I chose to write about the powerless rather than the powerful. I knew full well that the types of experiences and issues that I wished to chronicle would not bring grants from corporate foundations or rewards from politically timid college administrators. I knew that my work would make powerful enemies and that the friends it made would rarely have any resources with which to support it. In addition, I have to acknowledge that I sometimes created unnecessary difficulties for myself. Too often I was too proud to ask for help, too arrogant to understand that nearly everyone had something to teach me, and too frightened for my own future to see each petty battle along the way as anything other than a microcosm of the larger social crisis that had marginalized me and the people I cared about most. But I have to be honest. Attempting to teach and learn under these conditions has been excruciatingly painful. Nothing came easy, nothing came directly. Always there were the detours.

I taught colonial America and recent America, pre-industrial China and post-industrial Europe. My courses ranged from film theory to American slavery, from popular music and television to the European Enlightenment. Most of my students showed up in these courses by accident; they were pursuing degrees in other subjects and wound up in my classroom to fill a requirement or to fill an empty hour in their schedules. Some had come back to school in the mistaken belief that a degree would automatically entitle them to higher wages, while others found themselves in school because they had no jobs and nothing else to do with their time. They were a detour for me, but I was a detour for them too.

Yet sometimes, the long way around *is* the shortest way through. Everywhere I found more than a detour; I found people with something to teach me. My students ranged from prison inmates to Catholic nuns, from working-class evening school adults to young undergraduates at an exclusive women's college, from profoundly anti-intellectual technocrats seeking credentials in business to passionately committed graduate students with astounding gifts for intellectual work. Their knowledge was not always in the form I expected (and maybe not in the form I would have preferred), but it was real and compelling and significant. They came to me with stories in their heads—stories about their lives that exposed me to both the diversity and the unity of the American experience.

The stories my students told me resonated with the hurts of history. They exposed the unhealed wounds of decades of political turmoil and cultural change. They revealed the frustrations of Americans conditioned to expect happiness and security only to face disappointments and instability. Every area of human endeavor emerged as problematic in their stories—sexuality, romance, family, careers, race relations, ecology, and global politics all provoked uncertain and self-doubting stories. Sometimes their stories displayed a sadistic rage directed against groups identified as "others"—homosexuals, Iranians, Afro-Americans, intellectuals, and Asians. Sometimes their stories saw through that process of scapegoating and faced up to the hard facts about the American mainstream itself. But in all cases, these stories reflected the hurts of history.

Most compelling to me about the stories students brought to my classes was how sharply they differed from the dominant narrative then being fashioned within politics and popular culture. I began teaching at the end of the Carter presidency and the beginning of the Reagan years, a time when neo-conservatism clearly captured the dominant narrative about American culture. It was a time when Ronald Reagan's rhetoric turned the Vietnam War into America's "most heroic moment" rather than the "unjust and immoral war" that Dr. Martin Luther King, Jr. and others had described fifteen years earlier. It was a time when television programs like "Dallas," "Dynasty," and "Lifestyles of the Rich and Famous" stoked the fires of material desire, eclipsing the 1970s depictions of urban working-class life in "Kojak," "Good Times," and "All in the Family." It was a time when James Watt declared environmentalists the main threat to the environment while William Bradford Reynolds presented the preservation of white male rights as the main task of civil-rights law enforcement. Yet this dominant story was not what I heard from my students, even those whose political affiliations and career ambitions hinged on the success of the neo-conservative agenda.

Inside my classes and in discussions with students outside of them, I came to see that the dominant neo-conservative narrative of the 1980s conflicted with the experiences and memories of even those Americans who desperately wanted neo-conservatism to succeed. The Vietnam War caused too much pain to be reframed as a singularly heroic moment; such a story immediately summoned up its opposite—the collective recollection of the division and disillusion engendered by the war's terrible destruction of American and Vietnamese lives. In the context of the worst depression in America in forty years, glittering displays of wealth on television programs raised anxieties about the morality of the rich and the fate of the poor. The consciousnesses raised by the 1960s struggles for equality could not easily accept the protection of white male privilege as America's most important civil-rights task, especially given the context of the consequences of economic deindustrialization for female and ethnic minority wage earners and their children. Even those students who clearly benefited from the neo-conservatism of the 1970s and 1980s expressed deep doubts about the emerging world and their place in it.

But if my students would not buy the dominant narrative, neither did they accept the oppositional narratives one might have expected them to embrace. My students were not right-wing, they were not left-wing. They believed deeply in their own powerlessness. They never objected to my left-wing politics; what troubled them was that I had any politics at all, that I seemed to believe that humans operated out of any but the basest self-centered motivations. Their cynicism made them intensely critical of the dominant narratives, but left them unwilling to fashion alternatives, at least in discussions about politics and economics. But popular culture texts provoked a different response from them. They identified with television programs, films, and popular music in a way that they would not even consider about politics. These texts unleashed the memories and experiences suppressed by the dominant rhetoric of their private and public lives. Here hope was still an issue, and happiness was still possible. The gap between dominant political rhetoric and their lived experiences left them with enormous tensions and anxieties with no outlet for expression save in their responses to popular culture texts. Here was a sphere they saw as their own, a presentation of choices about the world that mattered to them, and in discussing these texts they brought forth the full passion and anger and hope that they repressed elsewhere. For them, too, the long way around was the shortest way through: a detour was the way to confront emotions very close to home.

As my students and I used popular culture texts from the past to gain insight into the complex stories defining our present identities, we found terrains of conflict and struggle in the most unexpected places and allies in the most improbable individuals. Not because these films, songs, and shows reflected our lives directly, but, rather, because they reflected the core contradictions of our lives indirectly enough to make discussion of them bearable.

It was not that any of these texts told our stories directly; rather, they enabled us to see the resemblances between our own stories and those of others, calling ever more attention to the structural unities that underlay seemingly diverse experiences. For example, the film *Flaming Star* (1960) featuring Elvis Presley as a young (and blue-eyed) American Indian growing up in a mixed-white and Indian family on the 1870s Texas frontier provoked a vigorous discussion. An older Chicano male remembered the film as a favorite in his neighborhood when it first came out because it detailed the anguish of having an ethnic identity that left one caught in the middle between warring ethnic groups. A middle-class housewife read the inter-racial family in the film as the kind of Aquarian voluntary community that the hippie communes of the 1960s tried to build. A working-class white woman identified with Presley himself and his character as an emblem of upward mobility for her class, a sign of the right to dream of something better in the face of all the rejections and disappointments around her. A young black male found the justifications of Indian resistance in the film as evocative of the black militant rhetoric he had grown up with in the 1960s. A radical lesbian viewed Presley as an androgynous image, a heroic subject that was neither completely male nor female, but that enabled one to choose the best of both identities. A young Chinese-American woman felt that the film demonstrated the immutable power of American racism and its determination to destroy any identities that do not fit the dominant image. A middle-class male attorney found the film dangerously tragic in its obliviousness to women's wishes and its celebration of reckless male heroism. The plurality of views provoked by this text left no one correct reading, but, instead, provided a locus of meanings intersecting around the content of the film and the lived experiences of its viewers.

Discussions about popular culture in my classes always seemed to become discussions about the relationship between the past and the present in American life and culture. The stories on the screen clashed with dominant political and historical stories, and the stories my students and I told often clashed with each other. But the very diversity of these stories helped map out the contours of what we had and did not have in common, and taken collectively they explained a lot about the American past and present. Provoked by these discussions, I found myself increasingly investigating the concrete contexts of popular culture production and reception. These investigations caused me to reframe my understanding of the roles played by discourse and ideology in social change; they led me to rethink the labor and social history I had been trained to do, while they provided me with tools for inquiries for which I had no training. Everywhere I found others engaged in the same kinds of inquiries, both professionally and avocationally. Eventually I found myself part of a field, part of "cultural studies" in a variety of disciplines. I discovered colleagues in anthropology, literature, sociology, music, and speech communication whose experiences with their disciplines and with scholarship in the 1980s led them to projects similar to my own. Our enterprise is still fragile and always imperiled, but it has an institutional existence now that we would have thought impossible a decade ago. Whether we make appropriate use of this institutional space will depend in large measure upon our ability to keep faith with all the students and colleagues who led us to this kind of inquiry in the first place, on our success in relating media texts to the social crises in which they are produced and received.

Exploring any part of the American past has its built-in risks. No amount of contextualization can obscure the grim realities of slavery, conquest, and genocide; no amount of mythologizing the "American way" can erase how hard life has been on this continent for so many people. On the other hand, the hard facts about America are not the only facts, the perpetrators of American aggression are not the only Americans. I am quite prepared to say that the ruling elites in America have committed quiet and systematic crimes and that they have been supported in those crimes by many ordinary citizens. But I am unwilling to let the history of monopoly, imperialism, racism, and sexism stand for the totality of American experience. When one examines American culture, one inevitably finds all the hard facts, but one also sees the earnest longings and heroic struggles for something different that have characterized the American past. This book is not one of those exercises that finds only the debased and distorted in American history and culture. For all its crimes, this is too good a country, its cultures too rich and varied and inspiring to justify that kind of pessimism, a pessimism that masquerades as critique but which is so one-dimensional that it ultimately serves as a form of collaboration with the oppressors.

* * * * *

I cannot possibly acknowledge all of the individuals who have contributed so much to my understanding of the issues outlined in this book, but I would like to thank my mother, Paulette Lipsitz, for all the support she has given me, as well as for the moral vision that forms the core of her own world view. At the University of Missouri-St. Louis I received the benefit of wisdom and friendship from Neal Primm, George Rawick, Peter Fuss, Charles Korr, Dick Miller, Gary Burns, Beth Kizer, Linda Kulla, Neda Hardin, Deland Edwards, Gerald Hall, Sister Anita Louise Frantz, and Katharine Corbett.

At the University of Houston-Clear Lake I had the privilege of team teaching and sharing an office with Edward Hugetz, whose intellectual power and cultural vision have left an indelible mark on me. At that same institution I also had the benefit of counsel and criticism from many good friends including Mitchell Aboulafia, Barbara Ellman, Don and Jean Quataert, Sandy Gabin, Bruce Palmer, Curt Smith, and Debbie Arnold. At Mount Holyoke College I had the opportunity to learn from wonderful colleagues including Daniel Czitrom, Don Weber, Edward Royce, William McFeely, and Fi Herbert.

In the summer of 1984 I attended a National Endowment for the Humanities seminar about television studies conducted by Nick Browne at UCLA. That summer changed my life; it provided me with the tools for cultural analysis that have become essential to my scholarship. I will always feel grateful to Professor Browne and to members of that seminar including Robert Deming, Mary Beth Haralovich, Phil Lane, John Leo, Beverly O'Neill, and Tom Zynda. In 1985 I attended my first meeting of the International Association for the Study of Popular Music and wish to express my appreciation for all that I have learned within that organization, especially from Reebee Garofalo, Charles Keil, Leslie Roman, Cameron McCarthy, Francois Gougeon, David Horn, Herman Gray, Josee Destrempes, and Line Grenier.

Ever since I started work at the University of Minnesota in 1986, I have felt that I have been in the right place at the right time. One could not ask for better colleagues in cultural studies than Susan Mc-Clary, Richard Leppert, David W. Noble, Lary May, Elaine May, John Mowitt, Bruce Lincoln, Rey Chow, and Maria Damon. Nor could one ask for better students than Wendy Kozol, Rob Walser, Csaba Toth, Joe Austin, and Betty Bergland. I would also like to acknowledge the help and criticism I have received from scholars across the country including Janice Radway, Michael M. J. Fischer, Horace Newcomb, Dana Polan, Mari Jo Buhle, Paul Buhle, Stanley Aronowitz, Elizabeth Long, Tom Dumm, Brenda Bright, Sharon O'Brien, Adam Sorkin and Lynn Spigel. Barbara Tomlinson has been generous with her time as a critic and editor; my work always benefits from her help.

With so many debts to pay for this kind of work, it is difficult to single out any individuals from among the rest. But Aaron Neville, Johnny Otis, Billy Peek, and Irma Thomas have not only taught me indispensable truths about American culture, they have also enabled me to live with the consequences of those truths. With deep respect and admiration, this book is dedicated to each of them.

Culture and History

1
Popular Culture:
This Ain't No Sideshow

In this great future, you can't forget your past.
Bob Marley

The late jazz musician Rahsaan Roland Kirk used to preface his performances with an unusual word of advice for the audience. A burly black man who often wore a stovepipe hat with a feather in it, and who frequently carried two saxophones (which he sometimes played simultaneously), Kirk would peer out at the crowd through dark sunglasses and growl, "This ain't no sideshow." Invariably people would laugh at the incongruity of this consummately theatrical individual denying his theatricality. Yet once Kirk began to play, discerning listeners grasped his point.

There was a show going on when Roland Kirk played music, but it was not a sideshow. Nearly everything that Kirk did and said, nearly everything that he played and sang called attention to his role as a black musician in a society controlled by whites. With bitingly satiric renditions of hymns like "The Old Rugged Cross," Kirk related the forms and conventions of popular music to their origins within the historical struggles of the Afro-American past. With mischievous wordplay his song "Blacknuss" called attention to the unequal relationship between the black keys and the white keys on the piano. Kirk's attire and stage behavior subverted conventional expectations about performance, and his aggressive humor exposed the tension between music as a commodity and music as an expression of lived experience.

What distinguished Rahsaan Roland Kirk's "show" from a "side-

3

show" was history. All his eccentricities called attention to his identity as a historical subject, a descendant of slaves and a victim of white racism, a human being forced to disguise his pain and anger within the outward appearances of a sideshow. In songs like "The Old Rugged Cross" and "Blacknuss," Kirk translated his experiences and aspirations into art, just as his ancestors had done when they fashioned spirituals, blues, and jazz out of the clash between Afro-American values and Euro-American racism. His stage antics played against the expectations of the audience because they revealed a sedimented layer of historical knowledge and historical critique beneath the surface appearance of novelty and performance. Within the commercial context of commodified mass culture, Rahsaan Roland Kirk created a history that could be hummed, a story of the past that relied on sharps and flats instead of on footnotes, and one that testified to the historicity of experience even while avoiding the linearity and teleology generally associated with historical narratives.

The elements of historical inquiry and explanation encapsulated in Rahsaan Roland Kirk's stage performance present both possibilities and problems. They testify to the importance of historical thinking as an organic and necessary way of understanding human experience, a mode of organizing ideas and interpretations that is as indispensable in everyday life as it is in scholarly research. Yet its location within popular culture gives Kirk's "history" an impressionistic, interpretive, and allegorical aspect. His art contained multilayered and heavily coded covert messages about the past, but for a large part of his audience, Kirk's music inevitably appeared as just another novelty and diversion within the seemingly autonomous realms of commercialized leisure.

Kirk's problem is our problem. The powerful apparatuses of contemporary commercial electronic mass communications dominate discourse in the modern world. They supply us with endless diversion and distraction mobilized to direct our minds toward advertising messages. They colonize the most intimate and personal aspects of our lives, seizing upon every possible flaw in our bodies, minds, and psyches to increase our anxieties and augment our appetites for consumer goods. Culture itself comes to us as a commodity. The artistry and historical consciousness of a Rahsaan Roland Kirk becomes obscured by our contexts of reception. We buy records and attend concerts, watch films and television commercials as a matter of course. Rarely do we ask about the origins and intentions of the messages we encounter through the mass media; sometimes we forget that artists have origins or intentions at all, so pervasive are the stimuli around us.

Yet mass communications also embody some of our deepest hopes and engage some of our most profound sympathies. People ingeniously enter those discourses to which they have access; the saxophone or the guitar, the stage or the camera can offer precious and unique opportunities for expression. For some populations at some times, commercialized leisure is history—a repository of collective memory that places immediate experience in the context of change over time. The very same media that trivialize and distort culture, that turn art into commodities, and that obscure the origins and intentions of artists also provide meaningful connection to our own pasts and to the pasts of others. But they do so only indirectly, constrained by the nonlinear biases of the electronic media as well as by a commercial matrix hostile to the kinds of empathy, inquiry, and analysis basic to historical thinking.

The presence of sedimented historical currents within popular culture illumines the paradoxical relationship between history and commercialized leisure. Time, history, and memory become qualitatively different concepts in a world where electronic mass communication is possible. Instead of relating to the past through a shared sense of place or ancestry, consumers of electronic mass media can experience a common heritage with people they have never seen; they can acquire memories of a past to which they have no geographic or biological connection. This capacity of electronic mass communication to transcend time and space creates instability by disconnecting people from past traditions, but it also liberates people by making the past less determinate of experiences in the present.

History and commercialized leisure appear to be polar opposites—the former concerned with continuities that unite the totality of human experience, the latter with immediate sense gratifications that divide society into atomized consumers. But both the variants of history and the forms of commercialized leisure familiar to us originated at the same time and for the same reasons. Both developed in the nineteenth century in response to extraordinary technological and social changes. Recognition of the common origins of history and commercialized leisure can explain the seemingly paradoxical tensions within Roland Kirk's music, while also helping to explain how the "remembering" of history and the "forgetting" of commercialized leisure form parts of a dialectical totality.

Commercialized Leisure and the Crisis of History

As literary critic Richard Terdiman has demonstrated, nineteenth-century industrialization and state-building entailed a massive disruption of traditional forms of memory. The instrumental mentality capable of building the political and industrial machines of that century had to countenance the destruction of tradition—the enclosure of farm lands, massive migrations to industrial cities, the construction of an interchangeable work force, and a consumer market free from the constraints of tradition. A sense of disconnection from the past united an otherwise fragmented and stratified polity, and consequently the study of the past took on new meaning. Terdiman notes that "history became the discipline of memory," whose task was to uncover "the crisis which inevitably entailed disconnection with the past as a referent."[1] Michelet, Dilthey, Bancroft, and the other great historians of the nineteenth century emerged to provide a sense of continuity and connection with the past in societies riddled with the ruptures and dislocations of modernity.

The beginnings of the electronic mass media in the form of the telegraph exacerbated the nineteenth-century crisis of memory. The telegraph enabled simultaneous communication for the first time, dissolving previous barriers of time and space. But that very simultaneity favored the agenda of ascendant industrial capitalism. The telegraph innately privileged the transmission of isolated facts like prices or recent events; it did little to convey context or continuity. Newspapers took on a new role with the stimulus of the telegraph, but it was a role geared toward commerce and change rather than to the preservation of cultural memory. The daily newspaper naturalized a kind of confusion in which the world seemed structured by isolated and discrete events; news became synonymous with change and more important than tradition.

A new kind of commercialized leisure emerged as a corollary to the telegraph in the United States during the late nineteenth century. Previously, churches, lodge halls, and community centers had served

6

as sites for theatrical productions designed to mark festive occasions like weddings and holidays. But urban taverns, dance halls, amusement parks, and theaters brought new meanings to culture. The new commercial theaters, and later variety, vaudeville, and motion-picture halls, needed no special occasions and no association with ritualized activities to justify plays, skits, and music. They carved away a new kind of social space for working-class people—buildings devoted exclusively to leisure activities. Theatrical performances became commodities sold to strangers for an agreed-upon price rather than collective creations by communities enacting rituals essential to group identity and solidarity.[2]

Of course, commercialized theater had existed since the sixteenth century in Europe. Jean-Christophe Agnew, among others, has delineated the complicated connections between the assumptions of theater and the values central to the capitalist marketplace, but in nineteenth-century America, theater, medicine shows, circuses, taverns, dance halls, amusement parks, and vaudeville-variety houses intervened in culture and society in especially important ways. They helped Americans make a decisive break with Victorian restraints, while at the same time blending an ethnically diverse working class into an "audience" with a unified language and sign-system.

The success of popular theater in nineteenth-century America aggravated the crisis of historical memory by further detaching culture from tradition. It institutionalized a kind of dissembling, one feared by philosophers as far back as Plato. To speak someone else's words or to wear someone else's clothes meant hiding one's own identity. In a world where ancestry, locality, and vocation determined social status and identity, the inherent disguise of acting threatened core values. Role playing in the theater suggested that identities could be changed, that one was not bound by bloodlines, nationality, or occupation. This contained the essence of egalitarian and utopian thought by challenging the legitimacy of static identities inherited from the past, but it also threatened a sense of authentic self-knowledge and created the psychic preconditions for the needy narcissism of consumer desire. On stage, actors deliberately speak and act inauthentically, off stage everyone learns to act, because everyone needs to take on ever-changing roles as a consumer and worker. As literary scholar Michael Bristol points out about the cultural crises posed by theater in Elizabethan England, "An actor is not just someone whose speech

7

is 'dissembling'; the deeper problem is that he is most valued for his ability to dissemble convincingly."[3] As commercialized theaters in nineteenth-century America helped destroy connections to the past, historical tableaux and dramas became common features within them, offering a fictive representation of what was being destroyed in reality. Thus the contents of theatrical productions sometimes ministered to the very wounds that their forms had helped to open.

Along with the telegraph and the daily newspaper, the theater helped reshape cultural memory and consciousness. Its role on behalf of the emergent industrial order helped mold a diverse population into a unified working and consuming force, but it also raised anxieties about the moral costs of disconnection from the past. To many critics, the "dissembling" of theater presented a challenge to established order and morality. These critics feared that nothing genuine or refined could come from a sphere of activity devoted to false representations and masked identities. Furthermore, they recognized that theatrical "time" presented an alternative to work time, pitting the pleasures of leisure against the responsibilities of labor. Theater attendance enabled individuals to play out fictive scenarios of changed identities, to escape from the surveillance and supervision of moral authorities and institutions. The fantasy world of the theatrical stage encouraged audiences to pursue personal desires and passions at the expense of their socially prescribed responsibilities.

Yet audiences embraced the new possibilities presented by commercial theater with enthusiasm. Unlike the wedding celebration or the community festival, the theater assembled an audience with no shared history, with no reciprocal responsibilities and obligations. Theatergoers in nineteenth-century America shared intimate and personal cultural moments with strangers. The unfamiliarity of the crowd with each other provided a kind of protective cover—a "privacy in public" whereby personal feelings and emotions could be aired without explanation or apology.[4] Women especially utilized the new popular culture as a way of escaping parental surveillance and patriarchal domination.[5] Using the borrowed legitimacy of theater's status as a form of cultural refinement, audiences flocked to the melodramas, vaudeville and variety shows, and later to motion pictures for decidedly unrefined productions and performances. In the theater, they encountered a world momentarily liberated from the sexual and emotional repressions of the nineteenth century. Theatrical performances provided an outlet for expression of the needs and desires for pleasure long suppressed by the normative constraints of Victorian America.[6]

The sexual repressions of the Victorian era created powerful anxieties and tensions that could not be confronted directly by "respectable" citizens. But theater productions offered audiences an opportunity to view the forbidden and to contemplate the unthinkable. This "freedom" came less in the form of true sexual emancipation, however, than through a redirection of frustrations. The unfilled desires and unconsummated lusts of theater audiences made them good customers for sexually suggestive images, no matter how coded, coy, or indirect. The theater offered immediate but transitory gratification. It turned sexual impulses and desires into symbolic commodities to be purchased from others. One bought a theater ticket to see a performance that depicted happiness and pleasures missing from one's own life. Pleasure itself could not be purchased as a commodity—at least not legally—but the image of pleasure represented in the theater could be obtained for a small price. Similarly, theatrical productions evoked other desires—for intimacy, for recognition, for connection to the past. But the very forms of commercial theater aggravated rather than salved the wounds they pretended to heal.

Yet the theater did encompass a kind of free space for the imagination—an arena liberated from old restraints and repressions, a place where desire did not have to be justified or explained. By establishing commodity purchases as symbolic answers to real problems, the theater also helped lay the groundwork for the consumer-commodity culture of our own day wherein advertisers and entrepreneurs offer products that promise to bring pleasure and fulfillment. The nineteenth-century theater may have emerged in part as a rebellion against sexual repression, but its greatest long-term significance lay in shaping the psychic and material preconditions for Americans to shift from a Victorian industrial economy to a hedonistic consumer-commodity economy. It would not be the last time that the commercial matrix in which popular culture was embedded worked to undermine its potential for educational or social transcendence.

9

Melodramas, vaudeville and variety shows, and motion pictures taught Americans to make a break with the discipline, sobriety, thrift, and sexual repression that formed the core of Victorian culture. Appropriate to an industrializing economy, Victorian values provided necessary preconditions for economic growth during the nineteenth century. They stressed the work ethic, personal responsibility, punctuality, and willingness to defer gratification necessary for life as an industrial worker. But by the 1890s, it appeared that Victorian culture had done its work all too well. The hard-working Americans who internalized Victorian values helped build a powerful industrial economy that produced more products than the domestic market could consume. Overproduction and underconsumption threatened the very survival of industrial capitalism in the 1880s and 1890s, as business failures led to massive unemployment and repeated financial panics. The "false promise" of the Victorian code, that sober self-management would lead to upward mobility, helped provoke general strikes and other forms of "aggressive festivity" among workers. To solve their many problems, business leaders had to move away from the production of capital goods like railroads and locomotives and start producing consumer goods for the domestic market. But as long as Victorian repressions inhibited desires for immediate gratification, consumers lacked the psychological makeup necessary for an economy oriented around ever-increasing purchases of commodities by individuals.

Commercialized leisure evolved out of the contradictions in late nineteenth-century capitalism. As I. C. Jarvie notes, motion pictures not only served as renewable commodities in themselves, but they also helped legitimate the consciousness necessary for purchasing other renewable commodities. The specialization of industrial capitalism requires individuals "detachable from tradition, family, and ascription." Jarvie argues that motion pictures encouraged people to see themselves as detached and autonomous consumers by replacing ritualistic community celebrations with leisure that could be purchased as a commodity and shared with strangers.[7] Between 1890 and 1930 American society underwent extraordinary changes, from a Victorian culture of thrift to a consumer-oriented culture of spending. By the 1920s, production of renewable commodities like automobiles and appliances played a more important role in the U.S. economy than production of nonrenewable capital goods like heavy

equipment and machinery. Economic historians have long understood the logic of this change for the interests of capital; building factories and locomotive engines brought enormous immediate profits,
but the market for them became saturated rather quickly. Consumer
goods did not need to last—indeed advertisers worked very dili-
gently to see to it that considerations of fashion and style would render old goods obsolete and engender a demand for new ones.

Scholars examining the transition from Victorianism to consumerism in the U.S. have concentrated on the idea of leisure as contested
terrain. Drawing upon the research of E. P. Thompson and Herbert
Gutman, they have emphasized the ways in which the transition from
agrarian to industrial life gave new meanings to work and play. In
pre-industrial society, agrarian labor could be done at one's own
pace and for one's own benefit. In the industrial workplace, factory
time replaced natural time, and unremitting labor measured by the
time-clock replaced the task-oriented work of the farm. No longer
could leisure be mixed in with work, and work itself became a more
prominent and a more alienating part of human existence. Just as the
centralized industrial work site replaced home labor, so commercial
establishments devoted to leisure-time pursuits replicated in the
arena of play the capitalist division of labor. Intense resistance
against these practices fueled strikes, sabotage, and other forms of
working-class self-activity throughout the era of industrialization, but
religious, medical, and legal authorities attempted to prevent revolt
by inculcating Victorian values within the character structure of the
work force, values championing repression, denial, thrift, chastity,
sobriety, and hard work. But like most forms of ideological legitimation, they contained severe internal contradictions. When workers
internalized Victorian norms, their labor produced a surplus of
goods that could not be consumed by a domestic market filled with
poorly paid thrifty self-denying individuals like themselves. When
workers *resisted* Victorian norms, their repressions and anger drove
them toward the only available source of pleasure—the illicit vices
offered for sale by the underworld.

Thus commercialized leisure both facilitated the triumphs of industrial capitalism and focused attention on their psychic and emotional costs. Commercial culture sought credibility with its audiences
by promising at least the illusion of connection with the past. But the
gap between lived experience and the false promises of popular cul-

11

ture always created the possibility for counter-memories, for ethnic, class, and regional music, art, speech, and theater. Culture itself contributed to retraining and reshaping the masses to serve the interests of capital, but also to articulating unfilled desires and expressing disconnection from the past. British cultural studies theorist Stuart Hall notes the contradictions in this process as well as the centrality of tradition as a contested category in the nineteenth century,

> Capital had a stake in the culture of the popular classes because the constitution of a whole new social order around capital required a more or less continuous, if intermittent, process of re-education. And one of the principal sites of resistance to the forms through which this 'reformation' of the people was pursued lay in popular tradition. That is why popular culture is linked, for so long, to questions of tradition, of traditional forms of life—and why its 'traditionalism' has been so often misinterpreted as a product of a merely conservative impulse, backward looking and anachronistic.[8]

The transformations in behavior and collective memory fueled by the contradictions of the nineteenth century have passed through three major stages in the United States. The first involved the establishment and codification of commercialized leisure from the invention of the telegraph to the 1890s. The second involved the transition from Victorian to consumer-hedonist values between 1890 and 1945. The third and most important stage, from World War II to the present, involved extraordinary expansion in both the distribution of consumer purchasing power and in the reach and scope of the electronic mass media. The dislocations of urban renewal, suburbanization, and deindustrialization accelerated the demise of tradition in America, while the worldwide pace of change undermined stability elsewhere. The period from World War II to the present marks the final triumph of commercialized leisure, and with it an augmented crisis over the loss of connection to the past. Popular culture has played an important role in creating this crisis of memory, but it has also been one of the main vehicles for the expression of loss and the projection of hopes for reconnection to the past.

What Is Popular Culture?

As historian Ramon Gutierrez observes, the term "popular culture" is a description crafted exclusively from the outside. The creators of popular culture do not think of themselves as operating within an endeavor called "popular culture"; they see themselves merely creating signs and symbols appropriate to their audiences and to themselves. It is only from the vantage point of Enlightenment ideals of "high culture" that something called popular culture can be seen to exist. In recent years, scholars have increasingly challenged the divisions between "high" and popular culture, and rightly so. Yet it is also clear that what we call popular culture differs markedly in its aims and intentions from the Enlightenment culture of "beauty and truth" idealized in the nineteenth century by Matthew Arnold, as well as from the isolated "folk" cultures studied by anthropologists and folklorists. In general, we have a better idea of what commercial culture *is not* (high art and folklore) than what it is. But we can identify some aspects of commercialized leisure that have come to define its conditions of possibility.[9]

Popular culture has no fixed forms: the historical circumstances of reception and appropriation determine whether novels or motion pictures or videos belong to a sphere called popular culture. Similarly, individual artifacts of popular culture have no fixed meanings: it is impossible to say whether any one combination of sounds or set of images or grouping of words innately expresses one unified political position. Images and icons compete for dominance within a multiplicity of discourses; consumers of popular culture move in and out of subject positions in a way that allows the same message to have widely varying meanings at the point of reception. Although cultural products generally reflect the dominant ideology of any given period, no cultural moment exists within a hermetically sealed cultural present; all cultural expressions speak to both residual memories of the past and emergent hopes for the future.

Rather than looking for innately emancipatory or hegemonic forms and meanings within popular culture, we would do better to study its "transformations," which Stuart Hall defines as

> "the active work on existing traditions and activities, their active reworking so that they come out a different way: they appear to 'persist'—yet, from one period to another, they come to stand in a different relation to the ways working people live and the ways they define their relations to each other, to 'the others' and to the conditions of life."[10]

In the United States since World War II, these transformations have coalesced around identifiable conditions of possibility. These conditions are not an "aesthetic," or a finite set of rules guiding artistic production and reception; they are not inherently "progressive" practices guaranteed to advance struggles against exploitation and hierarchy wherever they appear; they are not pure, authentic, or transcendent by themselves. They are historically specific elements within commercial culture that allow for the expression of collective popular memory and the reworking of tradition. Participation and investment, carnival, and a struggle for hegemony have provided significant conditions of possibility within American commercial culture since World War II. At times, all of these have created frames of reception consistent with dominant ideology, but they have also worked to hone and sharpen collective popular memory.

Sociologist Pierre Bourdieu's categories of participation and investment accurately characterize audience expectations from American popular culture since World War II.[11] Unlike "high culture" where a dogmatic formalism privileges abstraction over experience, the effectiveness of popular culture depends on its ability to engage audiences in active and familiar processes. Tania Modleski has demonstrated how television soap operas and game shows win credibility with viewers by turning into play the everyday work of nurturing families and making purchases, much as rodeo events or car customizing do for cowboys and mechanics.[12] Fredric Jameson describes popular songs as copies for which there exist no originals, texts whose popularity depends less on innovation or imagination than upon a sense of familiarity conducive to immediate audience appropriation.[13]

Traditions of participation and investment, combined with the internal biases of electronic mass media, tend to privilege forms of communication emanating from aggrieved and marginal communities. Sociolinguists Basil Bernstein, Leonard Schatzman, and Anselm Strauss have identified empathy, immediacy, and emotion as core components of working-class speech, and they have demonstrated how working-class speakers subordinate linear, individualistic, and analytic ways of speaking to stress nonlinear effects and collective emotions.[14] Rhetorician Kathleen Hall Jamieson points out that television favors a style of speaking that historically has been associated with women—an unself-conscious sense of self-disclosure about one's private self and an ability to integrate others into one's discussions—and that, conversely, the medium works against speech styles traditionally associated with men, which favor projection of the self against the environment.[15] The ever changing meanings and deliberate indeterminacies of subcultural slang undercut the authority of the word, replacing it with an appreciation of the inevitable metaphoricity of language. Such usage entails a break with the logocentric world of the Enlightenment in which univocal utterances and precise descriptions serve to fix final meanings and identities; at the same time it foregrounds a sense of language so new that it resembles postmodern poetry and so old that it echoes the ancient Nahuatl poet who insisted that "no one among us truly and finally speaks here."[16]

Melodrama presents a particularly significant form of participation and investment within American commercial culture since World War II. Melodrama emerged out of the same nineteenth-century dislocations responsible for the problem of historical memory and the rise of popular culture itself. It emerged as an expression of the inadequacies of Enlightenment language and art, displacing conventional narratives and reasoned discourse with broad physical gestures, tableaux, simple binary oppositions between good and evil, and plots resolved more by fate and sudden reverses than by human action. A precursor to film noir, the gothic romance, and the television night-time serial, melodrama established important subtexts within American popular culture. Television critic Jane Feuer points out that melodrama's unsatisfying endings resist the unproblematic closures of dominant narratives, while cinema scholar Laura Mulvey demonstrates how melodrama contains a critique of the cinematic apparatus itself by subjecting its protagonists to "the curious and prurient gaze of intrusive community, neighbors, friends, and family so that the spectator's own look becomes self-conscious and awkward."[17]

Carnival traditions have provided another important frame of reception for American popular culture since World War II. Bourdieu speaks of popular forms that "satisfy the taste for and sense of revelry, the free speaking and hearty laughter which liberate by setting the social world head over heels, overturning conventions and proprieties."[18] Literary critic Mikhail Bakhtin identifies these sensibilities as the essence of carnival—ritualized celebrations oriented around the passions of plenitude, inversions of the social order, and mocking laughter designed to "uncrown power." The dangerous "dissembling" that so troubled nineteenth-century opponents of popular theater, the anarchic anti-authoritarianism of the Marx Brothers, and the sense of entitlement to the good life enshrined in popular music and television all build upon the oppositional possibilities of carnival. Practices within popular culture like constituting the body as a site for decoration and style, valorizing the street as a locus of sociality and creativity, and inverting dominant icons to affirm a prestige from below also resonate with the legacy of carnival.[19] For Bakhtin, retentions of carnival laughter and display evidence a "materials memory," by which words themselves contain ideological traces from the past that take on renewed significance when they are appropriated in the present.[20]

Like participation and investment, carnival privileges certain social dispositions, but it has no intrinsic political meaning. Only in the context of a struggle for hegemony can the latent possibilities of collective memory be activated. The idea of "a struggle for hegemony" originates with the Italian Marxist Antonio Gramsci, who maintains that elites rule not merely by force but by "managed consent" as well, that they form "historical blocs" with other groups that make existing power relations appear natural and just. Some scholars emphasize the ways in which Gramsci's formulations explain how elites impose their will on society and turn potential rebels into unwitting accomplices in their own victimization. But hegemony is not just imposed on society from the top; it is struggled for from below, and no terrain is a more important part of that struggle than popular culture.

Cultural forms create conditions of possibility, they expand the present by informing it with memories of the past and hopes for the future; but they also engender accommodation with prevailing power realities, separating art from life, and internalizing the dominant culture's norms and values as necessary and inevitable. Politics and culture maintain a paradoxical relationship in which only effective political action can win breathing room for a new culture, but only a revolution in culture can make people capable of political action. Culture can seem like a substitute for politics, a way of posing only imaginary solutions to real problems, but under other circumstances culture can become a rehearsal for politics, trying out values and beliefs permissible in art but forbidden in social life. Most often, however, culture exists as a form of politics, as a means of reshaping

16

individual and collective practice for specified interests, and as long as individuals perceive their interests as unfilled, culture retains an oppositional potential. Fredric Jameson argues that the dominant culture can only presume to ease anxieties like disconnection from the past by calling attention to them in the first place, thereby running the risk of re-opening the very ruptures it seeks to close.[21] For Jameson, the best cultural creations present contemporary social contradictions in such a way as to suggest eventual resolutions of them, but even works that fall short of that goal retain the potential to play a role in the struggle for hegemony.[22]

The complicated relationship between historical memory and commercial culture, between the texts of popular culture and their contexts of creation and reception, resist conventional forms of cultural criticism. The coded, indirect, and allegorical aspects of popular culture, its inversions of speech and ideology, and its refusal to isolate art from lived experience (a source of corruption as well as social connection) baffle and frustrate critics trained in traditional Western aesthetics and criticism. Neil Postman indicts television as a force debasing public discourse in America because its claims are made with images rather than language. For Postman, the eclipse of language renders empirical tests and logical analysis "impotent."[23]

In a similar vein, Allan Bloom assures us that rock and roll music's entire meaning rests in its rhythm (as if there were only one), which he confidently explains is the "rhythm of sexual intercourse" (as if here, too, there were only one).[24] The equally uninformed Robert Pattison contends that rock music represents the "triumph of vulgarity," through mindless celebration of a debased primitivism. The nadir of Pattison's slipshod argument comes in his dismissal of the Silhouettes' 1958 hit record "Get a Job" as solipsism rejoicing "in the conclusion that language is meaningless." In actuality, the record became a hit during the recession of 1958, and the song's lyrics described the anxieties of looking for work when there are no jobs available. The scat singing of "nonsense" syllables that leads Pattison to see the song as meaningless plays upon well understood conventions within black music of imitating musical instruments with the human voice, a tactic that Louis Armstrong (to use just one example) employed brilliantly to punctuate some of the lyrics in his songs. In fact, Afro-American poets and writers including Bob Kaufman and Ishmael Reed have long drawn on the creative wordplay of scat sing-

ing as a vital source for their poetry and prose.[25] Like the anthropol
ogist some years back who decided that the *penitente* cults of New
Mexico were "mired in webs of iconographic confusion" because
their iconography made no sense to her, Pattison assumes that "Get
a Job" has no meaning because it is not expressed in language that he
understands. But like the many other errors of fact and interpretation
in Pattison's and Bloom's criticisms, these are beside the point because they stem from a larger conceptual error. Like Postman, Pattison and Bloom are so eager to tell us what popular culture does *not*
do (advance the agenda of the Enlightenment) that they fail to tell us
what popular culture actually *does* or how it is shaped by the economic and social matrix in which it is embedded.

Television provides an important test case for critics of popular
culture. As David Marc quips, the number of people who condemn
television are exceeded only by the number of people who watch it,
but it is difficult to understand or evaluate television's popularity
from most of the critical literature about the medium. This is not to
call for uncritical approval of everything or anything within popular
culture; it is merely to say that questions of connoisseurship and aesthetics need to follow rather than precede an understanding of how
the medium does its work within larger social contexts. Even if we
could safely dismiss every program on television as artistically worth-
less, we would still need to understand the ways in which television
presents the illusion of intimacy, how it intervenes in family relations, how it serves the consumer economy, and how its hold on the
viewing audience relates to the disintegration of public resources,
the aggravations of work, and the fragility of interpersonal relations
that characterize our lives. Furthermore, to function as a mechanism
of escape, television and other forms of popular culture often recu-
perate the very history that their content appears to erase. Certainly
the reach and content of commercial television provide ample
grounds for criticism. Television is both an advertising mechanism
and the primary discursive medium of our culture; it irreparably in-
scribes consumer desire and commercialism into the fabric of entertainment, news, and sports. Television colonizes intimate areas of
human sexuality and personality, exacerbating anxieties and fears to
sell more products. Its penetration into the home helps order domestic space, leisure time, and family identity, while its seemingly
endless flow reduces complex ideas and images to a melange of dis-

traction and trivilization. By addressing viewers as atomized consumers, the medium obscures experiences of race, region, class, and gender. By turning politics into entertainment, television transforms citizens into spectators and turns politicians into performers. Television critic Arthur Kroker may be unique in describing Ronald Reagan's State of the Union addresses as more like "Presidential holograms," than political speeches, but Kroker is hardly alone in noticing the ways in which artistic "representation" defined as the depiction of images has superseded political "representation" defined in relation to the distribution of power and resources.

Yet responding to television's popularity with blanket condemnation of its content misses the point; questions of connoisseurship focus too much on how television fails to meet critical expectations at the expense of understanding how television succeeds at intervening in the everyday life of the society it addresses. Like many popular music critics, television's detractors condemn the medium because they feel it debases an otherwise successfully functioning society. Without discounting the shallow vulgarity of the medium, it is important to note that television also reflects an already ongoing unraveling of social relations in society; its needy narcissism serves as a salve for the wounds of everyday life.

Guided by emotion and empathy, working through ritual and repetition, television's core vocabulary reflects its role as a therapeutic voice ministering to the open wounds of the psyche. As a "close-up" medium whose dramatic and social locus is the home, television addresses the inner life by minimizing the heroic while maximizing the private and personal aspects of existence. Where motion pictures favor the panoramic shot, television privileges the zoom shot, looking *in* rather than out. To represent conversation, film directors use the "shot-counter-shot" effect while television directors employ the tightly constructed "two faces east." Thus motion-picture conversation emphasizes the separations between people, while television depicts people as closely linked to one another. This vocabulary of television lends itself to certain kinds of representation—the empathetic nurturing of others that viewers feel while watching a soap opera or a game show, the nonlinear quick cuts and distractions of action/adventure and comedy programs, and the situation comedy's fixation on stars mugging for the camera which stresses individual moments rather than teleological closure. These all focus attention inward and undermine the psychic prerequisites for a public life, but they also reflect a society already turned inward by the rise of consumerism and the demise of a healthy public life.

For all of their triviality and frivolity, the messages of popular culture circulate in a network of production and reception that is quite serious. At their worst, they perform the dirty work of the economy and the state. At their best, they retain memories of the past and contain hopes for the future that rebuke the injustices and inequities of the present. It might be thought a measure of the inescapable irony of our time that the most profound intellectual questions emerge out of what seem to be ordinary and commonplace objects of study. It may well be that such a paradox exposes the decline of intellectual work and the eclipse of historical reason. But there is another possibility. Perhaps the most important facts about people and about societies have always been encoded within the ordinary and the commonplace. Rahsaan Roland Kirk had an eminently serious agenda, but little access to the arenas in which "serious" decisions about power and resources are contested. However, every time he picked up the saxophone (or saxophones), he made a statement about the past, present, and future. By examining the relationship between collective popular memory and commercial culture, we may be on the threshhold of a new kind of knowledge, one sensitive to contestations over meaning and capable of teaching us that a sideshow can sometimes be the main event.

2

Precious and Communicable: History in an Age of Popular Culture

At the end of her wonderful novel *My Antonia*, Willa Cather speaks about "the precious and incommunicable past."[1] Her formulation identifies historical work as necessary and indispensable, but always incomplete. We need to understand the past in order to make informed moral choices about the present, to connect our personal histories to a larger collective history. But that larger history can never be fully comprehended; the complexities and pluralities of the past always resist definitive evaluation and summary. Reconstructing the infinitely complex experiences of the past through the paltry bits of evidence about it available to historians inevitably renders some aspects of the past as incommunicable.

Those of us who teach history rarely think about history as "precious and incommunicable" in the sense that Cather means. Perhaps we walk into the classroom believing that history is precious, but find our students' disinterest in the subject so thorough that we despairingly conclude that it is incommunicable. Too often, we think of history as neither precious nor incommunicable, but rather as an inert body of facts to be retrieved by diligent scholarship and to be learned by rote memorization. Even historical methodologies that try to do justice to the pluralities of the past, that hone the necessary skills of empathy, imagination, and analysis basic to historical thinking confront resistant audiences. History as an academic subject and as a way of understanding the world appears increasingly in jeopardy, regarded inside and outside academia as exceedingly "incommunicable" but scarcely "precious."

In accepting the 1980 Nobel Prize for literature, Czelaw Milosz identified a "refusal to remember" as the characteristic vice of our time.[2] For Milosz, the horrors of history, of Nazi barbarism and Stalinist totalitarianism, loom so monstrously over the present that people find it easier to forget than to take on the burdens and responsibilities of remembering. Intellectual historian Russell Jacoby sees a similar erasure in the eclipse of historical memory. Totalitarianisms thrive on "social amnesia" in Jacoby's view, because people who have lost the ability to "think back" have lost the ability to think at all. "Society has lost its memory," Jacoby writes, "and with it, its mind."[3]

The rapid pace of change itself helps explain the crisis of historical understanding for some. Lawrence Grossberg describes the post-World War II era as an age of "postmodernity" where "change increasingly appears to be all that there is," where "there is no sense of progress which can provide meaning or depth and a sense of inheritance," and where "both the future and the past appear increasingly irrelevant; history has collapsed into the present."[4] John Berger—artist, novelist, and critic—makes a similar argument, contending: "Today what surrounds the individual life can change more quickly than the brief sequence of that life itself. The timeless has been abolished and history has become ephemerality. History no longer pays respect to the dead: the dead are simply what has passed through."[5] Whether due to the suppression of hard and unpalatable facts about the brutalities of the past (and present), or to the debilitating effects of incessant change, historians and history teachers today confront intellectual trends that include what the social historian Warren Susman characterizes as "a fundamentally antihistorical view of the world."[6]

The Neo-Conservative Critique of History

The contemporary crisis of historical thinking extends across the globe, and represents only a part of a larger crisis in the humanities and the social sciences about the uneasy relationship between "truth" and our accounts of it. But the most publicized efforts to address this crisis in the United States have posed the problem in parochial and technical terms. Lynne Cheney, Ronald Reagan's director of the National Endowment for the Humanities, issued a 1987 report

22

blaming history teachers and textbooks for shortcomings in student knowledge about the American past. Drawing upon a study commissioned by the Department of Education, *What Do Our Seventeen Year Olds Know?* by Diane Ravitch and Chester Finn, Cheney blasted "a system of education that fails to nurture memory of the past."[7] Cheney's well publicized remarks came in the wake of the substantial sales garnered by books by Allan Bloom and E. D. Hirsch, which also cite alleged deficiencies in student knowledge about literature and history that they blamed on the bad values and poor teaching strategies of instructors.

What unites these pronouncements by Cheney, Ravitch, Finn, Bloom, and Hirsch is their failure to connect arguments to evidence and their inability to address issues of context and power. Most of them presume (without proof) a previous golden age when students possessed mastery of historical facts and methods. All presume that the crisis of historical thinking begins in the classroom, not in the world outside, and that teachers can solve the problem merely by compelling children to memorize and recite the proper phrases. They ignore the suppressions of memory fostered by the public relations arms of totalitarian states East and West, the dizzying pace of change engendered by technological change and social dislocation, and the "crisis of representation" affecting not just history, but all of the humanities and social sciences. They find no fundamental difference between teaching the children of yesterday (at least those who could afford to stay in school)—who lived in homes where class, ethnicity, religion, neighborhood, and region all contained visible markers of the past—and children of today—who live in a world of electronic mass media, corporate transfers, and social pressures to obsess about contemporary fashions and styles so as not to be identified with any personal or collective past. In short, these "defenders" of historical thinking are themselves abysmal historians, unable to ground either their own analyses or their proposed solutions in the world of power relations, personal subjectivity, and change over time in which we all live.

It is not surprising that the Reagan administration and wealthy foundations representing corporate interests would sponsor such research. The very same Department of Education that tried to eliminate school-lunch programs and reduce loans to college students paid for Ravitch and Finn's study; the Olin Foundation supported

Bloom's writing, while Hirsch received funds from the Exxon Foundation. The resulting research makes no mention of the ways in which the deindustrialization of America in the 1980s undermines people's ties to the past and threatens their hopes about the future. It makes no mention of the ways in which the tax cuts of this decade that fuel merger manias and luxury spending sprees mandate a diversion of resources away from schools and universities, devastating support for new scholarship, library resources, and graduate programs in history. Even the technical educational recommendations emerging from these reports serve to narrow rather than broaden the scope of historical knowledge. They do not call for a reinvigoration of historical writing and teaching so much as they mandate censorship of the most interesting and most effective research methods developed within the historical profession over the past two decades.

Given the depth of their dissatisfaction with students and teachers, the neo-conservative critics make surprisingly few affirmative suggestions about how to improve the discipline. Ravitch and Finn offer a few common-sense "proposals" that merely codify the way history is already being taught. Cheney calls for textbooks like those "in the early decades of this century," which she characterizes as "filled with stories — the magic of myths, fables, and tales of heroes."[8] Hirsch offers a list of disconnected nouns for students to memorize on the dubious premise that the ability to recognize the items on his list constitutes "cultural literacy." These "remedies" might possibly encourage religious revivals, frenzies of uncritical nationalism, or unthinking acceptance of the dictates of authority figures, but they do nothing to solve the crisis of historical thinking. Indeed, they undermine the very cornerstones of historical research — appreciation of difference, understanding of context, and ability to make critical comparative judgments on the basis of empathy and evidence.

The neo-conservative educational critics champion heroic stories told from one point of view that make the power hierarchies of the present appear natural and inevitable. Bloom argues that "the contempt for the heroic is only an extension of the perversion of the democratic principle that denies greatness and wants everyone to feel comfortable in his [sic] skin [sic] without having to suffer unpleasant comparisons."[9] Cheney argues that "our history and literature give us symbols to share; they help us all, no matter how diverse our backgrounds, feel part of a common undertaking."[10] Hirsch claims that an agentless "history" has determined what we need to know about the past, and that no value judgments or ideologies have shaped the "common elements" available to us.[11] These assertions seek closure on the very possibilities that history opens up. For in historical research the "heroic" is a matter of context and perspective, what people have in common can be studied empirically rather than mandated from above, and it is understood that all information available to historians has been shaped by the ideological conditions of its origins and preservation. In addition, the true neo-conservative agenda becomes clear when these authors expound on the kinds of historical scholarship they wish to eliminate. Cheney claims that textbooks have become vacuous because they are preoccupied with concepts like "expanding environments" and "recognizing the interdependence among people."[12] In a 1988 report on the state of the humanities in America, Cheney airs her agenda more fully. While paying lipservice to the necessity of historical inquiry, Cheney defends her emphasis on the great books and great works in the Western tradition by asserting in decidedly ahistorical fashion that these works and the concepts of "truth," "beauty," and "excellence" that they embody are "timeless." Of course, because historical inquiry emphasizes how time and place are crucial determinants in the origins and uses of these works, to call them "timeless" is to ignore the insights historical study can provide. Cheney takes on the critics of Western tradition by quoting them out of context and misrepresenting their views — hardly a tribute to the effects of classical learning — and then she asserts, without benefit of comparative study, that we need to focus on Western civilization because it really is *better* than all other civilizations, past and present.[13] Bloom asserts that "the problem of getting along with outsiders is secondary to, and sometimes in conflict with, having an inside, a people, a culture, a way of life. A very great narrowness is not incompatible with the health of an individual or a people, whereas with great openness it is hard to avoid decomposition."[14] Hirsch contends that national cultures are contrived by intellectuals, and have no innate moral value, but they must be taught to the young because the modern nation state depends upon them.[15] Ravitch and Finn argue, "It is not coincidental that general knowledge of history and literature in the schools appears to be imperiled at the same moment that specialists in the uni-

versities devote themselves to arcane debates among deconstructionists, structuralists, neo-Marxists, and other specialized schools
and esoteric interpretations."[16] What is really no coincidence is that
Ravitch and Finn choose to ally themselves with mythical constructs
of history while venting their anti-intellectualism against methods
that seek true and useful accounts of the past by subjecting the forms
and contents of historical narratives to rigorous analysis.

What can we learn from a history like Cheney's, one that considers
concepts like "expanding environments" and "interdependence
among people" as vacuous compared to "myths, fables and tales of
heroes"? From a history like Bloom's that cultivates "a very great narrowness" to avoid the "decomposition" of openness? From Hirsch
who wants us to memorize stories and disembodied facts about the
past without worrying about whether or not they are true? From Ravitch and Finn who seek to silence discussion about the ways in
which every story about the past has been told from someone to
someone else in keeping with the interests of the speaker and the
listener? We certainly will not learn very much about the history of
the United States with its many conflicts and disagreements. The
"heroism" of westward expansion from the settlers' perspective may
have seemed like genocide to the Native American Indians. The
"progress" of American agriculture and industry might have appeared as naked exploitation to slaves and industrial laborers. The
inclusive story about immigrants coming to find freedom in America
excludes many blacks, Chicanos, and Native Americans who did not
come to America, but instead had America come to them. The icons
and images of our culture — that appear value-free to Hirsch — might
bear traces of oppression from the perspectives of women and ethnic minorities. Much recent scholarship has worked to open up these
differences, eschewing univocal heroic narratives for a multi-vocal
story more reflective of the experience of the American people as a
whole. The impetus for this recent scholarship has not been to divide
a unified society, but to understand existing divisions by tracing their
historical roots. Nor has the goal of this scholarship been what
Bloom calls "moral relativism" where the multiplicity of stories
means that no value judgments can be made. On the contrary, it assumes that value judgments can be made only on the basis of knowledge and evidence, that moral or political synthesis can be accom-

plished only by honest acknowledgment of what is being synthesized.

Thus the neo-conservatives are not so much against the way history is taught and written, as they are against the complex realities of American history itself. Their desire to elevate a few heroes from the past above their contemporaries, to suppress difference and disagreement, to accept uncritically the past and present as "givens" independent of human agency, rejects the complicated and plural history that has actually happened in favor of a mythical construct invented to impose cultural unity and obedience to the present government. Even worse, they profess to "save" historical inquiry by returning it to an uncritical glorification of the past and present, to an institutionalized cheerleading for the victors of the past, no matter how villainous or immoral they may have been. They laud history while fearing historical inquiry, because that inquiry might lead to critical reappropriation of the past by aggrieved groups. One might call this history a kind of ancestor worship, but its bias toward a certain kind of experience—white male upper-class experience— means that most of us are being called upon to worship not our own, but someone else's ancestors. We are being asked to imagine the past as a succession of military, political, and economic struggles beginning in antiquity and culminating in the "progress" manifested by the nation state in our own day. But at the same time we are being ordered to forget the hurts of history, the complicated struggles and deadly rivalries out of which real history is made.

Although their standards of evidence and argument tend to undercut their claims, neo-conservative critics often profess to ground their views on history within the traditions of the European "Enlightenment." This "project of man," beginning in the Renaissance, combined diverse developments in art and in the natural and human "sciences." Through a variety of intellectual devices ranging from the scientific method to perspectival painting to historical narrative, the Enlightenment created a subjectivity or point of view that has become synonymous to its adherents with the human subject. Thus the scientific advancements and artistic expressions of Europe are considered the best that humanity has ever achieved, and the story of the world told from the European point of view is presented as total world history.

All contemporary scholars and every reader of these pages has benefited from the Enlightenment in an extraordinary number of ways, but it is also apparent that this tradition has done a lot of harm. The instrumental view of nature behind the natural and physical sciences has led to exploitation of the environment and to an instrumentality inevitably directed against other human beings. The bourgeois perspective in painting constituted European males as the viewers and relegated females and non-Western people to the status of objects for viewing. Every day this power of the bourgeois "look," with its capacity for racial differentiation and sexual objectification, serves to humiliate and oppress human beings who suffer from the ideals of body image and the metaphors for activity and passivity (male vs. female) encoded within European visual traditions. The idea of history as synonymous with European "progress" has elevated a minute part of global experience to the center stage of history, while lumping all the rest into a kind of contextless "other," worthy of mention only when it impinges on the European consciousness. The popular and academic attack on history in recent years, especially by the very "structuralists" and "deconstructionists" that Finn and Ravitch wish to silence, has largely focused on the shortcomings of the Enlightenment and its legacy. It is to these perspectives that we now turn in our search for a precious and communicable past.

Textual Criticism and Historical Thinking

Post-structuralist and deconstructionist critiques of history revolve around the textual nature of historical narratives. Enlightenment standards of "objectivity" compelled traditional historians to remove their own voice from the text, to present evidence as if the facts "spoke for themselves." But instead of eliminating subjectivity, this method only disguised it. It tended to favor the written word over all other forms of human expression. It privileged the experiences of those with the power and position to leave behind documentary evidence about themselves, and it silenced those without access to the printed word. Post-structuralist and deconstructionist critics recognize that the "crisis of representation" stems from the "inevitability of representation," from the ways in which all facts are also interpretations singled out for notice because of some subjective judgment. They elect to analyze all texts, including historical narratives, to expose the hidden ideological biases built into any mode of representation.

Hayden White began leveling particularly effective critiques of history in the 1960s and 1970s. White wonders "why so much of modern fiction turns on the attempt to liberate Western man from the tyranny of the historical consciousness."[17] He concludes that writers understand history as just another text, one presuming to stand for collective world experience, but which in reality fabricates a chronological and teleological frame upon an infinitely plural and decidedly non-teleological reality. White echoes Nietzsche in his view that history prevents rather than permits informed action because it makes people feel "that they were latecomers to a world in which everything worth doing had already been done."[18]

Jacques Derrida's explorations into the inevitability of representation in language and the ways in which centralized perspectives silence difference provide linguistic reinforcement for textually oriented criticisms like White's. Derrida sees destructive binary oppositions as the core of the historical method, which in his view always counterposes continuity to rupture, the universal to the specific, without seeing ways in which they might overlap. In place of the traditional historical notions of time as chronological and teleological, Derrida offers temporality as "repetition with change." In this way, events do not just happen, but they are articulated and rearticulated in ways that illumine rather than suppress multiple differences.[19]

Michel Foucault's path-breaking research in the late 1970s and early 1980s brought the critique of history to a new level; Foucault demonstrates the ways in which the presumption of a common human history allows centralized structures of power to extend their reach into every level of human experience. Foucault sees historical narratives as irrevocably tainted with the language of power and control. He argues,

> The history which bears and determines us has the form of a war
> rather than that of language: relations of power, not relations of
> meaning. History has no "meaning," though this is not to say that it is
> absurd or incoherent. On the contrary, it is intelligible and should be
> susceptible to analysis down to the smallest detail—but this in

accordance with the intelligibility of struggles, of strategies and tactics.[20]

White, Derrida, and Foucault have influenced some post-structuralists to reject history altogether, to see it as simply another repressive vestigial remnant of the Enlightenment.[21] But it is possible to read White, Derrida, and Foucault in a different fashion; to see in their critiques a means of passing from one historical paradigm to another. Derrida himself concedes that "if the word 'history' did not entail in itself the motif of a final repression of difference, one could say that only differences can be from the outset and thoroughly historical." Richard Terdiman outlines how this might be established in his exemplary work on nineteenth-century French literature.[22] Terdiman supports Derrida's claim that language always involves metaphorical comparisons that should not be confused with the object under description. But Terdiman points out that historical accounts do not have to presume final and fixed meanings, that they can become important mechanisms for opening up and understanding the multiple possibilities contained in any one account. "The diachronic" claims Terdiman, "is the experience of time over difference," and consequently change over time offers a fundamental model for the study of difference. Precisely because the truth about the past is created by inquiry in the present, history is not just an inert body of facts from the past constraining the present. Instead, history can be a way of opening up the present, of seeing its multiple possibilities by exploring the "roads not taken" from the past.

Hayden White's more recent work acknowledges this power of historical narratives to open up rather than to constrain possibilities. White views the work of Fredric Jameson as particularly significant in this regard, because for Jameson "every present is at once a realization of projects performed by past human agents and a determination of a field of possible projects to be realized by living human agents in their future."[23] Thus Jameson holds on to the necessity of historical narratives without imposing on them the kinds of closure condemned by Derrida and Foucault. Jameson argues that even conventional narratives (historical and otherwise) with their "strategies of containment" which eliminate all but one resolution and which make that conclusion appear inevitable and necessary can be opened for investigation of the ideological possibilities they constrain. The implications of Jameson's work for historical scholarship are neatly summarized by Dana Polan, who points out that "we don't so much write *the* meaning of the period as a history of some possible meanings: we study what was able to emerge within, and against, what seems at first glance at least, to be a dominant field of social perception."[24]

Defenders of history like Polan, Jameson, and Terdiman are not simply calling for more stories. Each believes that the past imposes constraints on the present that cannot be wished away or imagined out of existence. To them, historical truth is neither subjective nor objective; rather, it consists of a dialectical interaction between the two. Knowing subjects (themselves shaped by historical contingencies beyond their control) construct the periodizations and cause-effect relationships characteristic of historical narratives, but they do so with a commitment to come as close as possible to an inclusive and collective truth. They do not presume the disinterested objectivity that blinds traditional historians to their own ideologies, nor do they let the fact that history appears in story form convince them that history is just stories. Instead, they accept retrospective narratives as useful tools, as ways of organizing and understanding evidence about experiences with change over time.

It may be impossible to bridge fully the gap between the post-structuralists and deconstructionists on the one hand and the historically grounded literary critics on the other. Textually oriented critics distrust the idea of a total human history, while the historically oriented critics insist on it. For the textualists, history is one of many texts that order and interpret experience; for the historians history can only be comprehended as a text, but it possesses an independent identity as "necessity," "absent cause," and the cumulative collective legacy of human ideas and actions. But even if no final reconciliation between the two camps is possible, the dialogue between them has enriched our understanding of history and enabled us to explore new methods of expressing historical consciousness. It suggests ways of teaching and learning history that avoid neo-conservative myth-making, Enlightenment pseudo-objectivity, and post-structuralist resignation.

History in an Age of Popular Culture

In his acceptance speeches at the 1980 and 1984 Republican National Conventions, and in his inaugural addresses in 1981 and 1985, President Ronald Reagan frequently invoked the American past. He located the origins of the American story in 1620 when the Pilgrims landed at Plymouth Rock. He talked about how "we" came to North America from Europe, how "we" tamed the wilderness and the frontier until settlement reached California, and how "we" fought two world wars and conquered space.[25] In his second inaugural address, the President compressed American history into a series of vignettes where

> a general falls to his knees in the hard snow of Valley Forge; a lonely President paces the darkened halls and powers, [sic] ponders his struggles to preserve the union; the men of the Alamo call out encouragement to each other; a settler pushes west and sings a song, and the song echoes out forever and fills the unknowing air.[26]

The President's speeches constructed the audience as historical subjects with a common past. They were asked to begin their story in Europe in 1620 and to see westward expansion, military triumphs, and space exploration as their common heritage. In so doing, the speeches reflected the "truths" of the popularly understood history of the United States.

But there were other truths that Reagan's address omitted. It denied the memory and perspectives of those Americans who traveled to this country from Asia or Latin America. It erased the experiences of those Americans who came in chains from Africa, or whose Chicano and Native American ancestors had their land stolen from them by "westward expansion." As many histories have done, his address presented the history of the American state as if it were the history of the American people. In so doing, it neglected the plurality of personal stories that shaped the American past.

In contrast, Jesse Jackson's speech to the Democratic National Convention in 1988 constructed the audience in a different fashion. Jackson spoke of his childhood experiences, growing up poor in South Carolina. He recalled how his grandmother could not afford to buy a blanket, so she sewed together a quilt out of all the patches of leftover and discarded fabric in the house. Jackson then used the construction of that quilt as his organizing metaphor about political power. The many groups who make up the American electorate, in Jackson's view, had only piecemeal resources. But joined together on "common ground," they could survive and prosper. Just as his grandmother had pieced together a quilt from different patches, Jackson urged workers, women, blacks, Chicanos, Native Americans, Asian-Americans, homosexuals and lesbians, senior citizens, and the handicapped to piece together a coalition that could encompass them all.

Jackson's speech constructed his audience on both the margins of society and at the center. His narrative about the past neglected the history of the state and claims about "the inevitable trajectory of progress" in favor of the ingenuity and effort of his grandmother. Rather than uniting his listeners in fictive identification with a unified past that they did not share, he contended that their very historical diversity and fragmentation united them in mutual interdependence.

At first glance it may appear as if Reagan's speech drew upon history while Jackson's relied on myth. After all, the president listed specific events and facts in chronological order, while the civil-rights leader recited a private story about a person unknown outside of her own immediate family. But on closer examination, it becomes clear that both speakers mixed myth and history in ways that dramatically illustrate the contested nature of historical memory in our time. While the text of Reagan's speech dealt with historical events, his credibility with the audience did not depend upon his skill as a historian. Rather, the images he invoked of westward expansion, world war, and space exploration activated deep layers of sentiment and emotion shaped by endless narratives—dime novels, motion pictures, television programs. The nature of "heroic" action, the inevitability of conflict, and the march of progress have been portrayed in popular culture over and over again; Reagan's skill as a politician rests in no small measure with his ability to understand and tap these structures of consciousness among Americans. Similarly, Jackson's seemingly innocent family narrative scarcely rested upon the superiority of quilts to blankets or on any actual shared memory of the process of quiltmaking. Rather, it rested on the audience's understanding of history, on its identification with experiences of deprivation and adaptation, and on a perception of difference and fragmentation. Jackson's metaphor would not have seemed credible to his audience if his grandmother's perseverance in the face of suffering did not em-

body the collective historical experience of the groups he was addressing. Nor would Reagan's "historical" allusions have worked
with an audience that was not already conditioned to accept the triumphs of the state as their own.

When confronted with competing versions of reality like Reagan's
and Jackson's, we have to rely on our understanding of evidence and
our understanding of our own interests. Historical research can determine whose story is more in keeping with the facts: which does a
better job of connecting the present with the past? Political analysis
can determine whose interests are served by each story: which legit-
imates decisions likely to help or harm us as individuals or as a society? But competing narratives are not just fights about the past, they
also serve to transform cultural identity and political dialogue in the
present. Both Reagan and Jackson wish to tap collective popular
memory and imagination, to make their political stances express the
values of America. But these values are not static, not bequeathed to
us willy-nilly by the accidents of history, as E. D. Hirsch would have
us believe. Rather, they are struggled over and contested every day
on innumerable fronts and in countless arenas. What we choose to
remember about the past, where we begin and end our retrospective
accounts, and who we include and exclude from them—these do a
lot to determine how we live and what decisions we make in the
present. Political speeches and history books provide two important
sites for that contestation; the texts and practices of popular culture
encompass the battle as well.

James Brown, the great black rhythm and blues singer, has made
millions of dollars in show business, has owned airplanes, motels,
and radio stations. Yet when asked to describe his career he points to
the scars on his pock-marked and discolored knees, damaged from
repeated full impact landings during his wild stage shows. "They
made my daddy crawl," Brown relates, "crawl under cars, behind
mules. Crawl all kinds of ways. Four years ago they made me go
down on my knees—my comeback they call it to prove that I could
still do it."[27] Brown's comparing his own suffering with his father's
adds historical, class, and racial dimensions to grievances that could
just as easily be discussed without reference to history, class, or race.
Yet the connection is real. Brown's suffering and mistreatment as a
performer have everything to do with who he is, with what class he
comes from, and with his racial identity. Even though his financial

success and popular acclaim separate him from his father's particular crises, he is too self-aware to ignore the ways in which history shapes his present-day experiences and subjects him to the same kinds of demeaning power realities that his father faced.

Bruce Springsteen is younger and wealthier than James Brown, an object of adulation, and a white male hero in a symbolic order that privileges white men. But he, too, finds remnants of history shaping his stance toward the world. "I grew up in this house where there was never any books or I guess anything that was considered art," he told a concert audience one night. Continuing, he explained that he had ignored most of what his teachers were trying to teach him in school, either because of the way they were teaching it or because he just wasn't interested. But then, Springsteen told the crowd

> when I got older I looked back and I saw that my father, he quit high school and went in the Army and he got married real young and picked up jobs where he could, workin' in a factory, driving a truck. And I look back at my grandfather and he worked in a rug mill in the town that I grew up in. And it seemed like we all had one thing in common and that was that we didn't know enough, we didn't know enough about what was happening to us. Like I'm thirty-one now and I just started to read the history of the United States. And the thing about it is, I started to learn about how things got to be the way they are today, how you end up a victim without even knowing it. And how people get old and just die after not having hardly a day's satisfaction or peace of mind in their lives.[28]

Pat Benatar's 1982 music video "Shadows of the Night" offered one of the first heroic narratives about women in the notoriously sexist music video field. Benatar fashioned a story about a 1940s woman war worker who sheds her daytime "Rosie the Riveter" work clothes to be airlifted behind Nazi lines for night-time commando raids and acts of sabotage. From all the icons and images of women in popular culture, Benatar chose to periodize her story in the 1940s, a time of importance to 1980s feminists because in that decade women worked outside the home for wages with societal and government approval. Positioning herself as a woman entering a male-dominated field in the 1980s, Benatar legitimated and explained her struggle by reference to the repressed self-activity of the last great opportunity for women workers.

This is not to suggest that James Brown, Bruce Springsteen, and Pat Benatar hold the answers to the contemporary crisis of historical thinking. Certainly quotations from other entertainers might lead in opposite directions, and even Brown, Springsteen, and Benatar are not always consistent about their relationships to the past. But the desire to connect to history, the impulse to pose present problems in historical terms, and the assertion of a temporal and social reality beyond one's immediate experience pervade popular culture in significant ways. I want to argue that the ruminations on the past reflected in the films of John Sayles, in television programs like *Crime Story*, in the novels of Eudora Welty and Toni Morrison, or in the music of John Cougar Mellencamp equal or exceed the quality of historical acumen represented in most political speeches or history textbooks. If by themselves they do not hold an answer to the crisis in historical thinking, they go a long way toward showing us where answers might be found.

The crisis in historical thinking is certainly real. The dislocations of the past two centuries, the propaganda apparatuses of totalitarian powers, disillusionment with the paradigms of the Enlightenment, and popular culture itself have all served to make the search for a precious and communicable past one of the most pressing problems of our time. But simply because historical inquiry has been reframed, it does not necessarily follow that it has been diluted. It is just that historical memories and historical evidence can no longer be found solely in archives and libraries; they pervade popular culture and public discourse as well. As Eudora Welty wrote about Willa Cather's own sense of the precious and incommunicable,

> In the world of her novels, history lies in persistence in the memory, in lost hidden places that wait to be found and to be known for what they are. Such history is barely accessible, the shell of it is only fraily held together, it will be loseable again. But the continuity is *there*.[29]

Popular Television

3

The Meaning of Memory: Family, Class, and Ethnicity in Early Network Television

In 1949, one of the first episodes of the nationally televised CBS network comedy *The Goldbergs* featured a rent strike by disgruntled tenants against a landlord who refused to make repairs. The premise of a rent strike grew logically from the show's setting. Molly and Jake Goldberg, their children Rosalie and Sammy, and Molly's Uncle David all lived together in a crowded Bronx apartment building filled with working-class Jews like themselves. During every episode, neighbors and relatives passed through the Goldberg apartment. They carried on conversations by shouting through windows and yelling into dumbwaiter shafts. The Goldbergs met their friends on the streets, they shared night-school classrooms and Lewisohn Stadium concerts with the extended kinship network of their neighborhood, and problems like a leaking roof or a defective elevator immediately became group concerns.

Seven years later, *The Goldbergs* became *Molly*. The Goldberg family moved away from Tremont Avenue in the Bronx and bought a house in the Long Island suburb of "Haverville." (City of "the haves" as David Marc points out, the opposite of "Hooverville.")[1] In Haverville, neighbors did not walk through the Goldberg apartment or converse with them through windows and airshafts. The streets became a locus of danger, the threatening alternative to the centrality of the suburban home. Instead of rent strikes and collective action, comic premises in "Molly" emerged from the relative isolation and alienation of the suburban setting. Consumer purchases and fears of installment credit took center stage. Adjustments to the expectations of strangers through dieting or home decorating provided major sources of comic tension. Even though the Goldberg family seemed more autonomous in Haverville than it had been in the Bronx, it now seemed strangely in jeopardy. New products made family keepsakes and memorabilia obsolete. New patterns of social acceptance made children the tutors to their inflexible and backward-looking parents. The new standard of living and opportunity for upward mobility secured by the Goldbergs for their children only served to push the children into a different world, one that mocked the foreign accents and archaic customs of the family.

The journey from the Bronx to Haverville, from an ethnic, urban, working-class, extended family and kinship network to a detached, single-family, suburban home was a journey from the past to the present. It relied upon the language, icons, and images of the ethnic immigrant past to explain the suburban consumer present. Between 1949 and 1956 millions of American families made the same journey, and they looked to programs like *The Goldbergs* for a reflection of their own circumstances. Television not only recorded migration to the suburbs, but it provided important economic stimuli and significant ideological justifications for that move. By looking at television programs like *The Goldbergs*, we can understand something of the dimensions of that transformation in American life, and we can gain important insight into how Americans explained drastic changes to themselves and to others.

The popularity of *The Goldbergs* coincided with that of other television situation comedies between 1949 and 1957 based on ethnic working-class family life. *Mama* depicted the experiences of turn-of-the-century Norwegian immigrants to San Francisco; *Amos 'n' Andy* portrayed blacks in Harlem. *The Honeymooners* and *Hey, Jeannie* showed Irish working-class families in Brooklyn. *Life With Luigi* concerned Italian immigrants in Chicago, and *Life of Riley* presented the adventures of working-class migrants to Los Angeles during and after World War II.[2]

The presence of this subgenre of urban, ethnic, working-class situation comedies on television network schedules seems to run contrary to the commercial and artistic properties of the medium. Television delivers audiences to advertisers by glorifying consumption, not only during commercial breaks, but in the programs themselves.[3] The relative economic deprivation of ethnic working-class households would seem to provide an inappropriate setting for the display and promotion of commodities as desired by the networks and their commercial sponsors. Furthermore, the mass audience required to repay the expense of network programming encourages the depiction of a homogenized mass society, rather than the particularities and peculiarities of working-class communities. Finally, as an artistic medium, television's capacity for simultaneity conveys a sense of living in an infinitely renewable present—a quality inimical to the sense of memory permeating shows about working-class life. Yet whether set in the distant past like *Mama*, or located in the contemporaneous present, the subgenre of ethnic, working-class, situation comedies in early network television evoked concrete historical associations and memories in their audiences.[4]

Anomalous to the commercial and artistic propensities of television, these programs also ran counter to the dominant social trends in the era in which they were made. They presented ethnic families in working-class, urban neighborhoods at the precise historical moment when a rising standard of living, urban renewal, and suburbanization contributed to declines in ethnic and class identity.[5] They showed working-class families struggling for material satisfaction and advancement under conditions far removed from the *embourgeoisement* of the working class celebrated in popular literature about the postwar era. They displayed value conflicts about family identity, consumer spending, ethnicity, class, and gender roles that would appear to be disruptive and dysfunctional within a communications medium primarily devoted to stimulating commodity purchases.

The dissonance between urban, ethnic, working-class situation comedies and their artistic, commercial, and historical surroundings might be explained by the persistence of artistic clichés and the conservatism of the entertainment business. Yet while four of these seven television programs previously existed as radio serials, radio popularity did not guarantee adaptation to television: many successful radio series never made that transition, and television networks actually made more profit from productions specially created for the new medium.[6] Even when radio programs did become television shows, they underwent significant changes of plot and premise. Television versions of urban, ethnic, working-class situation comedies placed more emphasis on nuclear families and less on extended kinship and ethnic relations than did their radio predecessors.[7] These

41

changes reflect more than the differences between television and radio as media; they illuminate as well significant transformations in U.S. society during the 1950s, and they underscore the important role played by television in explaining and legitimizing those transitions to a mass audience.

More than their shared history in radio or their reliance on a collective theatrical tradition from vaudeville and ethnic theater unites the subgenre of urban, ethnic, working-class situation comedies. Through indirect but powerful demonstration, all of these shows arbitrated complex tensions caused by economic and social change in postwar America. They evoked the experiences of the past to lend legitimacy to the dominant ideology of the present. In the process, they served important social and cultural functions, not just in returning profits to investors or by attracting audiences for advertisers, but most significantly as a vehicle for ideological legitimation of a fundamental revolution in economic, social, and cultural life.

The Meaning of Memory

In the midst of extraordinary social change, television emerged as the most important discursive medium in American culture. As such, it was charged with special responsibilities for making new economic and social relations credible and legitimate to audiences haunted by ghosts from the past. Urban, ethnic, working-class comedies provided one means of addressing the anxieties and contradictions emanating from the clash between the consumer present of the 1950s and collective memory about the 1930s and 1940s.

The consumer consciousness generated by economic and social change in postwar America conflicted with the lessons of historical experience for many middle-and working-class American families. The Great Depression of the 1930s had not only damaged the economy, it had also undercut the political and cultural legitimacy of American capitalism. Herbert Hoover had been a national hero in the 1920s, with his credo of "rugged individualism" forming the basis for a widely shared cultural ideal. But the Depression discredited Hoover's philosophy and made him a symbol of yesterday's blasted hopes to millions of Americans. In the 1930s, cultural ideals based on mutuality and collectivity eclipsed the previous decade's individualism, and helped propel massive union organizing drives, anti-eviction movements, and general strikes. President Roosevelt's New Deal attempted to harness and co-opt that grass-roots mass activity in its efforts to restore social order and recapture credibility and legitimacy for the capitalist system.[8] The social welfare legislation of the "Second New Deal" in 1935 went far beyond any measures previously favored by Roosevelt and most of his advisors, but radical action proved necessary if the administration was to contain the upsurge of activism that characterized the decade. Even in the private sector, industrial corporations conceded more to workers than naked power realities necessitated because they feared the political consequences of mass disillusionment with the system.[9]

World War II ended the Depression and brought prosperity, but it did so on a basis even more collective than the New Deal of the 1930s. Government intervention in the wartime economy reached unprecedented levels, bringing material reward and shared purpose to a generation raised on the deprivation and sacrifice of the Depression. In the postwar years, the largest and most disruptive strike wave in American history won major improvements in the standard of living for the average worker, through both wage increases and government commitments to support full employment, decent housing, and expanded educational opportunities. Grass-roots militancy and working-class direct action wrested concessions from a reluctant business and government elite—mostly because the public at large viewed workers' demands as more legitimate than the desires of capital.[10]

Yet the collective nature of working-class mass activity in the postwar era posed severe problems for capital. In sympathy strikes and secondary boycotts, workers placed the interests of their class ahead of their own individual material aspirations. Strikes over safety and job control far outnumbered wage strikes, revealing aspirations to control the process of production that conflicted with the imperatives of capitalist labor-management relations. Mass demonstrations demanding government employment and housing programs indicated a collective political response to problems previously adjudicated on a personal level. Radical challenges to the authority of capital (like the United Auto Workers' 1946 demand during the General Motors strike that wage increases come out of corporate profits rather than from price hikes passed on to consumers) demonstrated a social responsibility and a commitment toward redistributing wealth rare in the history of American labor.[11]

Capital attempted to regain the initiative in the postwar years by making qualified concessions to working-class pressures for redistribution of wealth and power. Rather than paying wage increases out of corporate profits, business leaders instead worked to expand the economy through increases in government spending, foreign trade, and consumer debt. Such expansion could meet the demands of workers and consumers without undermining capital's dominant role in the economy. On the presumption that "a rising tide lifts all boats," business leaders sought to connect working-class aspirations for a better life to policies that ensured a commensurate rise in corporate profits, thereby leaving the distribution of wealth unaffected. Federal defense spending, highway construction programs, and home-loan policies expanded the economy at home in a manner conducive to the interests of capital, while the Truman Doctrine and Marshall Plan provided models for enhanced access to foreign markets and raw materials for American corporations. The Taft-Hartley Act of 1947 banned the class-conscious collective activities most threatening to capital (mass strikes, sympathy strikes, secondary boycotts): the leaders of labor, government, and business accepted as necessary the practice of paying wage hikes for organized workers out of the pockets of consumers and unorganized workers in the form of higher prices.[12]

Commercial network television played an important role in this emerging economy, functioning as a significant new object of consumer purchases as well as an important marketing medium. Sales of sets jumped from three million during the entire decade of the 1940s to over five million *a year* during the 1950s.[13] But television's most important economic function came from its role as an instrument of legitimation for transformations in values initiated by the new economic imperatives of postwar America. For Americans to accept the new world of 1950s consumerism, they had to make a break with the past. The Depression years had helped generate fears about installment buying and excessive materialism, while the New Deal and wartime mobilization had provoked suspicions about individual acquisitiveness and upward mobility. Depression era and wartime scarcities of consumer goods had led workers to internalize discipline and frugality while nurturing networks of mutual support through family, ethnic, and class associations. Government policies after the war encouraged an atomized acquisitive consumerism at odds with the lessons of the past. At the same time, federal home-loan policies stimulated migrations to the suburbs from urban, ethnic, working-class neighborhoods. The entry of television into the American home disrupted previous patterns of family life and encouraged fragmentation of the family into separate segments of the consumer market.[14] The priority of consumerism in the economy at large and on television may have seemed organic and unplanned, but conscious policy decisions by officials from both private and public sectors shaped the contours of the consumer economy and television's role within it.

Commercial Television and Economic Change

Government policies during and after World War II shaped the basic contours of home television as an advertising medium. Government-sponsored research and development during the war perfected the technology of home television while federal tax policies solidified its economic base. The government allowed corporations to deduct the costs of advertising from their taxable incomes during the war, despite the fact that rationing and defense production left business with few products to market. Consequently, manufacturers kept the names of their products before the public while lowering their tax obligations on high wartime profits. Their advertising expenditures supplied radio networks and advertising agencies with the capital reserves and business infrastructure that enabled them to dominate the television industry in the postwar era. After the war, federal antitrust action against the motion-picture studios broke up the "network" system in movies, while the FCC sanctioned the network system in television. In addition, FCC decisions to allocate stations on the narrow VHF band, to grant the networks ownership and operation rights over stations in prime markets, and to place a freeze on the licensing of new stations during the important years between 1948 and 1952 all combined to guarantee that advertising-oriented programming based on the model of radio would triumph over theater TV, educational TV, or any other form.[15] Government decisions, not market forces, established the dominance of commercial television, but these decisions reflected a view of the American economy and its needs which had become so well accepted at the top levels of business and government that it had virtually become the official state economic policy.

Fearing both renewed Depression and awakened militancy among workers, influential corporate and business leaders considered increases in consumer spending—of 30% to 50%—to be necessary to perpetuate prosperity in the postwar era.[16] Defense spending for the Cold War and the Korean conflict had complemented an aggressive trade policy to improve the state of the economy, but it appeared that the hope for an ever-expanding economy rested on increased consumer spending fueled by an expansion of credit.[17] Here, too, government policies led the way, especially with regard to stimulating credit purchases of homes and automobiles. During World War II, the marginal tax rate for most wage earners jumped from 4% to 25%, making the home ownership deduction more desirable. Federal housing-loan policies favored construction of new single-family, detached suburban houses over renovation or construction of central-city multi-family units. Debt-encumbered home ownership in accord with these policies stimulated construction of 30 million new housing units in just twenty years, bringing the percentage of home-owning Americans from below 40% in 1940 to more than 60% by 1960. Mortgage policies encouraging long-term debt and low down payments freed capital for other consumer purchases, while government highway building policies undermined mass-transit systems and contributed to increased demand for automobiles. Partly as a result of these policies, consumer spending on private cars averaged $7.5 billion per year in the 1930s and 1940s, but grew to $22 billion per year in 1950 and almost $30 billion by 1955.[18]

Business leaders understood the connection between suburban growth and increased consumer spending. A 1953 article in *Fortune* celebrated the "lush new suburban market" which "has centered its customs and conventions on the needs of children and geared its buying habits to them."[19] For the first time in U.S. history, middle-class and working-class families could routinely expect to own homes or buy new cars every few years. Between 1946 and 1965, residential mortgage debt rose three times as fast as the gross national product and disposable income. Mortgage debt accounted for just under 18% of disposable income in 1946, but it grew to almost

55% by 1965.[20] To ensure the eventual payment of current debts, the economy had to generate tremendous growth and expansion, further stimulating the need to increase consumer spending. Manufacturers had to find ways of motivating consumers to buy ever increasing amounts of commodities. Television provided an important means of accomplishing that end.

Television advertised individual products, but it also provided a relentless flow of information and persuasion that placed acts of consumption at the core of everyday life. The physical fragmentation of suburban growth and subsequent declines in motion-picture attendance created an audience more likely to stay at home and to receive entertainment there than ever before. But television also provided a forum for redefining American ethnic, class, and family identities into consumer identities. To accomplish this task effectively, television programs had to address some of the psychic, moral, and political obstacles to consumption among the public at large.

The television and advertising industries knew they had to overcome consumer resistance. Marketing expert and motivational specialist Ernest Dichter observed that "one of the basic problems of this prosperity is to give people that sanction and justification to enjoy it and to demonstrate that the hedonistic approach to life is a moral one, not an immoral one."[21] Dichter later noted the many barriers inhibiting consumer acceptance of unrestrained hedonism, and he called on advertisers "to train the average citizen to accept growth of his country and its economy as *his* growth rather than as a strange and frightening event."[22] One method of encouraging that acceptance, according to Dichter, consisted of identifying new products and styles of consumption with traditional, historically sanctioned practices and behaviors. He noted that such an approach held particular relevance in addressing consumers who had only recently acquired the means to spend freely and who might harbor a lingering conservatism about spending based on their previous experiences.[23]

Insecurities and anxieties among consumers compelled network television to address the complex legacies of the 1930s and 1940s in order to promote consumption in the 1950s. In the middle of its appeals to change the world in the present through purchase of the appropriate commodities, commercial network television in its early years also presented programs rooted in the historical experiences and aspirations of diverse working-class traditions. From the evocations of the Depression era that permeated the world of *The Honey mooners*, to the recycled minstrel show stereotypes of *Amos 'n' Andy*, from the textured layers of immigrant experience underpinning the drama and charm of *The Goldbergs* and *Mama*, to the reenactment of immigrant histories in contemporaneous circumstances in *Life of Riley, Life With Luigi*, and *Hey, Jeannie*, the medium of the infinitely renewable present turned to past traditions and practices in order to explain and legitimate fundamentally new social relations in the present.

Family Formation and the Economy — The Television View

Advertisers incorporated their messages into urban, ethnic, working-class comedies through direct and indirect means. Tensions developed in the programs often found indirect resolutions in commercials. Thus Jeannie MacClennan's search for an American sweetheart in one episode of *Hey Jeannie* set up commercials proclaiming the virtues of Drene shampoo for keeping one prepared to accept last-minute dates and of Crest toothpaste for producing an attractive smile.[24] Conversations about shopping for new furniture in an episode of *The Goldbergs* directed viewers' attention to furnishings in the Goldberg home provided for the show by Macy's department store in exchange for a commercial acknowledgment.[25]

The content of the shows themselves offered even more direct emphasis on consumer spending. In one episode of *The Goldbergs*, Molly expresses disapproval of her future daughter-in-law's plan to buy a washing machine on the installment plan. "I know Papa and me never bought anything unless we had the money to pay for it," she intones with logic familiar to a generation with memories of the Great Depression. Her son, Sammy, confronts this "deviance" by saying "Listen, Ma, almost everybody in this country lives above their means — and everybody enjoys it." Doubtful at first, Molly eventually learns from her children and announces her conversion to the legitimacy of installment buying, proposing that the family buy two cars in order to "live above our means — the American way."[26] In a subsequent episode, Molly's daughter, Rosalie, assumes the role of ideological tutor to her mother. When planning a move out of their Bronx apartment to a new house in the suburbs, Molly ruminates about where to place her old furniture in her new home. "You don't mean we're going to take all this junk with us into a brand new house?" asks an exasperated Rosalie. With traditionalist sentiment Molly answers, "Junk? My furniture's junk? My furniture that I lived with and loved for twenty years is junk?" But by the end of the episode she accepts Rosalie's argument—even selling off all her old furniture to help meet the down payment on the new house and deciding to buy all new furniture on the installment plan.[27]

Chester A. Riley confronts similar choices about family and commodities in *The Life of Riley*. His wife complains that he only takes her out to the neighborhood bowling alley and restaurant, not to "interesting places." Riley searches for ways to impress her and discovers from a friend that a waiter at the fancy Club Morambo will let them eat first and pay later, for a cost of a dollar per week plus 10% interest. "Ain't that dishonest?" asks Riley. "No, it's usury," his friend replies. Riley does not borrow the money, but he impresses his wife anyway by taking the family out to dinner on the proceeds of a prize that he receives for being the one thousandth customer in a local flower shop. Though we eventually learn that Peg Riley only wanted attention and not an expensive meal, the happy ending of the episode hinges on Riley's restored prestige once he demonstrates his ability to provide a luxury outing for the family.[28]

The same episode of *The Life of Riley* reveals another consumerist element common to this subgenre. When Riley protests that he lacks the money needed to fulfill Peg's desires, she answers that he would have plenty of cash if he didn't spend so much on "needless gadgets." His shortage of funds becomes personal failure caused by incompetent behavior as a consumer. Nowhere do we hear about the size of his paycheck, relations between his union and his employer, or, for that matter, of the relationship between the value of his labor and the wages paid to him by the Stevenson Aircraft Company. Like Uncle David in *The Goldbergs* (who buys a statue of Hamlet shaking hands with Shakespeare and an elk's tooth with the Gettysburg address carved on it), Riley's comic character stems in part from a flaw which might be more justly applied to the entire consumer economy: a preoccupation with "needless gadgets." By contrast, Peg Riley's desire for an evening out is portrayed as reasonable and modest, as reparations due her for the inevitable tedium of housework. The solution to her unhappiness comes from an evening out, rather

49

than from a change in her work circumstance. Even within the home, television elevates consumption over production: production is assumed to be a constant, only consumption can be varied. But more than enjoyment is at stake. Unless Riley can provide Peg with the desired night on the town, he will fail in his obligations as a husband and father.[29]

A similar theme provides the crisis in an episode of *Mama*. The youngest daughter, Dagmar, "innocently" expresses envy of a friend whose father received a promotion and consequently put up new wallpaper in his house. "Why doesn't Papa get promoted?" Dagmar chirps, "Everyone else does." When Mama explains that a carpenter makes less money than other fathers, Dagmar asks if it wouldn't be smarter for Papa to work in a bank. Overhearing this dialogue, Papa decides to accept his boss's offer to promote him to foreman, even though he knows it will ruin his friendship with the other workers. The logic of the episode instructs us that fathers will lose their standing if they disappoint their children's desires for new commodities.[30] Shows exploring tensions between family obligations and commodity purchases routinely assert that money cannot *buy* love, but they seem less clear about whether one can *trade* material wealth for affection. Even the usually self-absorbed Kingfish on *Amos 'n' Andy* gives in to his nephew Stanley's wish for "a birthday party with lots of expensive presents," while Jeannie MacClennan's search for romance suffers a setback when a prospective suitor sees her shabby apartment with its antiquated furniture.[31] On *The Goldbergs*, a young woman is forbidden to marry the man she loves by her mother because her mother says "I didn't raise my daughter to be a butcher's wife."[32] Alice Kramden in *The Honeymooners* can always gain the upper hand in arguments with her husband by pointing to his inadequacies as a provider. In each of these programs, consumer choices close the ruptures in personal relations, allowing episodes to reach narrative and ideological closure.

One episode of *Mama* typifies the confusion between consumer purchases and family happiness pervading urban, ethnic, working-class situation comedies in early network television. "Mama's Birthday," broadcast in 1954, delineated the tensions between family loyalty and consumer desire endemic to modern capitalist society. The show begins with Mama teaching Katrin to make Norwegian meatballs, which she used long ago to "catch" Papa. Unimpressed by that accomplishment, Katrin changes the subject and asks Mama what she wants for her birthday. In an answer that locates Mama within the gender roles of the 1950s, she replies, "Well, I think a fine new job for your Papa. You and Dagmar to marry nice young men and have a lot of wonderful children—just like I have. And Nels, well, Nels to become president of the United States."[33] In one sentence Mama sums up the dominant culture's version of legitimate female expectations: success at work for her husband, marriage and childrearing for her daughters, the presidency for her son—and nothing for herself.

But we learn that Mama does have some needs, although we do not hear it from her lips. Her sister, Jenny, asks Mama to attend a fashion show, but Mama cannot leave the house because she has to cook a roast for a guest whom Papa has invited to dinner. Jenny comments that Mama never seems to get out of the kitchen, adding that "it's a shame that a married woman can't have some time to herself." The complaint is a valid one, and we can imagine how it might have resonated for women in the 1950s. The increased availability of household appliances and the use of synthetic fibers and commercially processed food should have decreased the amount of time women spent in housework, but surveys showed that homemakers spent the same number of hours per week (between 51 and 56) doing housework as had been the norm in the 1920s. Advertising and marketing strategies undermined the labor-saving potential of technological changes because they upgraded standards of cleanliness in the home and expanded desires for more varied wardrobes and menus for the average family.[34] In that context, Aunt Jenny would have been justified in launching into a tirade about the division of labor within the Hansen household or about the possibilities for cooperative housework, but network television specializes in less social and more commodified dialogues about problems like housework. Aunt Jenny suggests that her sister's family buy Mama a "fireless cooker," a cast-iron stove, for her birthday. "They're wonderful," she tells them in language borrowed from the rhetoric of advertising. "You just put your dinner inside them, close 'em up, and go wherever you please. When you come back your dinner is all cooked." Papa protests that Mama likes to cook on her woodburning stove, but Jenny dismisses that objection with an insinuation about his motives when she replies,

"Well I suppose it *would* cost a little more than you could afford Hansen."[35]

By identifying a commodity as the solution to Mama's problem, Aunt Jenny unites the inner voice of Mama with the outer voice of the television sponsor. Mama's utility as an icon of material selflessness would be compromised if she asked for the stove herself, but Aunt Jenny's role in suggesting the gift removes any taint of selfishness while adding the authority of an outside expert. Aunt Jenny's accusation of stinginess when Papa expresses reluctance to buy the stove encourages the audience to resent him for not making enough money and even to see his poverty as a form of selfishness—it denies his wife the comforts due her. In reality, we know that Aunt Jenny's advice probably contains the usual distortions of advertising claims, that even if the fireless cooker enabled Mama to go where she pleased while dinner cooked, it would bring with it a hidden set of tasks and demands like keeping the stove clean or having to prepare a wider variety of meals. But in the fantasy world of television, such considerations do not intervene. Prodded by their aunt, the Hansen children go shopping and purchase the fireless cooker from a storekeeper who calls the product "the new Emancipation Proclamation—setting housewives free from their old kitchen range."[36] Our exposure to advertising hyperbole should not lead us to miss the analogy here: housework is compared to slavery and the commercial product takes on the aura of Abraham Lincoln. The shopkeeper's appeal convinces the children to pool their resources and buy the stove for Mama. But we soon learn that Papa plans to make a fireless cooker for Mama with his tools. When Mama discovers Papa's intentions, she persuades the children to buy her another gift. Even Papa admits that his stove will not be as efficient as one made in a factory, but Mama nobly affirms that she will like his better because he made it himself. The children use their money to buy dishes for Mama (a gift hardly likely to leave her with less work), and Katrin remembers the episode as Mama's happiest birthday ever.

The stated resolution of "Mama's Birthday" favors traditional values. Mama prefers to protect Papa's pride instead of having a better stove. The product built by a family member has more value than the one sold as a commodity. Yet as was so often the case in these urban, ethnic, working-class comedies, the entire development of the plot leads in the opposite direction. The "fireless cooker" is the star of the episode, setting in motion all the other characters, and it has an un-questioned value, even in the face of Jenny's meddlesome brashness, Papa's insensitivity, and Mama's old-fashioned ideals. Buying a product appears as the true means of changing the unpleasant realities and low status of women's work in the home.

This resolution of the conflict between consumer desires and family roles reflected television's social role as mediator between the family and the economy. Surveys of set ownership showed no pronounced stratification by class, but a clear correlation between family size and television purchases. Households with three to five people were most likely to own television sets, while those with only one person were least likely to own them.[37] The television industry recognized and promoted its privileged place within families in advertisements like the one in *The New York Times* in 1950 that claimed, "Youngsters today need television for their morale as much as they need fresh air and sunshine for their health."[38] Like previous communications media, television sets occupied honored places in family living rooms and helped structure family time; but unlike other previous communications media, television displayed available commodities in a way that transformed home entertainment into a glorified shopping catalog.

Publicity about television programs stressed the interconnections between family and economy as well. Viewers took the portrayals of motherhood on these shows so seriously that when Peggy Wood of *Mama* appeared on the *Garry Moore Show* and invited questions from the audience, women asked her for advice about raising their families as if she were actually Mama, rather than an actress playing that role.[39] *The Ladies Home Journal* printed an article containing "Mama's Recipes," featuring photographs of Peggy Wood, while Gertrude Berg wrote an article as Molly Goldberg for *TV Guide* that contained her recipes for borscht and blintzes. "Your meal should suit the mood of your husband," Berg explained. "If he's nervous give him a heavy meal. If he's happy, a salad will do."[40] Actors on the shows also ignored the contradictions between their on-stage and off-stage roles. Marjorie Reynolds told *TV Guide* that she enjoyed playing Mrs. Chester A. Riley because, "I've done just about everything in films from westerns to no-voice musicals, and now with the Riley show, I'm back in the kitchen. Where every wife belongs."[41]

The focus on the family in early network-television situation comedies involved a special emphasis on motherhood. Images of long-suffering but loving mothers pervaded these programs and publicity about them. Ostensibly representations of "tradition," these images actually spoke to a radical rupture with the past: the establishment of the isolated nuclear family of the 1950s with its attendant changes in family gender roles. The wartime economic mobilization that ended the Depression stimulated an extraordinary period of family formation that was in sharp contrast to the experience of preceding decades. Americans married more frequently, formed families at younger ages, and had more children in the 1940s than they had had in the 1920s and 1930s.[42] The combination of recommendations for permissive childrearing and social changes attendant to increases in consumer spending isolated mothers as never before. Work previously shared with extended kinship and neighborhood networks now had to be done at home in isolation by machines. Childrearing took up more time and responsibility, but inflation and expanded consumer desires encouraged women to work outside the home for pay. When the conflicting demands of permissivism created guilt and feelings of inadequacy, outside authorities—from child psychologists to television programs—stood ready to provide "therapeutic" images of desired maternal behavior.

While placing special burdens on women, changes in family identity in the postwar era transformed the roles of all family members. As psychoanalyst Joel Kovel demonstrates, the decomposition of extended kinship networks made the nuclear family the center of the personal world, "a location of desire and intimacy not previously conceptualized."[43] Kovel argues that contemporary society encourages a kind of "needy narcissism" in individuals, structuring them as ideal consumers. In his view, participation in civil society can keep individuals from sliding back into total narcissism, but the separation of family from society in modern capitalism blocks access to the public realm. The family becomes the locus of all social demands, an institution lauded all the more in theory as its traditional social functions disappear in practice. The family appears to be private and voluntary, yet its isolation from neighborhood and class networks leaves it subject to extraordinary regulation and manipulation by outside authorities like psychologists and advertisers. The family appears to be the repository of mutuality and affection, but commodity

society has truncated its traditional functions into the egoism of possession. The family appears to maintain the privileges and authority
of patriarchy, but "like a house nibbled by termites," the outwardly
strong appearance of patriarchy masks a collapsing infrastructure no
longer capable of wielding authority in an increasingly administered
and institutionalized society. According to Kovel, the demise of the
traditional family creates a need for authority that becomes filled by
the "administrative mode"—the structure of domination that offers
commodities as the key to solving personal problems.[44] Sociologist
Nancy Chodorow draws a similar conclusion in her observation that
"the decline of the oedipal father creates an orientation to external
authority and behavioral obedience."[45] Chodorow also points out
that the idealization of masculinity inherent in the "distant father"
role in the nuclear family gives ideological priority to men, while
channeling resentment and rebellion against the power wielded by
the accessible and proximate mother. Kovel and Chodorow both
stress that these patterns are neither natural nor inevitable: they
emerge in concrete social circumstances where the nuclear family
serves as the main base of support for consumer society.[46]

Commercial network television emerged as the primary discursive
medium in American society at the precise historical moment when
the isolated nuclear family and its concerns eclipsed previous ethnic,
class, and political forces as the crucible of personal identity. Television programs both reflected and shaped that transition, defining the
good life in family-centric, asocial, and commodity-oriented ways. As
Todd Gitlin argues, "What is hegemonic in consumer capitalist ideology is precisely the notion that happiness, or liberty, or equality, or
fraternity can be affirmed through existing private commodity forms,
under the benign protective eye of the national security state."[47] Yet
the denigration of public issues and the resulting overemphasis on
the home contained contradictions of their own. If the harmonious
and mutually supportive family of the past granted moral legitimacy
to the consumer dilemmas of urban, ethnic, working-class families,
the tensions of the modern nuclear household revealed the emerging nuclear family to be a contested terrain of competing needs and
desires.

The structural tensions inherent in the "father-absent/mother-
present" family identified by Chodorow pervaded television portrayals of urban, ethnic, working-class life in the 1950s. Peg Riley, Alice

Kramden, and Sapphire Stevens heroically endure their husbands' failures to deliver on promises of upward mobility, and they earn the sympathy of the audience by smoothing over the consequences of the inefficiency of their spouses. Yet their nagging insistence on practicality also marks them as "shrews," out to undercut male authority. Male insensitivity to female needs forms the focal point of humor and sardonic commentary in these programs, as in the episode of *The Life of Riley* where Riley can't understand Peg's complaints about staying home all the time. "I can't figure her out," he tells his son. "She's got a home to clean, meals to cook, dishes to wash, you two kids to look after, floors to scrub—what more does she want?"[48] Few shows displayed hostility between husbands and wives as openly as *The Honeymooners*. (Even the title functioned as bitter irony.) When Alice employs sarcasm in response to Ralph's "get rich quick" schemes and his neglect of her needs, Ralph invariably clenches his fist and says, "One of these days, Alice, one of these days, pow! right in the kisser!" Coupled with his threats to send her "to the moon," the intimation of wife-beating remains a recurring "comic" premise in the show. Jackie Gleason told one interviewer that he thought many husbands felt the way Ralph did about their wives. And an article in *TV Guide* quoted an unnamed "famous" psychiatrist who contended that the program's popularity rested on male perceptions that women had too much power, and on female perceptions that male immaturity demonstrated the superiority of women."[49] *The Honeymooners* might end with a humbled Ralph telling Alice, "Baby, you're the greatest," but the show clearly "worked" because tensions between men and women spoke to the experiences and fears of the audience.

Structural tensions within families, women betrayed by irresponsible and incompetent husbands, and men chafing under the domination of their wives: hardly an ideal portrait of family life. These depictions reflected the fissures in a fundamentally new form of family, a form which increasingly dominated the world of television viewers. One might expect commercial television programs to ignore the problems of the nuclear family, to present an idyllic view of the commodity-centered life. But the industry's imperial ambition—the desire to have all households watching at all times—encouraged exploitation of real fears and problems confronting viewers. Censorship eliminated many possible topics, but family tensions and resentments offered legitimate and fertile ground for television programs. Individuals cut off from previous forms of self-definition and assaulted by media images encouraging narcissistic anxieties had insatiable needs to survey the terrain of family problems, to seek relief from current tensions and reassurance about the legitimacy of current social relations.

In order to create subjects receptive to the appeals of advertisers and to achieve ideological and narrative closure for their own stories, the creators of television programs had to touch on real issues, albeit in truncated and idealized forms. While they unfailingly offered only individual solutions to problems, the mere act of exposing the contradictions of the nuclear family created the structural potential for oppositional readings by viewers. Representations of generational and gender tensions undercut the legitimating authority of the televised traditional working-class family by demonstrating the chasm between the memories of yesterday and the realities of today. If the programs remained true to the past, they lost their relevance to current tensions. Yet when they successfully addressed contemporary problems, they forfeited the legitimacy offered by the past, making it easier for viewers to escape the pull of parochialism and parental authority embedded in the traditional family form. This clash between the legitimizing promise of urban, ethnic, working-class shows and their propensity for exposing the shortcomings of both past and present social relations extended beyond family issues and affected portrayals of work, class, and ethnicity as well.

Work, Class, and Ethnicity

Changes in the nature of working-class identity accompanied the changing roles of family and consumer in the 1950s. The decade of the 1940s had not only witnessed an unprecedented transformation in the nature of the American family, but it also encompassed an extraordinary social upheaval among workers, which labor historian Stanley Aronowitz has characterized as a period of "incipient class formation."[50] War mobilization reindustrialized the sagging U.S. economy and it reconstituted the working class. Migrations to defense production centers and breakthroughs by women and blacks in securing industrial employment changed the composition of the work force. Traditional parochial loyalties waned as mass production and full employment created new work groups on the shop floor and new working-class communities outside the factory gates. Mass strikes and demonstrations united workers from diverse backgrounds into a polity capable of sustained collective action. Of course, racism and sexism remained pervasive on both institutional and grass-roots levels, but the mass activity of the postwar era represented the stirrings of a class consciousness previously unknown in a proletariat deeply divided by ethnicity, race, and gender. By the 1950s, expanded consumer opportunities, suburbanization, and access to education offered positive inducements away from that class consciousness, while anti-Communism, purges of dissidents, and restrictions on rank-and-file activism acted negatively to undermine trade unions as crucibles of class consciousness. Yet retentions of the incipient class formation of the 1940s percolated throughout the urban, ethnic, working-class situation comedies of the 1950s.

Jeannie Carson, the star of *Hey, Jeannie*, began her career as a performer by singing to Welsh miners as they came out of the pits. Appropriately enough, her U.S. television series adopted a working-class locale — the home of Al Murray, a Brooklyn cab driver, and his sister, Liz.[51] The setting imposed certain structural directions on the program's humor, directions that gave voice to sharp class resentments. One episode contains Al Murray's efforts to hide his cab in a neighbor's garage so that he can take the day off from work to watch his beloved Dodgers play baseball at Ebbetts Field. Sensing Murray's dereliction of duty, the cab company president delivers a self-righteous harangue about the evils of such behavior to his secretary. Pontificating about the social responsibilities of a taxi-cab company, a "public utility," he asks his secretary if she knows what happens when one of his cabs is not operating. "No, what?" she inquires. "It cuts into my profits," he responds.[52] Humor based on such hypocrisy by employers has a long history in working-class culture, but it is rarely the subject of mass-media comedy. As the episode continues, the boss's secretary (in an act of solidarity) calls Liz and Jeannie to warn them that the boss is out on the streets looking for Al's cab. Jeannie takes the taxi out of the garage to prevent Al's boss from finding it there, but accustomed to driving in her native Scotland, she drives on the left side of the street and gets stopped by a police officer. The policeman discovers that she is an immigrant and remembering his own days as an immigrant from Ireland, lets her off with a warning. The resolution of the episode finds Jeannie getting to the ballpark in time to get Al back to the cab where his boss finds him and apologizes for even suspecting his employee of misconduct. The episode resonates with class consciousness, from the many acts of solidarity that get Al off the hook to the final victory over the boss—a victory gained by turning work time into play time and getting away with it. That kind of collective activity in pursuit of common goals appears frequently in the urban, ethnic, working-class situation comedies of the 1950s, in incidents ranging from the rent strike by tenants in *The Goldbergs* to community protests against a utility company's destruction of a favorite neighborhood tree in *Life With Luigi*.[53]

The workplace rarely appears in television comedies about working-class life; when it does, it usually signals seething class resentments. On one episode of *Mama*, Lars Hansen tells another worker that he prefers working for Mr. Jenkins to working for Mr. Kingsley because "Mr. Jenkins doesn't lose his temper so much." Mr. Kingsley also demands work speed-ups from his employees and he tries to pressure Papa into making the other workers produce at a faster pace.[54] In this episode, the workplace is a site where workers with common interests experience fragmentation. In *The Goldbergs*, even after Jake Goldberg graduates from his job as a tailor to become owner of a small dressmaking firm, work prevents him from enjoying life. Business pressures take him away from his family and prevent him from developing any recreational interests. When Molly's Uncle David starts playing pool, Jake confides that he never learned to play because "pool is a game that requires leisure." However, his business sense causes him to lean over the table, touch it, and murmur with admiration, "nice quality felt, though."[55] Jake's work brings in a bigger financial reward than Al Murray's cab driving or Lars Hansen's carpentry, but it still compels him to trade the precious minutes and hours of his life for commodities that he hardly has time to enjoy. Work as a noble end in itself is almost entirely absent from these shows. No work ethic or pride in labor motivates these workers. In fact, Ed Norton's pride in his job as a sewer worker provides a recurrent comic premise in *The Honeymooners*. The object of work in these programs consists of material reward to enhance one's standing within the family or to obtain some leisure-time commodity.

Not only does work appear infrequently in 1950s comedies about working-class life, but blue-collar labor often appears as a stigma, a condition that retards the acquisition of desired goods. The Kramdens' barren apartment in *The Honeymooners* underscores their barrenness as a childless couple; Ralph's circular bus route symbolizes the dead-end nature of his job and of his life which is going nowhere.[56] But even demeaning portrayals of working-class people sometimes contain contradictions, allowing for negotiated or oppositional readings. Advertisers and network officials lauded Chester A. Riley's "magnificent stupidity" as the key to the big ratings garnered by *The Life of Riley*. But that "stupidity" sometimes masked other sensibilities. At a fancy dinner where the Rileys are clearly out of place, they meet a blue-blood named Cecil Spencer Kendrick III. "You mean there's two more of you inside?" Riley asks. The audience laughter at his gaffe comes in part from resentment against the anti-democratic pretensions of Kendrick and his associates.[57] Similarly, when Riley's neighbor Jim Gillis tries to impress him with tales about the fancy food at an expensive restaurant, Riley gets Gillis to admit that crepes suzette are nothing more than "pancakes soaked in kerosene and then set on fire."[58] That capacity for unintentional insight also propels the malaprop-laden humor of Molly Goldberg. Who could dispute her self-sacrificing virtue when Molly vows to save money by purchasing old furniture: "I don't care how old, even antique furniture would be fine." She complains that her cousin has been gone for two weeks and that she hasn't seen "hide nor seek of him," and she warns her uncle that she will give him only one word of advice, and that word is "be sure." When Molly says that "patience is a vulture," or that "it never rains until it pours," her misstatements carry unexpected wisdom.[59]

Resentments about work, refusals to acknowledge the legitimacy of the upper classes, and creative word play abound in these programs, transmitting the texture of decades of working-class experience. Similarly, fraternal orders and ethnic lodges appear in television shows of the 1950s as a reflection of real historical experience. Historically, fraternal orders and mutual-aid societies offered essential resources to working-class people, often providing insurance, burial expenses, recreational facilities, and adult education at a time when neither the private sector nor the state accepted any of those responsibilities. Yet, in the urban, ethnic, working-class situation comedies of the early 1950s, the fraternal lodge appears as an archaic and anachronistic institution, a remnant of the past at odds with the needs of the contemporary family. Thus Lars Hansen's dinner guests from the Sons of Norway only produce more work for Mama.[60] Chester A. Riley wastes his time and money on the Brooklyn Patriots of Los Angeles, an organization set up to revere the world he left behind when he moved to the west coast. The Mystic Knights of the Sea provide Kingfish with a theater of operations for bilking his "brothers" out of their money, and for indulging his inflated sense of self-importance. The Royal Order of Raccoons keeps Ralph Kramden from spending time with Alice, and lodge dues eat away at his paycheck at the expense of his household. In one show Alice asks Ralph what benefit she derives from his lodge activities. With much bombast he informs her proudly that his membership entitles both of them to free burial in the Raccoon National Cemetery in Bismarck, North Dakota. With appropriate sarcasm, Alice replies that the prospect of burial in North Dakota makes her wonder why she should go on living.[61]

In organic popular memory, lodges may have retained legitimacy as sources of mutuality and friendship, but they represented an ideological threat to the consumer-and family-centered world of early network television. In an age when suburban tract housing replaced the urban ethnic neighborhood, when the state took on welfare functions previously carried out by voluntary associations, and when the home sphere became increasingly isolated from the community around it, the lodge hall became a premise for comic ridicule. The interests of television families took precedence over those of the lodge hall, and a binary opposition between the two seemed inevitable. Yet the very inclusion of the lodges in these programs demonstrates the power of the past in discourse about the present. Television programs validated the atomized nuclear family at the expense of the extended kin and class networks manifested in the fraternal order. When successful, these shows undercut the ability of the past to provide legitimacy for contemporary social relations. When unsuccessful, these shows called attention to the possibilities of other forms of community and culture than those that dominated the present.

Cultural specificity about working-class life provided credibility for early network television programs, but at the same time created problems for advertisers. Erik Barnouw points out that sponsors hardly relished the prospect of shows situated in lower-class environments (like the enormously successful teleplay *Marty*), because "Sponsors were meanwhile trying to 'upgrade' the consumer and persuade him to 'move up to a Chrysler,' and 'live better electrically' in a suburban home, with 'help from a friend at Chase Manhattan.' The sponsors preferred beautiful people in mouth-watering decor to convey what it meant to climb the socioeconomic ladder. The commercials looked out of place in Bronx settings."[62]

The working class depicted in urban, ethnic, working-class situation comedies of the 1950s bore only a superficial resemblance to the historical American working class. Stripped of essential icons of ethnicity and class, interpreted through perspectives most relevant to a consuming middle class, and pictured in isolation from the social connections that gave purpose and meaning to working-class lives, the televised blue-collar family summoned up only the vaguest contours of its historical counterpart. Even in comparison to depictions of class in other forms of communication like folklore, theater, music, literature, or radio, television presented a desiccated and eviscerated version of working-class life. Yet the legitimizing functions served by locating programs in working-class environments caused some attempts at authenticity that brought sedimented class tensions to the surface. While the producers of these shows hardly intended to direct viewers' attentions toward real ethnic and class conflicts, the social location of the writers and actors most knowledgeable about working-class life served to make some of these programs focal points for controversy. When producers took on the task of replicating working-class settings as a form of local color, they also burdened themselves with the contradictions of the communities that provided the color, as evidenced by the public controversies provoked by *The Goldbergs* and *Amos 'n' Andy*.

Part of the convincing authenticity of *The Goldbergs* came from actors and writers who developed their skills within the Yiddish theater and the culture that supported it. An organic part of that culture included political activists, among them Communists, socialists, and antifascists whose concerns found expression in a variety of community activities including the theater. Philip Loeb, who played Jake Goldberg, became the center of controversy when a right-wing anti-Communist publication accused him of subversive connections because of his appearances at antifascist rallies and his having signed a petition calling for the admission of Negroes into professional baseball. Afraid of threatened boycotts by anti-Communist groups, nervous sponsors and advertising representatives dropped their support of *The Goldbergs* and demanded that Gertrude Berg use her position as producer and star to fire Loeb. At first she refused, pointing out that Loeb had never been a Communist, but ultimately Berg gave in to the pressure and fired her co-star in order to keep her show on the air. Sponsors resumed their support after Loeb left the program in 1952, and *The Goldbergs* ran for four more years. Loeb received a $45,000 settlement in exchange for a promise not to sue the show for firing him, but he never worked again as an actor because producers viewed him as controversial. In 1956, Loeb committed suicide.[63]

Similarly, Mady Christians played Mama in the Broadway play *I Remember Mama*, but could not get the role on television. Anti-Communist pressure groups harassed Christians because she had worked on behalf of refugees from fascism in the 1930s and 1940s along with individuals accused of subversive associations. Blacklisted from her profession, Christians sank into a severe depression that friends felt sapped her strength and made her unable to overcome health problems that led to her death in 1951. Loeb and Christians dismayed advertisers, not because of their political views, but because their presence provoked political controversy and interfered with the illusions of a world without politics created by their programs. Like the real-life Goldbergs and Hansens of America, Philip Loeb and Mady Christians lived in a world made up of more than consumer purchases, a world where ethnicity connected people to important political issues. The controversy over their histories and the public attention directed toward them threatened to unmask the world of *Mama* and *The Goldbergs* as a created artifact, polarizing the audience and depriving television of its legitimating power.

Amos 'n' Andy contained similar, but more culturally explosive, connections. Stereotyped and demeaning portrayals of Afro-Americans have long constituted an obsessive theme in American theater (and, for that matter, in American life). Historian Nathan Irvin Huggins points out that the minstrel-show stereotypes enabled white society at the turn of the twentieth century to attribute to black people the very characteristics it feared most in itself. At a time when industrialization demanded a revolutionary transformation in behavfor, compelling Americans to accept Victorian values of thrift, sobriety, discipline, and abstinence, the minstrel show emerged to identify greed, gluttony, laziness, and licentiousness as singular traits of black people. These images worked to legitimate the emerging Victorian code by associating opposition to dominant ideology with the despised and taboo culture of Afro-Americans. The minstrel show "Negro" presented white society with a representation of the natural self at odds with the normative self of industrial culture. Uninhibited behavior could be savored by the id during the minstrel performance, but overruled afterward by the superego. The viewer could release tension by pointing to the minstrel show "darkie" and saying "It's him, not me." But the viewer came back, again and again. The desire to subjugate and degrade black people had political and economic imperatives of its own, but emotional and psychic reinforcement for that exploitation came from the ways in which racist stereotypes enabled whites to accept the suppression of their natural selves.

The centrality of racist images to white culture presented peculiar problems for Afro-Americans. Entry into white society meant entry into its values, and those values included hatred of blacks. To participate in the white world, blacks had to make concessions to white America's fantasy images. As Huggins notes, black people found it dangerous to step out of character, either on or off stage. The great black vaudeville entertainer Bert Williams embodied the absurd contradictions of this process: he donned blackface makeup to perform on stage—a black man imitating white men imitating black men. Williams' artistic genius and stubborn self-respect led him to inject subtle elements of social criticism into his act, but for most spectators, he merely reinforced their *a priori* conclusions about the stage Negro.[64]

The black cast of *Amos 'n' Andy* came out of the theatrical traditions that spawned Bert Williams, and they perpetuated many of his contradictions. As a successful radio program, the all-black world of *Amos 'n' Andy* had been performed mostly by its white creators (Freeman Gosden and Charles Correll). With the move to television, Gosden and Correll hired an all-black cast, but they faced protests from community groups. The National Association for the Advancement of Colored People and black actor James Edwards campaigned to have the program taken off the air because they felt it made the only televised presentation of Afro-American life an insulting one. The NAACP complained in federal court that black citizens routinely suffered abuse from whites addressing them as "Amos" or "Andy," and that the program defamed black professionals by presenting them as liars and cheats. In response, black actors employed on the program and a few black intellectuals defended *Amos 'n' Andy* as a harmless satire and an important vehicle for bring much needed exposure to black actors.[65] But Nick Stewart, who played the demeaningly stereotypical character "Lightnin' " on the television program, hated his role. Years later he told a reporter, "I saw it as an opportunity. I couldn't have learned without an opportunity to play these roles, but I saw how this was poisoning the black community."[66] Stewart used his earnings from *Amos 'n' Andy* to build the Ebony Showcase Theatre, an Afro-American community repertory group, but he felt that the kinds of racist imagery perpetuated by the program continued to make it difficult for black actors.

Placed in historical context, *Amos 'n' Andy* did for the values of the 1950s what the minstrel show accomplished for previous generations. Everything considered precious but contested in white society—like the family or the work ethic—became violated in the world of Kingfish. Ambition for upward mobility drew ridicule only when pursued by blacks. In a society nurtured on Horatio Alger stories about rising from rags to riches, this lampooning of a black man's aspirations served to release tensions about the fear of failure. It could redirect hostility away from the elite toward those on the bottom of society. When Kingfish pretends to be educated and uses grandiose language, the audience can howl derisively at his pretensions. But the same audience could glow with warm recognition when Mama Hansen uses her broken English to express her dreams for her son to grow up to be president. Ambition viewed as worthy and realistic for the Hansens becomes a symbol of vanity and weak character when voiced by Kingfish.

Consistent with the values of the 1950s as mediated through popular culture, family responsibilities—or neglect of them—define Kingfish even more than work or ethnicity. The glorification of motherhood pervading psychological and popular literature of the 1950s becomes comedy in *Amos 'n' Andy*. Wives named for precious stones (Ruby and Sapphire) appear anything but precious, and "Mama" in this show appears as a nagging harpy screaming invective at the cowerling—and emasculated black man. Kingfish shares Ralph Kramden's dreams of overnight success, but his transgressions against bourgeois morality are more serious. Kingfish has no job, his late-night revelries and lascivious grins hint at marital infidelity, and he resorts to criminal behavior to avoid what he calls "the horrors of employment." He betrays his family and cheats his lodge brothers (and by implication the "brothers" of his race) with no remorse. But his most serious flaws stem from neglect of the proper roles of husband and father. In one episode, Kingfish's late-night excursions cause his wife, Sapphire, to leave home and live with her mother. Kingfish misses her and orders one of his lackeys to find out where she has gone. When the report comes back that Sapphire has been seen entering an obstetrician's office, Kingfish assumes that he is about to become a father. In reality, Sapphire has simply taken a job as the doctor's receptionist, but the misunderstanding leads Kingfish to tell Amos how much fun he plans to have as a father. When Amos warns him that fatherhood involves serious responsibilities, Kingfish replies, "What you mean serious? All you gotta do is keep 'em filled up wid milk an' pablum and keep chuckin' em under de chin."[67] Kingfish's ignorance plays out the worst fears of people in a society with a burgeoning obsession with family. By representing the possibility of incompetent parenting, Kingfish provides the audience with a sense of superiority, but one that can be maintained only by embracing parental responsibilities. Lest we miss the point of the show, Kingfish and his friend Andy go to a clinic for prospective fathers where they learn to bathe a baby by practicing with a doll. Kingfish lets his slip under the water and "drown."[68]

Black protests made *Amos 'n' Andy* a much debated phenomenon, unmasking the calculation that went into its creation. In the context of the 1950s, when migration to industrial cities created greater concentrations of black political and economic power, these protests could not be dismissed casually by advertisers or the networks. Blatz Beer decided to drop its sponsorship of *Amos 'n' Andy* in 1954, knocking the show off prime-time schedules and into syndication until 1966 when another wave of protests made it untenable even in reruns. As the program most thoroughly grounded in ideologically charged historical material, *Amos 'n' Andy* lent itself most easily to critical historical interpretation and action. That capacity conflicted with the needs and desires of advertisers. But just with shows rooted in white working-class histories, structural contradictions in black working-class life also allowed for oppositional readings of the program's content. Black activist and author Julius Lester recalls his own formative experiences with *Amos 'n' Andy* in his autobiography in a quintessential example of reinterpreting hierarchically prepared and distributed mass culture. Ruminating on the seeming paradox of a home life that installed black pride into him, but that also encouraged him to listen to the antics of the Kingfish, Lester recalls

> In the character of the Kingfish, the creators of Amos and Andy may have thought they were ridiculing blacks as lazy, shiftless, scheming and conniving, but to us Kingfish was a paradigm of virtue, an alternative to the work ethic. Kingfish lived: Amos made a living. It did not matter that my parents lived by and indoctrinated me with the Puritan work ethic. Kingfish had a *joie de vivre* no white person could poison, and we knew that whites ridiculed us because they were incapable of such élan. I was proud to belong to the same race as Kingfish.[69]

Whether through the careful decoding exemplified by Julius Lester, or through the politicization of *Amos 'n' Andy* by mass protest, audience response to the program in some cases focused on the show's artifice and distortions of history. As was the case with *The Goldbergs*, the traditions needed to provide legitimacy for advertising messages surrounding *Amos 'n' Andy* contained sedimented contestation that undermined their effectiveness, and instead provoked negotiated or oppositional readings. Dominant ideology triumphed on television in the 1950s, just as it did in political and social life. But historically grounded opposition remained possible and necessary for at least part of the audience.

The realism that made urban, ethnic, working-class situation comedies convincing conduits for consumer ideology also compelled them to present alienations and aspirations subversive to the legitimacy of consumer capitalism. As Antonio Gramsci insists, ideological hegemony stems from the ability of those in power to make their own interests appear to be synonymous with the interests of society at large. But appeals for legitimacy always take place within concrete historical circumstances, in contested societies with competing interests. In a consumer capitalist economy, where unmet needs and individual isolation provide the impetus for commodity desires, legitimation is always incomplete. Even while establishing dominance, those In power must borrow from the ideas, actions, and experience of the past, all of which contain potential for informing a radical critique of the present.

Dialogue, Negotiation, and Legitimation: Method and Theory

Recent scholarship in literary criticism, cultural studies, and sociology offers investigative methods and theoretical frameworks essential to understanding the historical dialogue about family, class, and ethnicity in early network television. The literary criticism and "dialogic imagination" proposed by Mikhail Bakhtin demonstrates how all texts inherit part of the historical consciousness of their authors and audiences.[70] Cultural studies theorist Stuart Hall notes that commercial mass media seek legitimacy with audiences by effectively representing diverse aspects of social life including memories of past experiences, current contradictions, and potential sources of division and opposition.[71] Sociologist Jürgen Habermas observes that contemporary capitalist culture destroys the very motivations that it requires for the smooth functioning of the system, such as the work ethic or the willingness to defer gratification. Consequently, capitalist societies draw upon the borrowed legitimacy of cultural values and beliefs from the past, like religion or the patriarchal family, to provide the appearance of moral grounding for contemporary forces inimical to the interests of tradition.[72] Taken collectively, these approaches to culture provide a useful context for understanding the persistence of seemingly outdated and dysfunctional themes in early network television.

Bakhtin's analysis of text construction argued that communication does not begin in the present with a speaker or story, but, rather, that both speech and narrative come from a social matrix that is (at least in part) historical. Each speaker enters a dialogue already in progress; every work of art contains within it past, present, and future struggles over culture and power. Forms of communication from the past not only make current discourse comprehensible and legitimate, but they also imbed within the present a collective historical experience rich with contradictions. The producers of early network television worked in a new medium, but they addressed an audience acclimated to specific forms of comedy and drama that reflected, however indirectly, the real texture of past struggles and present hopes.

Structural unities underlie the seemingly divergent stories of different ethnic, working-class situation comedies. Viewers rarely saw Ralph Kramden's bus or Jake Goldberg's dressmaking shop, but the cameras introduced them to every detail of furnishing in the Kramden and Goldberg households. Difficulties encountered in the aircraft factory assembly line by Chester A. Riley or at the construction site by Lars Hansen paled in significance in contrast to the dilemmas of consumption faced in the Riley and Hansen families. The texture and tone of *Life with Luigi* and *Amos 'n' Andy* came from the ethnic worlds they depicted, but the plots of those shows dealt with the aspirations of individuals as if ethnic rivalries and discrimination did not exist. Instead, ethnics attain a false unity through consumption of commodities: Jeannie MacClennan learns to "be an American" by dressing fashionably and wearing the right makeup; Luigi Basco hopes to prove himself a worthy candidate for citizenship by opening a checking account and purchasing an insurance policy; Molly Goldberg overcomes her fears of installment buying and vows to live above her means, "the American way."[73] Comedies in this subgenre reflect Stuart Hall's contention that the commercial mass media tend to direct popular consciousness toward consumption and away from production. They present social actions and experiences as atomized individual events, fragmenting social groups into isolated consumers. They resolve the tensions confronting their audiences by binding them together in false collectivities defined for the convenience of capital accumulation.[74]

But Hall also shows that the imperial aspirations of the mass media lead to a disclosure of contradictions, allowing cultural consumers to fashion oppositional or negotiated readings of mass culture. To make their dramas compelling and their narrative resolutions dynamic, the media also reflect the plurality of consumer experiences. A system that seeks to enlist everyone in the role of consumer must appear to be addressing all possible circumstances; a system that proclaims consensus and unanimity must acknowledge and explain obvious differences within the polity, if for no other reason than to co-opt or trivialize potential opposition. Television, and other forms of electronic mass media, so effectively recapitulate the ideology of the historical bloc in which they operate that they touch on all aspects of social life—even its antagonistic contradictions. While the media serve to displace, fragment, and atomize real experiences, they also generate and circulate a critical dialogue as one unintended consequence of their efforts to expose the inventory of social practice.

Of course, mere disclosure of opposition does not guarantee emancipatory practice; ruling elites routinely call attention to "deviant" subcultures to draw a distinction between permitted and forbidden behavior. In urban, ethnic, working-class situation comedies in the 1950s, "deviant" traits, like Kingfish's aversion to work in *Amos 'n' Andy* and Lars Hansen's lack of ambition in *Mama*, taught object lessons about the perils of unconventional behavior. Yet the operative premises and enduring tensions in each of these shows revolved around the "otherness" of the lead characters. The "old-world" attitudes of newly arrived immigrants in *Hey, Jeannie* and *Life with Luigi* or the proletarian cultural innocence manifested in *The Life of Riley* or *The Honeymooners* led to comedic clashes that exposed the inadequacies and deficiencies of those on the margins of society. But at the same time, these clashes counterposed the conformity and materialism of the mainstream to the narratively privileged moral superiority of those with connections to the past. Traditional values and beliefs prevented protagonists in these shows from achieving success or happiness as defined by society, but those values and beliefs also facilitated a critical distance from the false premises of the present. As Gertrude Berg noted in an explanation of the popularity of her character Molly Goldberg, Molly "lived in the world of today but kept many of the values of yesterday."[75]

The complicated dialogue between the past and present embodied in Molly Goldberg underscores the complex role played by historical referents in early network television. The past that brought credibility and reassurance to family dramas also contained the potential for undermining the commodified social relations of the present. The Goldberg family interested advertisers because audiences identified their story as part of a precious collective memory resonating with actual experiences and lessons from the past. The Goldbergs could not be credible representatives of that past if they appeared to live amid the plethora of consumer goods that dominated commercials, or if they appeared uncritical of the consumer world of the present that made such a sharp break with the values of the past. Yet the Goldberg family had little value to advertisers unless their experiences sanctioned pursuit of commodities in the present. The creators of the program resolved this potential contradiction by putting the borrowed moral capital from the past at the service of the material values of the present. They acknowledged the critiques of materialism and upward mobility sedimented within the experiences of working-class families, but they demonstrated over and over again how wise choices enabled consumers to have *both* moral and material rewards. By positing the nuclear family as a transhistorical and "natural" locus for the arbitration of consumer desires, television portrayed the specific value crises of the 1950s as eternal and recurrent. By collapsing the distinction between family as consumer unit and family as part of neighborhood, ethnic, and class associations, television programs in the early 1950s connected the most personal and intimate needs of individuals to commodity purchases. They implied that the past sanctioned rather than contradicted the ever-increasing orientation toward shopping as the cornerstone of social life, an orientation characteristic of most media discourse in the postwar era.

The reliance on the past to justify controversial changes in present behavior forms the core of Jürgen Habermas's analysis of contemporary capitalism's "legitimation crisis." According to Habermas, the consumer consciousness required by modern capitalism revolves around "civil and familial-vocational privatism," a syndrome that elevates private consumer decisions over social relations and public responsibility. Individuals view their families as primarily centers of consumption and leisure, while they regard employment as primarily a means of engaging in status competition. Instead of the rooted independence demanded by traditional family and community life, contemporary capitalist society encourages an atomized dependence on outside authorities — on advertisers, self-help experts, psychiatric, educational, and political authorities. Clearly useful for purposes of capital accumulation, this process undermines traditional motivations for work, patriotism, and social relations, causing real crises for society. In addition, the infantile narcissism nurtured by this consumer consciousness requires validation by outside authorities, requires assurance that the impoverishment of work, family, and political life characteristic of late capitalism constitutes a legitimate and necessary part of progress toward a better life.[76]

For Habermas, the mass media play a crucial role in legitimation, but they do so imperfectly. The new forms of family and vocational consciousness cannot be justified on their own, but can be validated by invoking the moral authority of past forms of family and community. Thus the "work ethic" is summoned to justify a system based on commodified leisure. Mutual love and affection are called upon to sanction families that exist primarily as consumer units. The social relations of the past are used to legitimate a system that in reality works to destroy the world that created those historical relations in the first place. Consequently, the invocation of the past in the service of the present is a precarious undertaking. Tradition used to legitimate untraditional behavior may instead call attention to the disparity between the past and the present. Collective popular memory may see the manipulative use of tradition by advertisers as a conscious strategy, as an attempt to create artifacts that conflict with actual memory and experience. As Habermas cautions, "traditions can retain legitimizing force only as long as they are not torn out of interpretive systems that guarantee continuity and identity."[77]

Habermas provides us with a framework capable of explaining both the presence of historical elements in early network television shows and their limitations. In conjunction with Bakhtin's emphasis on dialogue and Hall's delineation of negotiation, Habermas's analysis explains how portrayals of traditional, ethnic, working-class families might have been essential for legitimizing social forces that undermined the very values that made those kinds of families respected icons in popular consciousness. At the same time, Habermas directs our attention to the fundamental instability of this legitimation process, to the ways in which audiences might come to see manipulative uses of the past as created artifacts at war with the lessons of history as preserved in collective popular memory.

After 1958, network television eliminated urban ethnic working-class programs from the schedule. Marc Daniels, who directed *The Goldbergs*, recalls that a changing society less tied to class and ethnicity demanded different kinds of entertainment, and certainly the emergence of ethnically neutral, middle-class situation comedies between 1958 and 1970 lends credence to his interpretation.[78] The entry of major film studios into television production in the mid-1950s also had an impact, since the working-class shows tended to be produced by small companies like Hal Roach studios. Major studio involvement in television production increased the proportion of action/adventure shows with production values ill-suited to the realism of urban, ethnic, working-class programs. In action and adventure shows, no embarrassing retentions of class-consciousness compromise the sponsors' messages and no social connections to ethnic history bring up disturbing issues that might make programs susceptible to protests and boycotts.

One might conclude that television and American society had no more need for urban, ethnic, working-class programs after 1958 because tensions between consumerist pressures and historical memories had been resolved. But the re-appearance of race, class, and ethnicity in 1970s situation comedies like *All in the Family, Chico and the Man, Barney Miller*, and *Sanford and Son* testifies to the ongoing relevance of such tensions to subsequent mass-media discourse. Michael Morris, who produced *Chico and the Man*, had spent eight years with Gertrude Berg as a writer, story editor, and director of *The Goldbergs* in the 1940s and 1950s. The programs of the 1970s reprised both aspects of the 1950s shows—legitimation through representations of working-class life and commodification through product-centered plot lines and portrayals of families divided by market interests. Like their predecessors, urban, ethnic, working-class shows of the 1970s mixed their commercial messages with visions of connections to others that transcended the limits of civil and familial vocational privatism. They held open possibilities for transcending the parochialisms of traditional ethnicity and for challenging the patriarchal assumptions of both extended and nuclear families. The same communications apparatus that presented consumerism as the heir to the moral legacy of the working-class past also legitimized aspirations for happiness and community too grand to be satisfied by the lame realities of the commodity-centered world.

In the early 1950s, an advertising instrument under the control of powerful monopolists established itself as the central discursive medium in American culture. With its penetration of the family and its incessant propaganda for commodity purchases, television helped erode the social base for challenges to authority manifest in the mass political activity among American workers in the 1940s. Yet television did not so much ensure the supremacy of new values as it transformed the terms of social contestation. As mass culture gained in importance as an instrument of legitimation, oppositional messages filtered into even hierarchically controlled media constructions like network television programs. The internal contradictions of capitalism fueled this process by generating anxieties in need of legitimation, and by turning for legitimation to the very beliefs and practices most threatened by emerging social relations. Thus every victory for the ideology of civil and familial vocational privatism can also constitute a defeat. Every search for legitimacy can end in the dilution of legitimacy by unmasking media messages as prepared and fabricated ideological artifices. Even successful legitimation fails to a degree, because the new social relations destroy their own source of legitimacy.

This is not to assume that the final outcome of television's ideological imperatives must be emancipatory. Inculcation of narcissistic desire coupled with destruction of traditional sources of moral restraint might well suit the needs of capital and produce a population eager for fascist authority. But structural conditions exist to make an alternative future possible. As Joel Kovel argues, "The point is not that people desire the administrative mode, it is rather that administration protects them against the desires they can not stand, while it serves out, in the form of diluted rationalization, a hint of the desire and power lost to them."[79] The separation of individuals from political and community life, combined with the destruction of cultural traditions that previously gave direction and purpose to individuals, might make status competition and "possession" of a secure family role all that much more attractive. Certainly the neo-conservatism of the 1980s seems to revolve around "protecting" the family from the increasing barbarism of society and upon shifting the blame for the social disintegration caused by civil and familial vocational privatism onto the opposition movements formed to combat it.[80] But the sleight-of-hand inherent in the neo-conservative position allows for other possibilities. Reconnection to history and to motivational structures rooted within it is both desirable and possible. More than ever before communication and criticism can help determine whether people accept the commodity-mediated desires that turn others into instruments and objects, or whether they build affirmative communities in dialogue with the needs and desires of others. By identifying the historical reality behind the construction of television texts in the early 1950s, we demystify their "organic" character and reveal their implications as created artifacts. We uncover sedimented critiques from the past and potential forms of opposition for the present and future.

The historical specificity of early network television programs led their creators onto dangerous ideological terrain. By examining them as part of our own history, we learn about both the world we have lost and the one we have yet to gain. Fredric Jameson claims that "history is what hurts, what sets inexorable limits to individual as well as collective praxis."[81] But the unfinished dialogue of history can also be what helps, what takes us back into the past to break its hold on the present. By addressing the hurt, and finding out how it came to be, we begin to grasp ways of understanding the past and ending its pain.

4

Why Remember Mama?
The Changing Face
of a Woman's Narrative

Almost every Friday night between 1949 and 1956, millions of Americans watched Rosemary Rice turn the pages of an old photograph album. With music from Edvard Grieg's "Holverg Suite" playing in the background, and with pictures of turn-of-the-century San Francisco displayed on the album pages, Rice assumed the identity of her television character, Katrin Hansen, on the CBS network program *Mama*. She told the audience about her memories of her girlhood, her family's house on Steiner Street, and her experiences there with her big brother Nels, her little sister Dagmar, her Papa, and her Mama—"most of all," she said, "when I remember that San Francisco of so long ago, I remember Mama."[1] Katrin Hansen's memories of her Norwegian immigrant, working-class family had powerful appeal for viewers in the early years of commercial network broadcasting. *Mama* established itself as one of CBS's most popular programs during its first season on the air, and it retained high ratings for the duration of its prime-time run.[2]

In December 1985, the Museum of Broadcasting in New York City presented a retrospective tribute to *Mama*, featuring a reunion with four members of the cast and crew. In the thirty years since the show had been broadcast, each of the featured guests had gone on to interesting and important careers. Rosemary Rice, who played Katrin, became a featured voice on many popular cartoons and children's records. Dick Van Patten, who played the Hansens' son Nels, went on to establish himself as one of America's best known father figures, through his acting role on the popular television show *Eight Is Enough*, and, as well, through his real-life role as father when his children achieved fame as actors and professional tennis players. Robin Morgan, who played Dagmar, became the author of several highly acclaimed books on feminism that established her as a leading thinker and spokesperson for the radical wing of the feminist movement. Ralph Nelson, the show's director, became one of the leading liberals in Hollywood as well as the creative genius behind magnificent motion pictures including *Lilies of the Field, Soldier Blue,* and *Charlie.* Despite their busy schedules and varied fields of endeavor, Rice, Van Patten, Morgan, and Nelson came together at the Museum of Broadcasting to pay tribute to their memories of *Mama.*

"Every show had a tear and a laugh, and every show taught you something," Rice remembered, adding that working on that series "Christmas didn't come just once a year, it came every Friday night." Van Patten talked about *Mama*'s enormous effect on his life: he named his first son Nels after his character on the show, and he secured his role on *Eight Is Enough* largely because producer Fred Silverman had watched *Mama* as a child and admired Nels. Morgan said that she had learned discipline, professionalism, and team play on *Mama,* and that those skills had been crucial to her success as a political activist. In addition, she discerned a connection between the show's content and her evolution into a feminist. "After all, this was *I Remember Mama,* not *Father Knows Best,*" she quipped, explaining that the scripts showed girls to be as important as boys, and that Judson Laire's characterization of Papa presented a strong, loving, but gentle male.[3] Ralph Nelson discussed how *Mama* prepared him for Hollywood by giving him the opportunity to direct both the regular cast and skilled guest performers including Paul Newman, Inger Stevens, Jack Lemmon, and Cliff Robertson. "When I did *Lilies of the Field* I followed the same structure as *Mama,* and I was quite conscious of it at the time."[4]

Through sympathetic laughter and applause, the audience at the Museum of Broadcasting symposium registered approval of all the praise for *Mama.* But the discussion took a bizarre turn when the audience began to question the speakers. One woman expressed her appreciation to the cast both for their remarks that evening and for their performances thirty years ago. She explained that while growing up she felt very alienated and unhappy with her own family, so she "adopted" the television Hansen family and pretended that they were her own mother and father, brother and sisters. Rosemary Rice responded, "We really were a family, we grew up together—we became a real family." Rice added that she attended classes at New York University while starring in the show and that she always showed her term papers to Judson Laire, who played Papa, because "I thought I should show my father my homework."[5] Robin Morgan indicated that the show helped provide a surrogate family for her as well. Her father had deserted her mother shortly after Morgan was born, providing her with a bitter early lesson about the family. But Judson Laire became a parental role model on and off camera for the young Morgan, and Peggy Wood encouraged her in her desire to become a writer, encouragement that she said, "meant a great deal to me."[6] Ralph Nelson recalled that *Mama* had helped reconcile him to his own family. As a teen-ager Nelson had argued constantly with his Swedish-American father, especially over the latter's racism and anti-Semitism. When his father tried to send him to a reform school, Nelson ran away from home and wandered all across the country. Not until he began directing *Mama* could he muster any affection or nostalgia for his background, but weekly contact with the fictional Norwegian Hansen family reconnected Nelson to his past. Then Nelson made a startling connection between his own negotiations with ethnic memory and those of Kathryn Forbes, the author of the original stories on which *Mama* was based. Nelson said that he had read somewhere that Forbes had fashioned a similar relationship to her own past through the Hansen family. Forbes was ethnically Norwegian, but she had spent much of her childhood in foster homes and felt deserted by her family. In her fiction, she "re-invented" her mother on the basis of the few stories she had heard about her grandmother and presented experiences that she wished had actually happened to her.

This projection of the Hansen family as part of the real family experiences of the woman from the audience, Rice, Morgan, Nelson, and Forbes turned the symposium into an exercise in a different kind of nostalgia from what had been planned. For one of the commonplace assumptions about *Mama* among contemporaneous critics and media historians has been that the show succeeded because it reflected the "real" family experiences precious to Americans. But the comments at the Museum of Broadcasting indicate that it played to another frame of reception as well—the past as people wish it had been rather than the past as they actually experienced it. The fact that so many of the speakers at the symposium treasured vicarious memories of a family life that none of them actually had, one that in fact ran directly counter to their own experience, illumines an important function of memory within popular culture in general—memory as managed *misappropriation*.

The popularity of *Mama* among people with unhappy family experiences might be seen as a quintessential example of the media's power to naturalize oppression. No one at the symposium expressed outrage at the program for presenting family life as sweeter and more loving than it actually was for them; instead they treasured a picture of the Hansens as normal and typical. One can well imagine the problems that might follow from this process—unrealistically high expectations about family relations, inability to anticipate problems that cannot be resolved by the final commercial, and the likelihood of blaming individual choices and behaviors for what in fact might be systemic problems between men and women or between children and adults. Indeed, as David Marc points out, much critical anger at the content of television programs revolves around these possibilities: critics understandably enough become alienated from a televised world in which nearly everyone is white and heterosexual, where no one sleeps on a mattress on the floor instead of a bed, where no one drives a used car, and where physical bravery and force always outperform moral courage and intellect.

But memory as misappropriation can have positive as well as negative consequences. It enables us to see beyond our own experience, rendering the oppressions of the past as contingent and unnecessary while modeling an alternate past, one as responsive to human wishes and desires as to the accidents of history. It says that biology is not destiny, that family and ethnicity can be sources of self-affirmation and connection to others, but only if they meet certain conditions of humane behavior. If our own personal pasts cannot be venerated as moral guides for the present, we must choose another from history or art and embrace it as our own. But such leaps cannot be fashioned purely from the imagination; the past has more informative power and more relevance to the present if we believe that it is what actually happened, because what people have done before they can do again, while what they imagine may never be realized. Even when misappropriated, memory has to appear credible, to resonate with lessons of some real past. *Mama* succeeded in that role because even its misappropriations resonated with the lessons of history. Because its core tensions exuded the truths of lived experience and memory, *Mama* enabled audiences to arbitrate the tensions facing them and to negotiate utopian endings.

It was not just the audience, cast, and crew of the television show *Mama* who made creative use of the Hansen family. From its inception in the Kathryn Forbes stories of the early 1940s, the narrative about the Hansen family has provided a particularly fertile field for misappropriation. As stories, a book, a broadway play, a radio special, a film, and finally as a television program, remembering Mama has engaged the revisionist energies of both artists and audiences. At each stage, alterations in narrative as well as in media responded as much to the larger political and ideological context as to dramatic necessities. Though they appear on the surface to be an uncontrollable obscuring of the historical record, the various versions of *Mama* represent in reality a creative adaptation of memory to arbitrate the indignities and alienations of everyday life. These changes were not always positive; some were obviously steps backward—regressive adaptations that precluded rather than promoted possibilities. But they demonstrate the indispensable dialogue with the past that accompanies any present, and they reflect the enduring potential of the past to help us see beyond the present even while speaking to its psychic and ideological preoccupations. The many incarnations of *I Remember Mama* reflected a continuing dialogue about the family and its proper social roles—a dialogue necessitated by extraordinary social changes between the early 1940s and the mid-1950s. Changes in the succeeding versions of these stories offer a significant index to the transformations in family life and family images in that period, as well as to the ways in which social pressures altered the forms and purposes of families.

This is not to argue that the many individuals involved in shaping the short stories, book, play, film, radio show, and television program about the Hansen family decided consciously to make their efforts relevant to contemporary affairs. Rather, it is to claim that commercial mass culture seeks credibility with its audience, at least in part, by arbitrating the ideological tensions created by disparities between cultural promises and lived experiences. As the core tensions facing families in society changed, intellectuals working in the culture industry participated in bending discursive practices to social realities, shaping their art to speak to current issues. Commerical pressures certainly contributed to their decisions: investors, editors, and advertisers had obvious stakes in supporting the status quo, and no doubt made their preferences known to those on the creative side of the enterprise. But more interesting than the conclusions and plot resolutions of these cultural artifacts are the oppositions that precede the conclusions, oppositions indicative of extraordinary contestation and confusion in society about family identity.

Operative Tensions in a Changing Narrative

As short stories, a book, and a Broadway play, the experiences of the Hansen family revolve around the legacy of the Depression. The operative tensions in the stories come from the mother's struggle to protect her family from hard times and from ethnic rivalries and hatreds. In the motion picture, the focus shifts to the differences between Mama and her daughters, to a story of a traditional mother raising independent daughters. The television program rescinds the independence enjoyed by the daughters in the film, presenting instead a narrative about threats to the family posed (or solved) by consumer goods. These three frames of reference responded to changes in American society at large—the remnants of the Depression in the early 1940s, the entry of large numbers of women into the workforce during World War II, and the rise of suburbs and increases in consumer spending in the early 1950s.

Kathryn Forbes published her first story about the Hansen family, "Mama's Bank Account," in the *Toronto Star Weekly* early in 1941. The *Reader's Digest* printed two excerpts from the story almost immediately upon publication, and Harcourt published an extended collection as a book titled *Mama's Bank Account*. The book received a warm welcome from reviewers and from the reading public; even the War Department deemed it worthile and wholesome reading, purchasing 50,000 copies for soldiers overseas. The success of *Mama's Bank Account* inspired the play "I Remember Mama" by John Van Druten, which opened in 1944 and ran for 713 performances. Both the book and the play depict Mama as an effective manager of the family's finances, successfully maneuvering around illness, unemployment, and the demands of the children so that she does not have to "go to the bank" and withdraw their savings. When Katrin's success as a writer eventually brings in some surplus cash, Mama can finally admit that there is no bank account, that she talked about one so that the children would be shielded from how desperate their financial circumstances actually were. Now they can go to the bank, but to open an account for Katrin's money, not to use up their "savings."

Forbes's book tells about a battle between family and the economy; it delineates the ways in which poverty threatens love. Mama's resolute courage in the face of deprivation connects her to the "Madonnas of the Fields"—the strong and courageous farm women made into icons by 1930s FSA photographers. In this ethos, women attain beatific status by keeping families together in the face of the Depression. *Mama's Bank Account* also revolves around ethnicity: retracing the steps taken by immigrants to find common cause in a new land filled with not-so-friendly strangers. Mama draws upon her special knowledge and skills rooted in the old country to help her children succeed in America.

The story of the bank account forms the core of the Hansen family narrative, touching effectively on historical memories about the Depression—especially its threats to the survival of families and the new roles demanded of women by changing economic circumstances. In the book, Papa turns to carpentry only after failing as a farmer; in the play he responds to Katrin's desire to be a writer by asking how much writers earn. But a subtext of ethnicity in the book and play also addresses the collective memory of the audience. Trade-union organizing drives and new political coalitions ranging from the New Deal to the Communist Party's popular front transformed the meaning of ethnicity in the 1930s, and the unity of the war effort eclipsed some internal ethnic rivalries. In Forbes's book, Katrin enrolls in a school where anti-foreign prejudice makes her sensitive about her Scandinavian background. At one point the principal complains about the immigrant children enrolling in his school, fulminating "Italians, Jews, what next? Negroes or even Orientals?" Katrin feels like an outsider—her only friend is an Italian-American girl—and she fears total humiliation when Mama is asked to take her turn with the other mothers and cook a meal for the class. Katrin worries that Mama's Norwegian meatballs will draw more anti-foreign ridicule, but when her classmates and teachers love Mama's cooking, Katrin sees that she can be accepted in American society by offering it her ethnic gifts instead of hiding them.[7]

The ethnic component of *Mama's Bank Account* appealed to actress Mady Christians. Born in Vienna in 1900, Christians first acted in her father's German-American theater productions in New York and spent much of the '30s as both an actress and an activist on behalf of refugees from Nazi persecution. When she heard that Rodgers and Hammerstein were thinking of basing a Broadway play on the book, Christians asked for the part. They eventually decided not to do the play, but they mentioned her interest to John Van Druten, who wrote his adaptation to the stage with her in mind and made sure that she got the part (along with a young Marlon Brando cast as Nels).[8] But even in its first incarnations, sharp contradictions divided the fictional representations of the Hansen family and the lives of the artists responsible for it. Forbes wrote what most critics and viewers considered "realistic" accounts of Norwegian-Americans, even though she had no real first-hand knowledge of them, and she fashioned a touching portrayal of family life despite herself having a fragile marriage that ended in divorce in 1946 on the grounds of her husband's "extreme mental cruelty."[9] Similarly, for all Christians' conviction about *I Remember Mama* as testimony to the immigrant presence in America, she was passed over for the film and television roles as Mama because as the Cold War deepened, her work with the American Committee for the Protection of the Foreign Born drew the ire of xenophobic anti-communists. A parade of "investigators" harassed Christians about her political affiliations, and both the film and television industries blacklisted her even though no evidence of "disloyalty" ever surfaced.[10]

If the story, book, and play versions of the Hansen family's adventures coalesced around New Deal mutuality, director George Stevens's 1948 film *I Remember Mama* focused on the rooted independence of immigrant daughters raised by traditional mothers.[11] Dewitt Bodeen's screenplay retained the emphases on gender, class, and ethnicity pervading previous versions of the Hansen story, but adapted them to the dominant social tensions of the war and postwar periods. As film scholar Andrea Walsh points out, the film reflected the "pressure to grow up" facing young girls in the 1940s, at a time when millions of men served overseas and millions of women embraced new roles as war workers. Within the discourse of the day, *I*

Remember Mama steered a middle way between hysterical anti-feminist tirades (like Philip Wylie's *Generation of Vipers*) that charged domineering mothers with destroying the independence of American children, and the emerging war and postwar feminist consciousness stimulated by women's success in securing and maintaining war production jobs. The film featured Mama as a source for reconciliation, as a means of proving that threatening changes could be resisted while one accommodated to progress.

Indeed the entire film *I Remember Mama* presents threatening contradictions and then shows that they are not contradictions at all. For example, an opposition between family and money pervades the narrative. Mama has to supervise the budget to see that her family survives, with financial crises popping up at every turn—her daughter Christine needs an operation, a boarder pays his rent with a bad check, her sister Trina has no dowry, her Uncle Chris leaves them nothing in his will. But love proves superior to money. Mama mediates in an argument between her Uncle Chris who has the money and a doctor who has the expertise to secure the operation for her daughter. She teaches her children that the works of literature left behind by their deadbeat boarder are worth more than money. Along with Uncle Chris she neutralizes issues of pride and honor to enable her sister to marry a man who does not insist on a dowry. She finds that Uncle Chris spent all his money on charities for crippled children, and she uses that fact to encourage her son Nels to be a doctor and carry on his uncle's good works. Although Mama works within the home for her family, the narrative suggests that her work has great economic value even though she does not succumb to the self-centered greed of the work world.

Lessons about greed dominate one particularly important exchange between Katrin and Mama. Shortly after Mama makes her only consumer purchase in the film, a bouquet of violets, Katrin promises her "When I'm rich and famous . . . I'll buy you just lovely clothes: white satin gowns with long trains on them and jewelry. I'll buy you a pearl necklace."[12] Mama replies that she prefers her *solje*, her brooch, to a pearl necklace. Her immigrant loyalties confuse the American daughter who protests that Mama must want to be rich. When Mama replies that being rich is like being ten feet tall, "good for some things—bad for others," Katrin asks why she came to America if not to be rich. Mama tells us, "We came to America because they

are all here all the others. Is good for families to be together."[13]
The exchange about the superiority of a *solje* to a pearl necklace and
the pre-eminence of family over wealth prefigures a crucial scene
which marks Katrin's maturation into an adult. Katrin admires a
dresser set in a store window, even though Mama warns her that
what Katrin takes to be ivory is probably just plastic. But Katrin persists, hinting about the dresser set for her high-school graduation
present. Mama and Papa had intended to give her the *solje*, but pres-
sured by their daughter's consumer desire they pawn the brooch to
buy her the dresser set. At this point younger sister Christine intervenes, scolding Katrin for her selfishness and reminding her that
with Papa on strike their parents could hardly afford the present she
wanted. "Why I don't believe you even know what they're striking
for. Do you? All you and your friends can talk about is the presents
you're going to get. You make me ashamed of being a girl."[14] Humbled by Christine's priorities, Katrin pawns the dresser set and returns the *solje* to Mama and Papa who reward her passage to adult
responsibility by letting her drink coffee with them.

Yet for all its privileging of love over money, *I Remember Mama*
ultimately validates love as one way of securing happiness *and*
money. Mama's old-fashioned female identity provides the key
breakthrough for Katrin's aspirations to become a professional
writer. When Katrin despairs because her stories have been rejected
and complains that she needs the critiques of an expert, Mama uses
her traditional skills to launch her daughter's career. Seeing a picture
of "famous author" Florence Dana Moorhead in the paper, Mama decides that Moorhead looks like a woman "who likes to eat." Mama
visits the author's hotel, and at first appears to be totally out of her
element in its magnificent lobby. But she bravely locates Moorhead
and explains that her daughter needs criticism from a writer. Initially,
Moorhead refuses, but when Mama offers to share her recipe for de-
licious Norwegian meatballs, Moorhead relents and provides the advice that proves decisive to Katrin's later success. When Katrin sells
her first story, she buys Mama a new coat with her earnings. Katrin
may reject plastic consumer goods in favor of a family heirloom, but
her mother's skills become validated only when they demonstrate
their ability to open doors in the outside world.

The ambiguous resolution of the tension between family and
money in *I Remember Mama* resonates with the value crises about

female identity in the 1940s. Confronted with unprecedented opportunities in the job market and fundamentally new definitions of social
responsibilities, women of the 1940s could turn to *I Remember
Mama* and see that they did not have to disown the past to participate
in the present, nor did they have to surrender opportunities in the
present out of a misplaced fidelity to the past. Their mothers' traditional skills paved the way for the independence of the present; the
moral dilemmas of the present could be kept under control by seeing their continuities with the past. Thus Katrin can have a career, but
it is one composed of writing about her family, thereby maintaining
her female identity. Katrin works at home, writes for love (of her
mother) rather than for money, and measures her success by assist-
ing her mother's work within the family rather than by any narcissistic gratification. On the other hand, Mama encourages Katrin, Christine, and Dagmar to have careers rather than talking to them about
marriage; she provides an example of sisterly solidarity when she defends Uncle Chris's wife from accusations of promiscuity; and she
comes to the aid of Aunt Trina, scorned for taking so long to marry.
Mama pays lip service to the authority of Papa and Uncle Chris, but
she takes action as an independent woman centering her concerns
on the welfare of others. She rejects the false lures of consumer
goods and gossip, while revering education, creativity, and mutuality.
Yet that very identity was a construct of the possibilities of the 1940s,
and when women's roles underwent serious alterations in the late
1940s and early 1950s, the next incarnation of the Hansen narrative
reflected those drastic changes.

A successful special performance of *I Remember Mama* on the Lux
Radio Theater helped convince CBS and General Foods to make a
television version for the 1949–1950 season. An instant success, the
program often appeared among the ten "most-watched" shows, enjoying an eight-year run before its cancellation in 1957. While retaining the main contours of previous versions, the televised *Mama*
shifted focus from ethnicity, class, and gender, using those categories
largely as a foil for a more pressing social problem—the family as
unit of consumption. Just as economic realities during the war encouraged an emphasis on the gender-centered aspects of Forbes's
stories, expansion of the consumer market in the 1950s made commodity purchases the core dramatic and narrative issue of the program.

Structural changes in cast and setting reflected external social changes each time *I Remember Mama* reached a new medium. In the stories and book, the Hansen family lived in a large house with seven boarders. The play and film whittled down the size of the house and featured only one boarder. The television program showed the Hansens as a modern nuclear family, owning their own house, without boarders. Forbes's original stories mentioned four aunts for the family to contend with; the play and the film showed three; the television program mentioned two, but tended to show only one. The Hansen family had four children in the stories, book, play, and film, but only three on television. In the print versions of the family's saga, Papa Hansen had failed as a farmer before becoming a carpenter. In the play and film his decision to participate in a strike represents an important chapter in the family's history. But the television show made no mention of failed business ventures and trivialized its few references to strikes. Ethnic rivalries provided significant tensions and taught important lessons in the book and the short stories, but they tended to disappear from the stage, screen, and television versions.

Changes in casting and plot no doubt owed something to the demands of different media and their attendant time constraints. Yet most of these changes also represent clear ideological and social changes as well. Over two decades and five forms of media, the Hansens changed from an ethnic working-class family deeply enmeshed in family, class, and ethnic associations, to a modern nuclear family confronting consumption decisions as the key to group and individual identity. Similarly, the spheres of action reserved for women change considerably from one version to another. In the stories and book, Mama uses her culinary skills to help her daughter win acceptance from classmates who made fun of her Scandinavian heritage. In the 1940s film, Mama uses those same cooking skills to advance her daughter's aspirations to become a writer. But in the 1950s television show, Mama's skill at cooking only provides hints to Katrin about how to get a husband. As the possibilities of the 1940s became transformed into the gender prison of the 1950s, Mama directed her daughter away from a career and toward a husband. Predictably, the child dropped from the family when it shrank for the television version was Christine, an independent, intelligent, and ambitious adolescent whose sisterhood, class loyalties, and integrity had provided important guidance for Katrin.

Not that career ambitions totally disappeared from the television program. But they changed. Katrin voices ambitions to become an actress instead of a writer. She actually becomes a secretary, and in the last episode of the program, becomes a full-time wife. She then receives Mama's *solje* as a gift, a reward for choosing her proper female role, unlike the film which rewarded her choice of history over consumer goods. Similarly, in the book and film, Katrin's brother Nels seeks to become a doctor because he wants to follow in the footsteps of his Uncle Chris who helped people by giving away all of his money to lame children in need of operations. In the television program, Nels's ambition to become a physician stems from a desire to own consumer goods and to socialize with "better" people.

The changing role of coffee as an icon in both the film *I Remember Mama* and the television program *Mama* maps the ideological difference between the two versions. In the motion picture, Katrin is allowed to drink coffee when she rejects the dresser set in favor of the *solje*, proving her maturation into adulthood by rejecting consumer goods in favor of tradition. In the television program, tradition serves only to legitimate consumer goods; the entire Hansen family story serves as a lure to bring the audience commercial messages by the program's sponsor, Maxwell House coffee. The narrative sequence that framed every episode of *Mama* demonstrates the centrality of advertising messages and their importance in establishing narrative and ideological closure. As soon as Katrin Hansen introduced the show with the words "I remember Mama," a male narrator announced, "Yes, here's Mama, brought to you by Maxwell House coffee." The camera then panned away from the photograph album to show Mama (played by Peggy Wood) making coffee for the Hansen family in their turn-of-the-century kitchen. The authority of the male narrator's voice established a connection between the continuity of family experiences and the sponsor's product, between warm memories of the past and Mama making coffee in the kitchen. In this progression, the product becomes a member of the Hansen family, while tradition and emotional support become commodities to be secured through the purchase of Maxwell House coffee. The sponsor's introduction announces ownership of the television show *Mama*, but it also lays claim to the moral authority and warmth of motherhood itself.

Coffee drinking also appeared in the dramatic narratives of the show with amazing regularity. In the very first episode, Katrin opens the program with a reminiscence about Mama and Papa drinking coffee in the family kitchen, and subsequent episodes feature the beverage as a means of calming down upset children, as a catalyst for conversations among women, as a requirement for receiving company, as a break from housework, and as an aid to clear thinking and problem solving.[15]

The magical attributes of coffee prepare viewers for equally respectful treatment of other commodities. In keeping with the economic imperatives of commercial television, *Mama* touted not only its sponsors' products, but an entire attitude about consumption as well. In one episode the children make home-made presents for Mama's birthday—a bread box, a pen wiper, and a bookmark. But Katrin tells them "those things don't count," and she argues instead for "a bought present." When Nels needs a new suit for his Sunday School graduation, Mama wants to alter one of Papa's, but her son insists on a "bought" suit. The children demand the purchase of goods that are "necessities" to them, but seem foolish to their parents—a telephone, a victrola, a magic-lantern slide projector, a pedigreed dog. But in these matters, the children are always right: a telephone that the family cannot really afford proves instrumental in securing a job for Papa; a victrola purchased to mollify the children shows Papa's boss that he is a music lover and worthy of promotion; a picture in the newspaper of Dagmar with her dog motivates yet another employer to offer work to Papa.[16] Unlike the film in which Katrin's own creativity (nurtured by Mama) enabled her to contribute to the family economy, on television consumer goods themselves mysteriously add to rather than subtract from the family's wealth. The lessons from the film about the false lure of consumer goods become inverted. On television products have no false glitter; instead they establish the necessary preconditions for continued familial ties.

Commodities not only help the family's financial status on *Mama*, they also minister to emotional needs. When an elderly neighborhood woman dies, Mama's social club delegates her to buy flowers for the deceased. But Mama learns that the woman's grandson is heartbroken because his grandmother had promised to buy him a tricycle before she died. Mama uses the flower money to buy the boy his gift and signs the birthday card from his grandmother. "Tricycles are better than flowers," she tells the club, "they last."[17] Grandmothers with the audacity to die before delivering desired toys to their grandchildren share the problem confronting all parents in *Mama*: the loss of face precipitated by inadequate performance as a consumer. In one episode Nels works as a toy salesman in a department store and confronts a bricklayer who cannot afford the expensive electric train that his son desires. Nels suggests a less expensive model, but the father bristles at the idea that he cannot provide the best for his child. Nels buys a raffle ticket for the train in question, and when he wins he gives it to the young boy because he remembers how he never got over his own disappointment at not receiving a pony when he was younger.[18] When Mama is not asked to join an elite social club, Papa fears it is because of his lowly job as a carpenter, and he wonders if his failures do not also explain Dagmar's exclusion from a prestigious dancing school the year before.[19] Papa's self-doubts receive reinforcement from his children. When Nels cannot afford to make long-distance calls to his girlfriend, he decides to start a business, cautioning his partner that they must be serious about upward mobility. "We can't be like my father. I don't even know what he ever came to this country for."[20] The blurred distinction between dramatic content and advertising messages in *Mama* did not just depend upon indirect ideological influences; sometimes the connection was intentional. Gordon Webber of the advertising agency that handled the show's accounts wrote several scripts for the show, and a 1954 memo from assistant producer Doris Quinlan to the producer, head writer, and director of the program reveals a sometimes conscious connection to product-plugging as Quinlan reminds her co-workers

> *Good Housekeeping Magazine* is coming out next month with a spread on "Mama." As you know, we have told them for some time we would make use of the magazine on the program. Could we please try to keep this in mind. It does not have to be anything elaborate. For example, the next time Katrin or Dagmar is looking at a pattern or a new dress, can they not use *Good Housekeeping* and mention it by name? We have a period copy of the magazine.[21]

Yet for all its embrace of consumer-commodity society, *Mama* still depended upon its ability to evoke the moral legitimacy of the past for its success in the present. Katrin Hansen's retrospective narrative

and the pictures from the family album reassured viewers by depict
ing events that had already happened in the emotionally secure confines of the audience's collective childhood memories and imagina-
tions. This false authenticity encouraged viewers to think of the
program as the kind of history that might be created about their own
homes. A CBS press release during the program's first broadcast season proclaimed, "On *Mama*, we try to give the impression that nobody is acting," and went on to claim success for that effort, quoting
an unnamed viewer's contention that the show depicted a real family
because "nobody but members of a real family could talk like that."[22]
Free from the real history of ethnic, class, and gender experience,
the history presented on *Mama* located its action within the personal
spheres of family and consumer choices. Within these areas, realism
could be put to the service of commodity purchases, as when the narrator followed his opening introduction with a discussion about how
Mama in her day "had none of the conveniences of today's modern
products" like Minute Rice, Jello, or Maxwell House instant coffee.[23]
Thus the morally sanctioned traditions of hearth and home could be
put to the service of products that revolutionized those very
traditions—all in keeping with Ernest Dichter's advice to his fellow
advertising executives: "Do not assert that the new product breaks
with traditional values, but on the contrary, that it fulfills its traditional functions better than any of its predecessors.[24]

Stability and Rupture in a Women's Narrative

In the 1970s, literary and film critics began to stress the conservative
functions of narrative. They charged that narrative closure worked to
forestall social change, to inculcate a distrust for contradiction and
conflict in readers and viewers. These critics argued that some narratives, especially in popular literature, film, and television, posed
imaginary solutions to real social problems, gave the appearance of
openness but allowed only one possible solution, in fact teaching inevitability. In some ways, the Hansen family narrative, even in its
many incarnations, could serve as evidence for that line of argument.
Its inscribed ideological content taught tolerance and self-help as solutions to the ethnic and class divisions of the Great Depression, favored a rooted independence as an arbitration of changes in wo-

men's roles in the 1940s, and presented consumer purchases as the key to family happiness in the 1950s. But narrative closure is not so easy to achieve. It is difficult to soothe anxieties without first aggravating them, and impossible to predict in any given case whether the emotional appeal of closure will silence the questions and criticisms provoked by narrative's evocation of the real hurts of history.

One significant failure to ensure narrative closure in the television program *Mama* may illumine more general principles. The single strongest ideological element in the transfer of the Hansen story to television came from the focus on the home. Television shifted the site of popular culture reception away from the public theater to the home, and both commercial and creative personnel thought of it as a medium where "families watched families." Yet as feminist literary critics have observed, the notion of the home as a safe haven from society encompasses some dramatic contradictions, for the glorification of domesticity traditionally draws legitimacy from the idea of the home as the moral center of society, as a social institution whose influence extends outward.[25] On *Mama* the narrative need to reaffirm the Hansen home as such a center of morality opens up rather than contains social contradictions. In one Halloween episode, delinquent street toughs harass the Hansens, throwing stones at their house. When Papa captures two of the youths, Mama serves them cider as they wait for the police to arrive. One asks her, "How do you think we feel when we look in windows and see kids eating ice cream and ducking for apples and stuff like that?" Mama says, "Like throwing stones ... I would too."[26] Mama tells Katrin to invite her friends over, and instead of turning the youths over to the police she invites them to join the party. Even Mama can feel the pain of economic deprivation, her class loyalties connecting her to the youths despite their decidedly unfamilial behavior.

Even the pursuit of consumer goods takes on some odd wrinkles because of the role of the home as the moral center of society. When the Hansens purchase a telephone that they cannot afford, Papa's boss fires him, claiming that a man who could afford such luxuries does not need work as badly as the other men. But Mama does not believe him. She says (in her accented television Swedish-English), "No, Lars, he do it because he do not like you to have same things that he has. That is not nice thing to say about Mr. O'Hara or any man, but is true. That is why we keep telephone, because I do not ever want anyone in this house to be afraid of men like Mr. O'Hara."[27] In this context, acquisition of consumer goods is no longer posed as a universal private need, but, rather, it becomes part of a class-conscious sense of entitlement to the good things in life. Awareness of a larger world outside the home also produces criticism of the home itself. In one episode Katrin bristles at the constant surveillance of her close-knit extended family and expresses a desire to move to Los Angeles to enjoy some freedom. Even though the plot reaches narrative closure by showing Katrin that her gossipy family protects her from malevolent strangers, the suffocating confinement of family identity leaves a bitter residue to the episode.

Similarly, *Mama* could glorify domesticity only by "containing" the allure of work outside the home. A parade of glamorous opera singers, cultured heiresses, and famous female actresses and writers tempt Katrin and her sister in ways that make Mama appear uninteresting, at least temporarily. Mama herself discloses the negative side of her life. She is jealous of women with public roles and fearful that they will attract Papa's interest. "I am someone who cooks and sews and makes the beds and takes care of the children, but when Lars sits and smokes his pipe and thinks thoughts they are not always of me."[28] Another time she complains after a frustrating day of housework, "Sometimes I wish I was an old maid. What does a family mean? Work. And who appreciates it?" Again, the resolution of these shows reassures us that Mama is loved and valued for her work, but for any given viewer the ruptures opened by the show might carry as much impact as the narrative resolution.

Frankfurt School Marxist T. W. Adorno claims that the culture industry opens such ruptures only to close them, that it disciplines all potential opposition by showing the possibility and then the futility of criticism. But as long as ruptures and closures accompany each other within media texts, at least the possibility of oppositional readings remains alive. One reason for that possibility comes from the contradictions of those fashioning the narratives. The tension between the ideological imperatives of commercialized leisure and the need for making the narratives credible creates a space for the airing of historical memories and contradictions. The sources of "authenticity" for these artists often belie the narrative closures and preferred readings demanded from their work. Earlier we saw how Rice, Morgan, Forbes, and Christians created parts of the Hansen narrative both with and against the grain of their own experiences; some of the contradictions about social reality and family roles evident within *Mama* resonate with the tension between life and art for its two main creators, writer Frank Gabrielson and director Ralph Nelson.

As the chief writer for *Mama*, Frank Gabrielson created some of the warmest and most touching images of family harmony in the history of television. But his own behavior often conflicted with the values that he projected onto the screen. His wife sacrificed her own career in radio to allow him to move to Hollywood and work as a writer for Twentieth Century Fox, and she supported him with her earnings when he could not find paying work. But Gabrielson abandoned his wife and young daughter in 1947, shortly before securing his position on *Mama*. As head writer he often took the entire cast out to dinner at expensive restaurants while neglecting to send alimony checks to his own family. His writings beautifully portrayed a kind of family loyalty and responsibility that had nothing to do with his own life. "He created the ideal family out of what we were not," observes his daughter, Hale Lamont Havers.[29] But however reprehensible his behavior, Gabrielson obviously drew upon his unhappy family experiences in his scripts. "Audiences are willing to accept the idea that good things are not the only things that happen in families," he told one interviewer, citing in particular an episode where Mama fears she will lose Papa's interest if she wears the eyeglasses that have been prescribed for her.[30]

Gabrielson's writing not only disclosed the contradictions of domesticity, with Ralph Nelson's encouragement it also used the moral concerns of the Hansen household to critique society. An episode about Halley's comet provided a pretext for airing concerns about nuclear war metaphorically; the presence of a Chinese laundryman provoked a lesson about the evils of racial prejudice, and an episode set during World War I gave Mama an opportunity to question the "glories" of war and the enthusiasms of uncritical nationalism. Nelson viewed his own liberal politics and his commitment to acting as part and parcel of a rebellion against his father's values, and he welcomed opportunities to combine the two. Censorship pressures within the industry only redoubled his resolve. Executives from a company that bought large amounts of commercial time on television once warned Nelson that he was to hire "no communists, no socialists, and we're even thinking of eliminating Democrats."[31] But he did not give in to that pressure, joining Martin Ritt in refusing to sign a loyalty oath. Nelson told the network, "There's nothing in my background that's subversive, and the loyalty oath is unconstitutional."[32] Like the creators of earlier incarnations of the Hansen family narrative, Nelson and Gabrielson developed the contradictions within *Mama* because those contradictions formed an important part of their lives. Their work both resisted and reinforced dominant ideology by highlighting operative ideological tensions in the social context in which their art appeared.

The serial nature of television situation comedies and the recombinant nature of popular culture texts inhibit premature closures. Narrative devices that fix meanings in other media leave them unstable and subject to revision on television. When combined with the continual changes in social life characteristic of our era, they contain the possiblity for opening up previously closed discussions. It is certainly possible that the Hansen family narrative served the interests of patriarchy, capitalism, and the state, but it is also possible that it exposed contradictions conducive to resistance to those institutions. As long as people's needs and desires remain unsatisfied, the prospects for narrative and ideological closure are always incomplete. As the old people used to say in the days of slavery, "You can hide the fire, but what you gonna do with the smoke?"

Popular Music

5

Against the Wind: Dialogic Aspects of Rock and Roll

Nothing is absolutely dead: every meaning will have its homecoming festival.

Mikhail Bakhtin

All music is derivative. It's built on what people did before.
Joe Perry of Aerosmith

Literary critic Bakhtin's observation has special significance for popular music.[1] As much as any other art form, popular music depends upon the recovery and re-accentuation of previous works. Bakhtin developed his concept of "dialogic" criticism to explain how popular carnival traditions influenced the content of writings by Rabelais, Pushkin, and Dostoevsky; his theories have been most often applied to the written word. Dana Polan and Horace Newcomb have applied dialogic criticism to cinema and television, respectively, but music critics have been strangely unresponsive to the implications of Bakhtin's work for their own discipline. Popular music is nothing if not dialogic, the product of an ongoing historical conversation in which no one has the first or the last word. The traces of the past that pervade the popular music of the present amount to more than mere chance: they are not simply juxtapositions of incompatible realities. They reflect a dialogic process, one embedded in collective history and nurtured by the ingenuity of artists interested in fashioning icons of opposition.

According to Bakhtin, culture is cumulative, a barrier reef constructed out of the choices and negotiations of everyday speech. Everyone enters a dialogue already in progress; all speech carries within it part of the social context by which it has been shaped. The dialogic model sees artistic creation as innately social and innately historical. As Richard Terdiman observes

> Dialogism in other words, is a memory model. It seeks to recall the semantic and social history carried by a culture's language, but which tends to be forgotten, to be blanked, in the characteristic form of cultural mystification since the revolutions of the nineteenth century.[2]

The novel drew Bakhtin's particular attention because of its "polysemic" nature—filled with contradictory voices representing the contradictions of social life. Popular music contains many of the features that attracted Bakhtin to the novel. Its "voices" resonate with the vernacular and sacred traditions of the past, incorporating musical and linguistic figures into readily understood icons and images. Bakhtin saw characters in a novel as representing different ideological responses to European culture; lyrical and musical elements in American popular music can be seen as standing for attitudes and "character zones" in the present. Bakhtin's novelists drew upon popular traditions of carnival laughter as a way of mocking and uncrowning power, of crying out for a just world; contemporary musicians draw upon the language and traditions of the postwar, urban, working-class subcultures that gave birth to rock and roll. Just as the European novel never lost touch with the popular traditions it seemed to eclipse, popular music has never been totally severed from the energy and imagination of the postwar American industrial communities in which it originated.

Four contentions form the core of my argument about the dialogic nature of rock and roll music. First, the presence of the past in rock and roll music has meaning beyond the lure of nostalgia and the persistence of artistic clichés. Second, the experiences of the past help shape both the structure of music and the intentions of artists. Third, the origins of rock and roll music in the postwar American industrial city infuse the music with certain democratic and egalitarian propensities. Finally, while no cultural form has a fixed political meaning, rock and roll music has been and continues to be a dialogic space, an arena where memories of the past serve to critique and change the present.

The Dialogic Challenge to Anthropological
and Semiotic Criticism

Explaining exactly how musical notes create their powerful affect is one of the most daunting problems facing cultural critics. Musicologists tend to take a formalistic approach, transposing musical creations into mathematical schemas and evaluating them on the basis of their complexity and originality. This approach tends to present the critic as the maximally competent listener, and it tends to portray the relationship between audiences and musical pieces as abstract, detached, and technical. Even with European classical music for which this method was devised, the traditional musicological approach has serious deficiencies, but it is a disaster when applied to popular music. The aesthetic intentions of popular-music composers and their relationship to their audiences are completely different from what confronts a classical-music composer. A popular-music audience expects entry and engagement with the work of art in a way that classical audiences do not (or at least do not any longer, although they once did). What might seem technically competent or original within classical music might seem dangerously unfamiliar or offputting to a popular-music audience. Finally, the interpellation of popular music into everyday life through dancing, repetition, and background noise makes engagement with it fundamentally different from music composed for the concert hall or refined stereo system.

Anthropological and semiotic criticism have emerged among popular-music critics as the two primary alternatives to musicological formalism. The anthropological approach focuses on the uses and effects of popular music in the everyday lives of listeners, while the semiotic approach identifies the underlying structural unities that determine the ideological consequences of popular music's production and reception. Anthropological and semiotic critiques offer indispensable insights about popular music, but they tend to obscure both affect and agency. They obscure affect either by ignoring the music entirely and focusing on the social processes it fosters, or by accounting for affect with a formalism of their own which assigns static social meanings to musical figures regardless of their context of creation or reception. Such critiques obscure agency by reifying the complex social interactions that create popular music into abstract

101

structures like "the rock and roll apparatus" or "the sociology of youth." Disturbing elements of Parsonian sociology and Geertzian anthropology in anthropological and semiotic criticism further elide human agency by presenting culture as a way for societies to stabilize themselves as total systems. Thus all oppositional practice becomes a way of letting off steam and of reconciling potential dissidents back into a total social structure that remains unified by virtue of the stories it tells itself. At any given moment societies may secure stability through culture, but over time we can see that some features of culture are ascendant and others descendant, that some serve the interests of dominant groups while others serve to educate and agitate aggrieved populations. Without an adequate sense of culture as conversation and contestation, without an adequate understanding of historical change, anthropological and semiotic critiques of popular music tend to degenerate into recycled formalism in their appraisals of music, and into recycled "consensus" social science in their judgments about society.

Dialogic criticism offers a means of transcending some of the limits of musicological, anthropological, and semiotic approaches to popular music. It connects affect to agency, and grounds social and ideological choices within the life worlds and collective memories of actual historical subjects. It shows how part of "what popular music is" can be found in "how popular music came to be," but it also avoids the twin pitfalls of formalism and essentialism. Dialogic criticism eschews formalism by finding meaning not in forms themselves, but in how forms are put into play at any given moment to re-articulate or dis-articulate dominant ideology. It avoids essentialism by evaluating cultural practice as an ongoing dialogue responsive to the demands of both past and present, rather than as a fixed inventory of practices to be approved or disapproved. Thus the problem for dialogic criticism is not whether rock music is oppositional or co-optive, but rather how it arbitrates tensions between opposition and co-optation at any given historical moment. Similarly, the dialogic evaluation of music forms like heavy metal, country music, reggae, or punk depends less on an identification of their core structures than upon the ways in which they mediate between past and present for their audiences.

The importance of the dialogic approach can best be demonstrated by what happens to even the best anthropological and semiotic criticism when it fails to account adequately for history, affect, and agency. Lawrence Grossberg, E. Ann Kaplan, and Simon Frith have written eloquent and intelligent works on rock music that have established them as the pre-eminent academic critics in the field. Yet all three have also been led to incomplete or erroneous judgments about rock and roll because their methods do not allow for sufficient consideration of music-making as a dialogic process.

Grossberg locates the reception of rock music within a historical time frame, but one that signals the end of history. He explains, "As history becomes mere change—discontinuous, directionless and meaningless—it is replaced by a sense of fragmentation and rupture, of oppressive materiality, of powerlessness and relativism."[3] Kaplan describes the MTV television channel as "part of a contemporary discourse that has written out history as a possible discourse," and she claims that the channel's teen-age audience "is constituted by the station as one decentered mass that absorbs all the types indiscriminately—without noting or knowing their historical origins."[4] Certainly the disorientation and fragmentation that Grossberg and Kaplan describe are part of the consciousness of our time. But the crisis of memory to which they allude is not new; indeed, it has been the constitutive problem of bourgeois society since the nineteenth century.[5] As Fredric Jameson points out, historical epochs like our own do not reflect one sense of history or one sense of values, but instead reflect many simultaneous ways of living and many simultaneous stories explaining life from the vantage point of competing interests.[6]

Compare the ahistoricity of rock critics Grossberg and Kaplan with the perspectives of rock artists Chuck D of the rap group Public Enemy and David Bowie, rock's "great chameleon." Chuck D says, "You have people saying, 'But the problems of the past are over, let's not even think about it.' But the problems growing out of hundreds of years of slavery remain for millions of black people and the only way I see them overcoming the problems is through education and networking."[7] David Bowie points out, "In our music, rock 'n' roll, the blues are our mentor, our godfather, everything. We'll never lose that, however diversified and modernistic and cliché ridden with synthesizers it becomes. We'll never ever, be able to renounce the initial heritage."[8] A rapper like Chuck D and a spectacular performance artist like David Bowie juxtapose seemingly incompatible

forms from the past and present in their art in a way that would satisfy the most demanding postmodern appetites. But their art also remains connected to the social formations in which they first developed. Chuck D's deployment of the past is expressly political, while
Bowie's relates specifically to music. But both serve to illustrate the
pervasive presence of the past in and around popular music, even in
an age of postmodernism. Of course, Grossberg and Kaplan would
be correct to contend that at any given moment audiences of Chuck
D and David Bowie might have no meaningful knowledge of the past,
but that is a far different matter from saying that audiences are posi-
tioned outside history, or that maximally competent listeners could
not discover meaningful historical connections in their work.

Simon Frith sees historical traces in popular music, but finds them
completely reactionary and defeatist. Citing Greil Marcus, Frith presents rock music's core tension as a battle between ambition, style,
adventure, risk-taking, and a refusal to be satisfied on one hand, and
a feeling for roots, history, "a dependence on community and tradition, the acceptance of one's lot" on the other. Frith's equation of
roots, history, community, tradition, and "acceptance of one's lot"
neglects the ways in which the past often serves as a critique of the
present, as a refusal of one's lot and an assertion of entitlement to
something better. Bruce Springsteen, John Cougar Mellancamp, and
Bob Seger often use the past in that way, but Frith dismisses the
meaning of such works simply because they are rooted in the past.
"By the end of the 1970s," Frith explains, "there was no music a rock
musician (however young) could make that did not refer back, primarily, to previous rock readings; the music was about itself now,
whether it liked it or not—this was obvious even (perhaps especially) in the work of a skilled rock naturalist like Bruce Springsteen."

Thus for Frith, references to the past are innately conservative, but
if they are not conservative then they are to be dismissed because
they are really about music, not about society. Yet one reason for
popular music's powerful affect is its ability to conflate music and
lived experience, to make both the past and present zones of choice
that serve distinct social and political interests. Frith's one dimensional view of the past becomes most evident in his dismissal of
country music as "a conservative form carrying a conservative message," the music of people whose "dignity derives from their passiv-

ity," with only one lyrical message "We're a loser." Aside from the anti-working class and anti-intellectual prejudices shaping such a description, it suffers from a lack of historical knowledge about the traditions of the white working class, of populism, Evangelical Protestantism, and the labor movement, and their impact on the historical imagination of country music. This is not to take the opposite view and say that there is nothing conservative about country music, but, rather, to assert that progressive and conservative elements interact in any memory of the past, and that the specific contexts in which these elements are deployed, rather than their focus on the past or present, determines their social meaning.

The same kind of one-dimensional either/or approach that enables Frith to reduce a reverence for tradition to "acceptance of one's lot," and which finds only a single message of defeatism and conservatism in country music, leads him to misunderstand rock and roll texts as well. Challenging what he terms "an unproblematic relationship between social experience and musical expression," Frith points out that under conditions of commodified mass culture "the sounds that fill our lives are always made *for* us," and that consequently "we hear music as natural and think nothing about how it came to be made that way." An unproblematic relationship between musical expression and social experience should be challenged, but Frith opposes it with an equally unproblematic assumption of rupture between cultural expression and history. For example, he claims that the materiality of human voices comprises an essential element in rock and roll music, and that "the only way" we can explain Elvis Presley's appeal is "not in terms of what he 'stood for,' socially or personally, but by reference to the *grain* of his voice." Obviously, we need more than one explanation to account for Presley's popularity, but to claim that the primary factor is the pitch and timbre of his voice is to totally overlook the context in which that voice was received. As I have argued, social context is the matrix of production and reception of popular music. For example, Bruce Springsteen remembers the voices he heard on the radio while growing up, but was struck by their social claims as well as by their "grain." Dave Marsh recounts Springsteen's words to a concert audience,

> I started reading this book, *The History of the United States*, and it seemed that things weren't the way they were meant to be — like the

way my old man was living, and his old man, and the life that was waiting for me—that wasn't the original idea. . . . But even if you find those things out, it's so hard to change those things. And it wasn't until I started listening to the radio, and I heard something in those singers' voices that said there was more to life than what my old man was doing and the life that I was living. And they held out a promise, and it was a promise that every man has a right to live his life with some decency and some dignity. And it's a promise that gets broken every day, and in the most violent way. But it's a promise that never, ever dies, and it's always inside of you.[9]

This is not to argue that grain of voice is an irrelevant category, but rather to demand that any formal musical device be studied to understand how it produces its desired affect for concrete historical subjects. Frith's neglect of the historical contexts of musical creation and reception leaves him with largely formalistic criteria for musical analysis and interpretation. He attributes the appeal of reggae music to "the music itself—its lack of a hierarchy of sounds, its depth of pulse," contending that "it didn't express anything else, some prior reality, but was the structure of experience, for musician and audience alike."[10] Frith contends that British punk music of the 1970s "no more reflected directly back on conditions in the dole queue than it emerged spontaneously from them," claiming that "punk was an effect of formal conventions, a particular combination of sounds."[11] According to Frith, black music's popularity depends on its "immediate and democratic" nature which he claims means that listeners "need no special training or knowledge to appreciate it," because "the qualities that are valued in spontaneous music making are emotional rather than technical."[12] Frith is to be commended for his interest in the music itself; indeed it is a tribute to his integrity as a scholar and his acumen as a critic that he writes so sensitively of the ways in which music affects the senses. But his laudable desire to avoid crude reductionism, to resist the temptation of treating music as *merely* a direct reflection of social and historical tensions leads him too far in the opposite direction. Frith understates the importance of musical and historical traditions in the construction of rock and roll. For example, black musicians need great technical skill and knowledge to make emotional contact with discerning audiences. The raw energy of punk music draws at least part of its power from a very real social crisis of the 1970s that threatened the futures of the young, and the hypnotic depth that Frith celebrates within reggae music owes a great deal to its functional role within aggrieved communities. It is one thing to assume an unproblematic relationship between musical expression and social experience, and quite another to see music as social, as a part of collective historical memory and continuing social dialogue.

It is not just the music that becomes one dimensional when anthropological and semiotic critics neglect dialogic and historical evidence. The complex interactions of the pop music world, their competing agents and ideologies, become flattened into a stable and seemingly monolithic system. True to his Parsonian methdology, Frith states the case most baldly: "The music doesn't challenge the system, but reflects and illuminates it."[13] Grossberg and Kaplan find more oppositional practice and potential within rock and roll than does Frith, but they see ideological incorporation into commodity society as the ultimate effect of popular-music consumption. Grossberg argues that rock and roll provides a diversion from the meaninglessness and boredom of contemporary adolescence by positioning "insiders" (white music listeners) as "outsiders" (rebels, hedonists, undifferentiated "others") "even while they exist within the hegemony."[14] For Kaplan, MTV is "symptomatic of Reagan's America in its unquestioning materialism," and the very structures of music video calls up a "desire for plenitude" that can only be filled by the consumer economy.[15]

Frith, Grossberg, and Kaplan also seem united in their views about the persistence of racism and the superficiality of black-white interchanges within rock and roll. Frith notes, "One of the most obvious features of rock'n'roll and street life, is how poorly racially integrated it is, how much it still reflects the problems of white leisure and white youth."[16] Grossberg claims that "the production and reception" of rock and roll by white youths severed the music from its country and blues origins, and made it the locus of a boundary within social reality "marked only by its otherness."[17] Kaplan argues that "the largely white middle-American audience to which MTV gears itself are uninterested in black bands, and this we must attribute to cultural codes that shape this group in Reagan's America."[18] Critics who attribute all the power in the world to the rock-and-roll apparatus, to its ability to construct comprehending and obedient subjects, strangely enough blame the audience rather than the commercial apparatus for the appearance of sexism, racism, and class hierarchies in popular music.

The portrayal of popular music as an enclave of conservatism, as a stimulus for consumer desire, and an agent of white racism is not incorrect, but it is incomplete. Popular culture is indeed a site for the iteration and reiteration of dominant values, commercialized leisure does provide distraction and diversion rather than fulfillment. But the very sites where ruling ideologies can be articulated are also the places where they can be disarticulated. As Stuart Hall writes

> Popular culture is neither, in a "pure" sense, the popular traditions
> of resistance to these processes; nor is it the forms which are
> superimposed on and over them. It is the ground on which the
> transformations are worked.[19]

Dialogic criticism insists that we understand "the ground on which the transformations are worked" by locating them within their proper historical context. Messages about commodity desire or racism within popular music enter a dialogue already in process. On the one hand, systematic exercises of power throughout society encourage expressions in popular culture reflective of economic, racist, and sexist hierarchies. On the other hand, oppositional traditions deeply embedded within the past and present lives of concrete historical subjects work to undermine dominant ideologies and to stimulate real and imagined alternatives. Thus racism in popular music needs to be seen in the context of other social institutions — of the systematic re-segregation of schools, neighborhoods, and recreation areas that has accompanied the assault on "public" space during the neoconservative ascendancy of the 1970s and 1980s. Similarly, the pervasiveness of commodity form and materialism in popular music needs to be assessed within the context of older traditions about plenitude and the good life — for example, the luxuriant boasting of blues and country-music songs that stake a claim on the good life for ordinary people. No articulation has meaning by itself: we need to see the ways in which it mediates between lived experience and desire, between the realities of the present and the blasted hopes of the past. Most important, we need to learn the language, to detect the exact nature of the dialogue that we have all entered.

Perhaps the best test case of the dialogic method concerns the persistence of working-class forms and images within rock and roll music. The anthropological and semiotic critics are also in accord about the class content—or lack of it—in rock and roll music. Grossberg argues, "The fact that particular forms of rock and roll, and even perhaps rock and roll in general, have specific class roots does not necessarily say anything about its reception and social effects in particular contexts."[20] Frith minimizes the working-class origins of rock-and-roll music and musicians, claiming that "to be a rock musician is, indeed, to be detached from a class background."[21] Kaplan acknowledges the significance of rock-music videos stressing social commentary in working-class settings, but insists that "the placement of the videos within the 24-hour televisual flow often eliminates any possible effectiveness."[22] Yet having specific class roots means that rock and roll contains specific class imagery, with biases toward specific class ideologies. Artists themselves may no longer be part of the working class when they achieve success as musicians, but the dialogue from which they emerge, and the one they maintain with their fans, prevents them from becoming completely detached from their class backgrounds. To credit the "24-hour" visual flow with totally suppressing the class content of popular music is to present capitalism's most grandiose self-inflated image of itself as reality and to underestimate greatly the guile and skill of artists who come from a tradition that has repeatedly placed oppositional messages in media unreceptive to popular control.

The creation of musical affect always takes place within a historical context. Musical forms have meaning only as they can be interpreted by knowing subjects. An inventory of the basic vocabulary of rock and roll reveals something about the triumphs of class hierarchies, of racism, sexism, materialism, and individualism, but it also identifies an unfinished dialogue about the potential of oppositional traditions. By looking at the music itself, we can find dialogic traces of the past and discern their enduring utility in the present.

What the Notes Mean: The Core Vocabulary of Rock and Roll in Social and Historical Perspective

Little Richard's "Good Golly Miss Molly" provides the quickest introduction to the vocabulary of rock-and-roll music. It employs a three-line, twelve-bar blues structure with an AAB rhyme scheme, uses call and response between instruments and voice, displays falsettos and similar "impure" tones, relies on blues chord progressions and blue notes, utilizes a rolling bass line in 8/8 time, and expresses a playful wit and joyous hedonism in its lyrics. These forms have displayed tremendous affective power; they undergird a music that has attained popularity around the globe. But they come from concrete historical circumstances; they emerged to express specific ideological positions; and they retain a bias toward those positions as they are played and interpreted today.

The three-line, twelve-bar blues echo the dominant forms of traditional West African poetry with their characteristic AAB rhymes. Little Richard sings "Good Golly Miss Molly, you sure like to ball" two times, and then completes the verse with a third line that comments on the first two—"when you're rockin' and a rollin,' you can't hear your mama call." Throughout the song, instrumental bursts "answer" and "respond" to the vocalist's "call." This antiphony, or "call and response," also originated in Africa and survived in North America in work songs and in responsive singing in churches. Rather than striving for "pure" tones as defined by the Western measured scale, Little Richard's singing involves leaps of register into high-pitched falsettos as well as an assortment of slides and growls down the scale. African languages characteristically vary meaning by changing tone register and that continent's musics draw upon the entire range of sounds open to the human ear, rather than merely upon the precisely measured vibrations that count as notes in the West. Part of the dynamic tension felt by listeners to "Good Golly Miss Molly" comes from the presence of "blue" notes—flatted thirds, fifths, and sevenths on the Western scale and by the I-IV-V blues chord progressions. These forms evolved within American popular music as a result of the efforts by Afro-Americans to "bend" the notes of western instruments to conform to the harmonies of African traditions. "Good Golly Miss Molly" also displays rhythmic properties of African derivation. Underneath the vocals, the band plays a rhythmic 8/8 time featuring the "rolling bass" notes popularized by "boogie woogie" piano players in the 1930s. The drummer complements this basic rhythm with accents and afterbeats that give the song a polyrhythmic quality reminiscent of African music.

Obviously, the Africanisms in "Good Golly Miss Molly" contain traces of America's most oppressive labor system—chattel slavery.

But more than origins are at stake here. The musical figures and lyrical choices represented by those song forms testify to ongoing beliefs about music and society that form an important subtext of rock-and-roll music. Historically, Afro-Americans have treasured African retentions in speech, music, and art both as a means of preserving collective memory about a continent where they were free and as a way of shielding themselves against the hegemony of white racism. As long as Africa existed, as long as African forms contrasted with Euro-American forms, white racism was a particular and contingent American reality, not an inevitable or necessary feature of human existence. But music with retentions of African culture have long held enormous appeal for American whites as well. Pre-industrial values endured longer in Afro-American culture than among more privileged groups because slavery and racism prevented black assimilation. White workers, whose own ancestors had been farmers or peasants, made a painful break with the past as they journeyed from field to factory. Industrial culture demanded regular disciplined work, competition, thrift, individualism, and delayed gratification. Residual elements of opposition to industrial values had to be purged from most Euro-American workers, but Afro-Americans maintained a closer connection to the pre-industrial world. Thus working-class whites could find a consistent and eloquent critique of individualism and competition in Afro-American culture which also displayed a humane and human alternative to industrial values in its music.

Dialogic criticism draws out the world view of Afro-American music and explains how musical devices use affect to create ideological coherence. Critical methods that ignore history can obscure the subjectivity of black music and grossly misrepresent white audience reception. For example, Robert Pattison's analysis of selected song lyrics leads him to claim

> White rockers adopted black bluesmen as their primitive ideals
> because there were no Navahos or Samoans available for the role.
> Most Americans have never met an Indian, but the black man is a
> ubiquitous American presence—thought to be primitive in his dark
> skin, his poverty, his strange dialect, his mysterious African origins. In
> the white man's imagination, he is only a few generations from the
> jungle and therefore the perfect candidate to be the realization of the
> Romantic idea of the primitive.[23]

Native American Indians and viewers of western films might wonder what kind of evidence leads Pattison to assume Americans incapable of turning Indians into popular culture icons. Those who study the various stereotypes of blacks in American popular culture might wonder how Pattison has decided that only *one* of them—the primitive—influences reception of black music. But to make these valid objections is to draw attention away from Pattison's central, and certainly false, presumption—that black music has nothing to say, that its entire creative meaning comes from the twisted imagination of white listeners who do not hear the music, but instead project on it a frame of reception designed for nineteenth-century European poetry. Pattison's conclusion is based solely on his investigations into song lyrics. He does not consider the music or its audiences. He projects himself as the ideal, maximally competent listener (actually reader), capable of articulating a "truth" unknown to the artists and audiences themselves.

In historical practice, black music has emphasized community, creativity, and criticism. Constant repetition of familiar forms like call and response encourages a close relationship between artists and audiences in collaborative cultural creation. Music that explores the entire range of possible sounds open to voice and instruments stresses individual creation and emotion in contrast to the mechanical system of notation in Western music that demands replication of standardized "pure" notes. The rhythmic complexity of Afro-American music encourages listeners to think of time as a flexible human creation rather than as an immutable outside force.

The glorification of pleasure and play in song lyrics serves as implicit and sometimes explicit criticism of a society that places primary emphasis on the duty of labor. The sense of time conveyed within Afro-American music directly contradicts one of the main disciplining forces of industrial culture. Before the rise of the factory, people generally worked at their own pace for their own purposes, disciplined by necessity or desire, but not by the time clock. Industrial labor brought the clock and its incessant demands into the workplace and into the home; days became divided into units of working time and individuals lost control over the nature, purpose, and duration of their labor. Controlling workers accustomed to pre-industrial values was the primary focus of management for over one hundred years. Despite rewards of high wages and punishments including the threat of starvation, workers never wholeheartedly embraced time-work discipline, and their culture reflected that refusal. Instead of the regular beat that measured time by the clock, working-class musics embraced polyrhythms and irregular time signatures as a way of realizing in culture the mastery over time denied workers in the workplace. Prison songs like "The Cryderville Jail" were changed to "Hard Times in the Mill," where every hour marked another indignity. Rock-and-roll musicians built on that tradition, rhythmically and lyrically. If nineteenth century workers marked every hour with mention of another indignity at work, rock and roll songs offered fantasies about partying or making love around the clock. Bill Haley's "Rock Around the Clock" and Chuck Berry's "Reelin' and Rockin' " became rock anthems by inverting the icon of the clock and using it to measure out doses of pleasure instead of units of labor.

Incorporating elements of Afro-American music into their own cultures enabled white working-class musicians to taste in culture what they missed in life. Incorporating elements of Afro-American music into rock and roll enabled middle-class people to draw upon their own sedimented traditions and receive a working model of "the good life" at odds with the hegemonic norms of industrial society. At least in music, harmony with others could replace competition, work and art could be united in creative labor, and the repressions of the industrial workplace could be challenged by the uninhibited passions of love and play.

The historical revolt against hierarchy and exploitation that gave voice to the Afro-American devices at the heart of rock-and-roll music also account for the many other retentions in popular music of vernacular working-class cultures. Rock-and-roll songs stressed continuity and community by reworking familiar melodies. Bill Haley and His Comets reached the middle class with "Rock Around the Clock" when the film *Blackboard Jungle* used it as its opening theme, but the song had a long history in the collective memory of the audience in that its basic structure appeared in country music ("Move It On Over" by Hank Williams, 1953), in rhythm and blues ("Cornbread" by Hal Singer, 1948), and in New Orleans parade music of indeterminate age ("Second Line"). The basic pattern of the Bo Diddley beat pervading so many songs from "Bo Diddley" (Bo Diddley, 1955), to "Not Fade Away" (Buddy Holly, 1957; Rolling Stones, 1964), "Willie and the Hand Jive" (Johnny Otis, 1958), "Marie's the Name" (Elvis

Presley, 1961), "Mickey's Monkey" (Miracles, 1963), and the Strange
loves' "I Want Candy" (1965) originated even earlier in a traditional
children's clapping and rhyming game, "Shave and a Haircut."

One of the most frequently imitated rhythm-and-blues songs,
Johnny Ace's 1955 "Pledging My Love," came straight out of country
music through "Down in the Valley," "Send Me Some Loving," and
"Birmingham Jail." The Rivieras' 1964 "California Sun" remade
Chuck Berry's 1959 "Broken Arrow," but "Broken Arrow" essentially
copied "Old MacDonald." Children's rhyming games provided the
lyrics for Lee Dorsey's 1961 "Ya Ya" and Shirley Ellis's 1964 "The
Name Game" and 1965 "Rubber Dolly." Cheerleaders at a football
game in Florida yelling "Our team is red hot, your team ain't doodley
squat" gave Billie Emerson the inspiration for his 1955 hit "Red Hot,"
a song covered a year later by rockabilly artist Billy Lee Riley.[24] Bo
Diddley's 1959 "Say Man" and "Say Man, Back Again" drew upon the
street-corner insult game, the dozens. The "bragging tale" of black
folklore found expression in the music of blues singer Muddy Waters's 1954 "Hootchie Cootchie Man" as well as in white artist Johnny
Rivers's 1965 "Seventh Son."

Songs with references to familiar folk tales and sagas or to everyday speech or street-corner games tended to include listeners in a
community of improvisation and elaboration. The songs came from
life and easily blended back into it. As the members of the audience
remembered and repeated, they ritualistically confirmed the com-
monality of everyday experience. Direct references to working-class
legend and folklore framed the dialogue within rock and roll. Afro-
American street singers in St. Louis's rough Chestnut Valley district in
the 1890s sang a tale of romance and revenge titled "Frankie and
Johnny." White country-music singer Jimmie Rodgers recorded a
version of "Frankie and Johnnie" in the 1930s, and it appeared in
rock-and-roll songs by Brook Benton (1961), Sam Cooke (1963), and
Elvis Presley (1966). Another Afro-American ballad of the same era
told about the "bad man" Stacker Lee, who emerged as a staple of
black folklore and as the hero of rock-and-roll songs by Lloyd Price
(1958), Wilson Pickett (1971), and Tommy Roe (1971). The traditions
of southern storytellers like Brother Dave Gardner and Jimmie Drift-
wood infused the lyrics of hit songs by Ray Stevens and Johnny Hor-
ton, while black folktales, legends, and word games permeated
records by Louis Jordan, Screamin' Jay Hawkins, Chuck Berry, and

Huey Smith and the Clowns. These folk retentions survived because of their appeal as narratives, but also because they marshaled the resources of the past as part of defining identity in the present.

Very few rock-and-roll songs addressed social issues directly, but their roots in working-class folklore traditions enabled them to encode social messages in metaphorical form. The definitive folk song of American working-class history has more likely been "John Henry" than "Solidarity Forever," but there is a lot of solidarity in workers singing about John Henry, the man who was better than a machine and who died trying to prove it. Social protest in rock and roll grew from that tradition. Gospel singer Bessie Griffin illumines this protest sensibility in a story about her childhood. Griffin explains that she used to sing hymns and spirituals as a way of challenging authority in her family. When scolded, she never talked back but would start singing "I Been 'Buked and I Been Scorned" or "Sometimes I Feel Like a Motherless Child," until one day her grandmother said "I know what you doing."[25] Griffin learned covert resistance from a culture that had developed it into a fine art under circumstances that prevented them from posing more direct challenges to power. Griffin's community may have paid a terrible price for their inability to confront oppression directly, but they also preserved their dignity and self-worth by asserting faith in some kind of ultimate justice. The same spirit pervaded rock-and-roll songs that celebrated the triumphs of clever tricksters over more powerful foes, from the De John Sisters' 1958 "Straighten Up and Fly Right" to Chuck Berry's 1958 "Jo Jo Gunne" to the Coasters' 1959 "Run Red Run."

Another form of encoding protest came in a series of songs with special meaning for particular reception communities. Chuck Berry's 1956 "Brown Eyed Handsome Man" enjoyed great popularity among blacks who knew that he meant brown *skinned* handsome man. The Five Keys' 1954 "Ling Ting Tong" (and its many cover versions) employed the slang of marijuana users, while seemingly mysterious references in the Jaynetts' 1963 "Sally Go 'Round the Roses" described a lesbian relationship to maximally competent listeners. Oppressions of class, age, and gender also provoked indirect forms of protest. Chuck Berry's 1956 "Too Much Monkey Business" equated frustrations at work, school, home, and in the army—attributing them all to the "monkey business" imposed on individuals by outside authorlty. Eddie Cochran's 1950 "Summertime Blues" drew a connection between youth, dependency, sexual repression, poverty, and the political impotence of youth. Three songs from 1956 illustrate resistance to alienated labor by contrasting it with leisure: Little Richard's "Rip It Up" boasts about spending Friday's paycheck on a wild Saturday night rather than saving it; Carl Perkins's "Blue Suede Shoes" invites the listener to take any of the singer's other material goods but to leave him his treasured subcultural symbols, his shoes; and Fats Domino's "Blue Monday" justifies the weekend spree by comparing it to having "to work like a slave all day" during the week. Women singers in the early 1960s highlighted the unfair constraints and double standards applied to females in a number of songs ranging from Jan Bradley's 1963 "Mama Didn't Lie," Sandy Posey's 1966 "Born a Woman," and Leslie Gore's dialectical 1963 trilogy "It's My Party," "Judy's Turn to Cry," and "You Don't Own Me."

From its tradition of social criticism to its sense of time, from its cultivation of community to its elevation of emotion, rock-and-roll music embodies a dialogic process of active remembering. It derives its comedic and dramatic tensions from working-class vernacular traditions, and it carries on a prejudice in favor of community, collectivity, and creativity in its very forms and constructs.

History and Rock-and-Roll Criticism

Literary critics Richard Terdiman and Allon White have emphasized the degree to which the dialogic approach is "a memory model," and therefore innately historical. The formal properties of rock-and-roll songs developed in response to concrete historical conditions rather than to a pre-established aesthetic agenda. To understand such songs in context, it is necessary to see how they shaped and reflected historical changes, particularly in regard to the rapid growth and immediate decline of the American industrial city in the 1940s and 1950s.

In essence, I argue that industrial labor created the preconditions for rock and roll, and the first rock-and-roll artists, entrepreneurs, and audiences came out of wartime working-class communities. Defense production for World War II attracted millions of rural whites and blacks to industrial cities, and the interactions between their cultures in the urban setting created rock-and-roll music. On the factory floor, at the neighborhood tavern, and on the radio, workers heard music previously restricted to limited audiences. Country music and blues interacted with jazz, pop, and ethnic music to form a new synthesis. Defense production centers like Los Angeles, Detroit, and St. Louis experienced enormous increases in population during World War II. Blacks left the South in large numbers during the 1940s, and during the war years alone 750,000 whites moved to Los Angeles and more than 200,000 moved to Detroit. Overcrowding created new realities in defense production centers. In Beaumont, Texas the housing shortages reached such levels that workers rented beds for eight-hour shifts, and the mounting piles of garbage in the streets led city officials to send hogs through the alleys in the hope that they would eat garbage and lessen dangers to public health. Crowded neighborhoods and buses created face-to-face contacts among previously separated groups. The new urban realities of the 1940s sometimes led to violence, but they also allowed for new cultural exchanges that would have been impossible in prewar America.

Black migrations to industrial cities during and after the war had profound cultural implications. Middle-class American popular music, dance, and dress reflected Afro-American influences as never before, and previously marginalized aspects of black and white southern culture influenced the national culture as never before. Following the most convenient railroad routes, black workers from the Southeast tended to migrate to the Baltimore, Philadelphia, New York corridor. Those from the Mississippi Delta and mid-South took the Illinois Central to Memphis, St. Louis, and Chicago, or took the Louisville and Nashville line to Cincinnati, Indianapolis, and Detroit. Blacks from Texas and Louisiana went to Los Angeles and San Francisco. As a result, east-coast music owed its structure to the music of the Southeast, Chicago's music encompassed the music of the Delta, and California music during and after the war contained a heavy dose of Texas blues.

Many of the black blues artists whose music prefigured rock and roll participated in these migrations and developed their music while employed as defense workers. John Lee Hooker moved from Mississippi to St. Louis and then to Detroit where he worked as a janitor in one of Chrysler's defense plants. Fellow Mississippians Muddy Waters and B. B. King followed the same pattern of rural-urban migration; Waters worked as a truck driver in Chicago, while King labored at construction jobs in Memphis. Lowell Fulson grew up in Oklahoma and Texas, but journeyed to Oakland, California to work in the wartime shipyards. Texas musicians Charles Brown, T-Bone Walker, and Amos Milburn all moved to the west coast to find factory jobs during the war.[26]

The white country-music artists who played crucial roles in creating rock-and-roll music also took part in those wartime migrations. Hank Williams came from rural Alabama to work in the Mobile shipyards. Elvis Presley's family left Tupelo, Mississippi after the war when his father found employment in Memphis's expanded industrial plant. Bob Wills brought his band from Texas to southern California to play for the transplanted "okies" and Texans drawn west by that region's burgeoning war production factories.[27]

When country music and blues mixed to form rock and roll, industrial cities became centers of the new music, and black and white workers became its leading performers. Fats Domino worked in a Louisiana factory making bedsprings. Chuck Berry worked on the General Motors assembly line in St. Louis. Little Richard washed dishes in the Greyhound Bus Station in Macon, Georgia. Bill Haley learned country music and blues in industrial Detroit, and worked as a disc jockey in Chester, Pennsylvania, a shipyard production center. Elvis Presley drove a truck for the Crown Electric Company in Memphis, and Buddy Holly pursued a career in music as an alternative to his part-time jobs in high school as a bricklayer and steel-manufacturing worker in Lubbock, Texas.[28]

Why did young workers from all over the country participate in the creation of rock and roll music? One strong motivation came from the desire to leave behind the alienations and indignities of work; a career in music could be the alternative to a career washing dishes. Working-class people have long pursued upward mobility through careers in show business that required disassociation from ethnic and class roots. This process involved something different. Raised in the newly desegregated environments of industrial cities, these artists represented a synthesis of historical traditions that had previously been kept apart. Rather than embracing the existing alignments within American popular culture, they sought recognition as part of something new—something infinitely more democratic and pluralistic than existing popular music.

The major recording companies dominating the music industry in the 1940s and 1950s largely ignored the earliest expressions of rock and roll. Secure with their rosters of famous artists and their connections to radio stations and promoters, they detected no demand for a new music. But small entrepreneurs in working-class communities noticed that their customers wanted to hear country music and blues, and so they began to establish small recording companies as sidelines to their regular businesses. More than four hundred new record labels came into existence in the years immediately following World War II, and these labels pioneered the recording of rock and roll music.[29]

Syd Nathan started King Records in Cincinnati because he observed the demand for music by war workers shopping at his department store. Another store owner, Herman Lubinsky of Newark, New Jersey, established Savoy Records to produce music for "the man with the dinner pail and the lady over the washtub."[30] Bob Geddins owned a music store in Oakland, and decided to create his own product by recording Johnny Fuller (a mechanic at Sears) and Lowell Fulson (a shipyard worker). Phil and Leonard Chess operated a night club in a working-class area of Chicago, and the title of their first release on their Chess label—Andrew Tibbs's "Union Man Blues"— gave some indication of the intended audience for their records. Saul Bihari, who operated juke boxes in Los Angeles, formed Modern and RPM Records along with his brothers because the major labels failed to keep him supplied with the kinds of music his customers wanted to hear. Sam Phillips in Memphis had been a radio engineer and owned a small recording studio where he produced records by black and white workers and sharecroppers. Phillips initially leased songs by Ike Turner, Junior Parker, and Howlin' Wolf to other labels, but he eventually started his own Sun Records featuring the music of Elvis Presley, Jerry Lee Lewis, and Carl Perkins.[31]

These small firms succeeded because they identified the cultural preferences of working-class audiences. New recording techniques (magnetic tape, 45 rpm and long-playing records) lessened the capital requirements for entry into the business and made it possible to record without a big studio. The newly acquired purchasing power and cultural interests of the working class, both products of wartime prosperity, created a demand that was invisible to the established firms in the music business. During the late 1940s, five companies essentially dominated the industry, but cut off as they were from working-class audiences and their tastes, these companies failed to anticipate the tremendous appeal of rock and roll. They regained control of the record industry by 1959, but only after a bitter battle with the independent companies making rock-and-roll records.

The Middle Class Encounters Rock and Roll

Because rock-and-roll music developed in highly concentrated urban markets, it became accessible to the middle class in a way that had not been true of blues and country music. The radio stations and record stores that specialized in rock and roll reached audiences previously unaware of working-class cultures. Young whites especially requested music by black artists as well as the blues/country fusions evident in "rockabilly" performances. Less tied to the history of racist norms than their parents, witness to a hybrid black/white culture all around them, and profoundly alienated by the oppressive conformity of 1950s popular culture, they embraced working-class music as their own.

That generation of teen-agers occupied a pivotal position in U.S. history. As the first generation of young people with money of their own to spend without necessarily having to work, they had the freedom to reject the values of their parents and to seek out cultural alternatives. Raised in times of unprecedented consumer affluence, they found more meaning and value in working-class culture than in the signs and symbols of their own emerging middle class. In part, they simply sought escape from the stifling blandness of 1950s popular music, but they also developed their preferences as people anticipating life in an increasingly bureaucratic and conformist society. In a culture that recommended obedience to all authority and lauded the "organization man," they sought autonomy, emotion, and authentic connection to others in the cultures of the working class.[32]

The process of "prestige from below" that infused middle-class fascination with rock and roll had been prefigured during World War II with subcultures that developed around "zoot suits" and "bop talk."[33] The zoot suit (draped coats, pants wide at the knee and narrow at the ankle, wide lapels, pleats and cuffs in the pants) originated in black and Chicano communities, but became a symbol of rebellion that spread to middle-and working-class whites. By wearing zoot suits, young people identified with the dress of the poor rather than the rich, and flaunted their alienation from the surrounding culture.[34]

Closely allied with the zoot-suit culture, bop talk originated among black jazz musicians. Their slang favored internal rhymes (a zoot suit with a drape shape and a reet pleat might impress a slick chick), inverted meanings (something "crazy" really made sense, "cool" people used an aloof posture to hide great passion), and relied on African retentions (a hip cat had the requisite knowledge about life—as one would expect from a term derived from the Wolof word "hipicat," meaning one who has his eyes open).[35] The popularity of bop talk as American slang severed its organic connection to black nationalism, but it remained identified with drugs, hostility to work, and a vaguely un-Christian attitude—a perfect expression of opposition to middle-class norms.

Rock-and-roll musicians often utilized the legacy of bop talk. Elvis Presley billed himself as "The Hillbilly Cat" early in his career, and Buddy Holly and his first singing partner, Bob Montgomery, advertised themselves as "Buddy and Bob—Western and Bop." Berry Gordy's first song-writing success for Jackie Wilson bore the title "Reet Petite," and Jerry Lee Lewis remembers the jazz anthem "Hey Ba-ba Re-Bop" as one of the formative influences on his music. From Carl Perkins's hit "Boppin' the Blues" to Alvadean Coker's "We're Gonna Bop," the word had a magic power for rock-and-roll pioneers. In addition, they made full use of the internal rhymes of bop talk in titles like "See You Later Alligator," "Tutti Frutti," "Ready Teddy," "Money Honey," "Boney Moronie," "Lean Jean," and "Skinny Minnie." These variations of bop talk may have misunderstood its original connotations, but they maintained its rebellious posture, its playfulness with words, and its capacity to create an oppositional in-group.[36]

By pursuing black music, working-class whites explored forbidden ground as did middle-class whites pursuing working-class music. The lure proved greater than the risks to people like Elvis Presley, who listened to Big Bill Broonzy and Big Boy Crudup at home, even though his parents scolded him for listening to that "sinful" music. Buddy Holly also embraced a music and a culture not designed for him. After he toured with a rock-and-roll caravan of stars, Holly's mother asked him if he got along with the Negroes in the other bands. "Oh we're Negroes too," he responded, "we get to feeling like that's what we are."[37]

People who made their living from rock and roll in the early 1950s recognized the ways in which the music helped break down barriers of race and class. Jerry Wexler, a producer for Atlantic Records, described the culture of rock and roll as neither black nor white, but as "southern proletarian." Yet many of the audiences that Wexler observed consisted of college students at elite southern schools; if their culture could be termed proletarian, it was by deliberate identification, not by birth.[38] In St. Louis, Chuck Berry found himself popular with middle-class, white audiences even though he had lived his whole life within a segregated ghetto and even though his music drew mainly upon the blues. At his first, paying musical jobs with the Johnnie Johnson trio in 1953, he noticed many young whites in the audience which struck him as odd "since a lot of white people were afraid to enter a black community."[39]

Consumption of mass popular culture always involves varied motivations and complex choices, and it is difficult to account fully for any specific consumer choice. But at least part of the motivation for the middle-class white youth adoption of Afro-American and working-class music as their own in the 1950s stemmed from a collective judgment about the demise of the urban industrial city and the rise of the suburb. At the very moment that residential suburbs increased class and racial segregation, young people found "prestige from below" by celebrating the ethnic and class interactions of the urban street. Visible markers of class and ethnic identity disappeared as the single-family, detached suburban home replaced the multi-family dwellings of ethnic neighborhoods, as network television eclipsed the neighborhood movie theater, and as a culture of consumption and conformity encouraged standardization of dress and behavior as the entrance requirements into the burgeoning, corporate white-collar world. Mass communications, upward mobility, and the anti-foreign atmosphere fueled by hysterical anti-communism and exaggerated "patriotic" Americanism left many middle-class youths without tangible ties to their own pasts. Facing a choice between the sterile and homogeneous suburban cultures of their parents or the dynamic street cultures alive among groups excluded from the middle-class consensus, a large body of youths found themselves captivated and persuaded by the voices of difference. Mass consumer culture had become so hegemonic that middle-class young people flocked to the cultures of the dying industrial city for connection to the past, for emotional expression, and for a set of values that explained and justified rebellion.

Defenders of middle-class morality and spokespersons for the major record companies recognized the ideological and economic threats to the status quo embodied in the new music. The Artist and Repertoire Director at Columbia Records, Mitch Miller, predicted the rapid demise of rock and roll, damning it as "the comic books of music." A Catholic Church official in Boston claimed that "the suggestive lyrics of rock'n'roll records are a matter for law enforcement agencies." Frank Sinatra told a Congressional investigating committee that rock and roll constituted "the most brutal, ugly, desperate, vicious form of expression it has been my misfortune to hear," adding that the "lewd" lyrics of rock and roll made it "the martial music of every sideburned delinquent on the face of the earth."[40] The actual musical selections that aroused the ire of these businessmen, clergy, and performers might seem quite tame by today's standards, but the musical censors of the 1950s (like their New Right counterparts in the 1980s) raised the specter of sexuality and its threat to youth as a cover for their real concerns—the "transgressions" perpetrated by middle-class white youths when they embraced "prestige from below" and undercut the ideological hegemony of their own race, class, and family. The anti-rock critics were (and are) no doubt sincere in their revulsion at rock and roll's refusal to separate romantic love from sexual pleasure, but this refusal to separate mind and body is merely one manifestation of an even more "menacing" refusal, that of a symbolic system which insists on "naturalizing" the socially constructed divisions and hierarchies between black and white, rich and poor, male and female. For in choosing truck drivers, dishwashers, and sharecroppers as cultural heroes, middle-class white youths challenged the legitimacy of the emerging corporate-suburban culture and validated the pluralities and ambiguities of the dying industrial city.

Thus the 1950s brought a revolution in popular music, but also provoked a counter-revolution. The major record labels and their allies attempted to regain control over the content of popular music, while business and government leaders continued their assault on the social formations that gave rise to working class leadership in popular culture. By 1959, both groups had succeeded. At first, the major labels ignored rock and roll, but when independent producers reaped the benefits of the increased sales generated by the new music, the big companies began issuing "cover" versions of rock songs performed by pop artists. The cover system made money: with their advertising and distribution powers, the big labels could see to it that their versions enjoyed broader exposure than the originals. But royalties and publication rights went to outsiders under the cover system, and an unpredictable network of artists and small entrepreneurs remained the driving force in the music industry. The popularity of independent artists like Sam Cooke, Jerry Lee Lewis, Little Richard, and Chuck Berry on small labels persisted despite efforts by the majors to "invent" new white and middle-class rock stars like Tommy Sands, Tab Hunter, and Pat Boone. RCA signed Elvis Presley and smoothed off the rough edges of his style for mass distribution, but even then it was specifically Presley the star under contract to RCA that they pushed, not the broader musical culture which had produced him.

Failing to "cover" rock and roll, the music companies then tried to destroy it. Working in tandem with radio-station chains, they encouraged smaller radio playlists (top 40 radio) which had built-in advantages for the big companies with their established connections to station managers. With fewer records on the air, marginal, innovative, or controversial music tended to be squeezed out. This practice rationalized production and minimized risks of new styles by saturating the air with the blandest common denominators of mass taste. When top 40 radio came in, much of the rougher, wilder, blacker, and more working-class music disappeared from the radio.

Limited playlists also encouraged "payola," bribes to disc jockeys for playing certain records. Although the big companies engaged in payola, their resources made them less dependent on it than were the smaller labels. Big companies could count on their contacts and interlocking business relations with radio networks, their influence with advertisers, their ability to supply or withhold future products, and their economy of scale to get their records played. Congressional investigators looking into payola virtually ignored the big firms; their targets were the independent labels likely to feature the harder-edged rock and roll. Government investigators harassed disc jockey Alan Freed and drove him out of the business for his acceptance of $30,000 in exchange for playing some of the wild rock-and-roll music that made his show popular, but the Congressional committee had only words of praise for clean-cut and middle-class Dick Clark, with his heavily white and pop playlists. Clark owned stock in record companies and publishing houses whose songs he played on his own shows, yet investigators saw nothing suspicious in the $500,000 in salary and stock or the estimated $25 million in free advertising that Clark derived from his dual role as nationally televised disc jockey and record-company impressario.[41]

Censorship and monopoly within the music industry pervade the history of rock and roll, but critics lacking a historical perspective too often miss their significance. For example, Steve Chapple and Reebee Garofalo, in their *Rock'n'Roll Is Here To Pay*, provide extensive documentation of malicious corporate distortion of rock-and-roll music. But Simon Frith misunderstands their argument, accusing them of objecting to commercial culture itself because of an unrealistic devotion to music as "art" or "folk culture." Despite Chapple and Garofalo's evidence (and that available from other sources), Frith contends, "There is, in fact, less conflict between art and commerce in rock than in any other mass medium," and "commerce is then a serious constraint only at this lower level, for musicians getting into the business."[42] Knowledge of the history of rock and roll indicates otherwise. One thinks of John Fogerty cheated of his royalties and left without a record contract for nearly a decade, of Boston unable to release new records at the peak of its popularity because of contract disputes with its label, or of Irma Thomas, the "soul queen of New Orleans," who records for the tiny Rounder label, despite more than twenty years of exquisite performances. Thomas says, "I know that unless you're on a major label that's spending megabucks for promotion, you haven't got a snowball's chance in hell of getting a record played on radio."[43] These examples from the 1980s underscore the pernicious effects of commercialism on rock-and-roll music, effects that are the rule rather than the exception in a business where more performers *lose* money than make money, but where publishing houses and recording conglomerates almost always increase their wealth. This pattern emerges from the historical record, and it validates rather than disproves the allegations of anti-corporate rock critics.

One need only look at the fate of the 1950s rockers caught up in the whitewashing of popular music that propelled Clark to prominence. In addition to the Congressional committee that lauded Clark, other government agencies also participated in cleaning up rock and roll. The army drafted Elvis Presley at the peak of his popularity, cut his hair, and took him out of circulation for two years. Presley's willingness to let the state borrow his prestige and turn him into a symbol of "patriotism," and his affiliation with RCA enabled him to withstand further harassment. Other artists were not as fortunate. Local prosecutors, the Federal Bureau of Investigation, and the Department of Justice persecuted Chuck Berry for acts that would have been overlooked if they had been committed by a mainstream entertainer. Berry eventually served twenty months in federal prison for allegedly engaging in voluntary sexual relations with a prostitute that he met while on tour. Jerry Lee Lewis faced a media blackout after marrying his fourteen-year-old cousin. But Elvis Presley faced no legal consequences when upon meeting fourteen-year-old Priscilla Beaulieu in Germany, he had her come live with him in Memphis at the age of sixteen.

Record companies and the government exaggerated rock and roll's threat to middle-class morality in the 1950s, but they did not invent it. Unquestionably, the performers and their music did violate middle-class norms. Elvis Presley's gyrations on television (copied from Bo Diddley's stage show) brought a defiant sensuality and unbridled hedonism into American living rooms. Chuck Berry drove big pink Cadillacs and Lincolns, and appeared in public in the company of white women. Little Richard's screeching falsetto, exuberant stage antics, and sexual ambiguities drew upon historical antecedents among black entertainers, but appeared shocking to much of the white middle class. Whether by active conspiracy or enlightened self-interest, the system struck back effectively at the rock-and-roll threat, using the protection of the family as justification to reinforce sexual repression, racial separation, and class divisions—elements that characterized most of the emerging corporate culture.

During the heyday of rock and roll, the percentage of best-selling records by black artists increased from 3 in 1954 to 29 in 1957. After 1959, the percentage declined every year. Sales of all records increased by as much as 36 percent each year between 1955 and 1959, but sales leveled off until 1964. As the industry became whiter and more middle class, its sales declined. But the major companies destroyed their independent competitors and regained their share of the record market.[44]

Yet rock and roll remained alive in working-class neighborhoods of industrial cities. In New Orleans it reached great artistic heights in the early 1960s on the strength of records by Lee Dorsey, an automobile-body repairman; Irma Thomas, a waitress and department store clerk; and the Neville Brothers—Art, an elevator operator; Aaron, a longshoreman; and Cyril, who cleaned box cars and grave yards.[45] Lee Dorsey later remembered his days in New Orleans as marked by a healthy confusion about whether he wanted to be an auto-body repairman who sang, or a singer who did auto-body work.[46]

In New York, young, middle-class and working-class, white songwriters like Carol King, Neil Sedaka, Cynthia Weil, Barry Mann, Doc Pomus, and Mort Shuman drew upon the changing nature of the working class to reinvigorate rock and roll. Inspired by the influx of Hispanic workers in that city and the attendant popularity of musicians Tito Puente, Ray Barretto, and Mongo Santamaria, such songwriters fashioned a series of Latin-tinged rock-and-roll songs for black singers such as the Drifters, Shirelles, and Isely Brothers. Pomus and Shuman even deliberately inverted the words of "Save the Last Dance for Me," making it sound like the English of a non-native speaker.

Despite this enduring working-class urban presence, and despite the occasional entry onto the best-seller charts of rockabilly survivors like Dorsey Burnette or blues veterans like Lloyd Price, popular music between 1959 and 1964 became whiter, blander, and less working class each year.[47] It took the stimulus of the "British Invasion," spearheaded by the Beatles and Rolling Stones, to restore the viability and profitability of the record industry—by reviving the very same American urban, working-class sounds that had been gradually purged from American popular music over the previous five years.

British groups acknowledged their lineage to urban working-class rock and roll. The Beatles "covered" and remade the Isley Brothers' "Twist and Shout," Chuck Berry's "Roll Over Beethoven" and "Rock and Roll Music," Carl Perkins's "Match Box" and "Honey Don't," and Larry Williams's "Slow Down." The Rolling Stones remade Chuck Berry's "Come On" and "You Can't Catch Me," Irma Thomas's "Time

Is On My Side," Marvin Gaye's "Hitch Hike," and Sam Cooke's "Little Red Rooster." The Stones took their name from a Muddy Waters song on Chess Records, and their song "2120 S. Michigan Avenue" paid tribute to the records made at the Chess Studios located at that address in Chicago in the 1950s. John Lennon directly quoted Chuck Berry's "You Can't Catch Me" in his "Come Together," and early Beatles records contained an encyclopedia of Chuck Berry guitar licks, Buddy Holly harmonies, and Little Richard falsettos.

The British invasion of 1964 won a new middle-class audience for rock and roll. Working-class forms seemed less threatening to middle-class morality when interpreted by cute, middle-class, white, British males whose good humor always left open the possibility that they might be joking. Of course, the music lost something in this transformation, but it retained much of importance as well. The collective memory of the audience located these sounds in a context of powerful social associations with rebellion, emotion, and sensuality. Just as zoot suits and bop talk lost some of their original meaning but nonetheless remained valuable as icons of opposition to middle-class subcultures, the recycled rock and roll of the 1950s proved important to the consciousness of middle-class youths of the 1960s. For artists and audiences alike, the starting point of self-identity came from identification with the working-class cultures that created rock and roll.

By the late 1960s, a hippie counterculture coalesced around rock-and-roll music and around a group of values inimical to the traditional concerns of the middle class. Hippies glorified pleasure while resisting work, championed the supportive community over the rugged individual, and responded to a nation at war with proclamations of faith in peace and love. Men adopted long hair, jewelry, and a level of ornamentation and display in dress previously associated with women; women wore comfortable clothing that conformed to the natural contours of the human body rather than to the fashion world's idealized female shape. Middle-class and affluent young whites moved to poor neighborhoods and imitated Afro-American hairstyles and the political rhetoric of the black community. All of these acts of rebellion had severe limits, and in its own way the hippie counter-culture mirrored many of the consumerist values of the society at large. But in attempting to reclaim the physical space of the abandoned inner city and to champion the cause of urban prestige from below, it represented a real rebellion in dialogue with the traces of previous working-class cultures and urban life.

Nothing better illustrates the sedimented, urban working-class traces in 1960s counter-culture better than the personal histories of its two leading symbols, Jimi Hendrix and Janis Joplin. Hendrix grew up in Seattle where his father worked on aircraft assembly lines, as a gardener, and as a steel worker. While still a teen-ager, Hendrix toured with black rock acts like Little Richard and the Isley Brothers and with white and mixed groups including Joey Dee and the Starlighters and Bobby Taylor and the Vancouvers. Hendrix derived his musical vocabulary from the blues which he learned while a foster child living with a family of transplanted Texans in Berkeley, California, and while touring with Ike Turner and Albert King. Like Elvis Presley Hendrix grew up in a public housing project, part of a working-class family, and became famous for fusing black and white music. He adapted traditional blues techniques to contemporary technology with his use of feedback, wah-wah pedal, and simulation of the human voice on guitar. His virtuosity and apocalyptic sensuality had powerful appeal for middle-class youths eager to blot out the ugly realities of everyday life.

Like Hendrix, Janis Joplin became popular both for her music and for her ability to symbolize new values. As a white child in industrial Port Arthur, Texas, she listened to records by blues singers Odetta and Leadbelly to vent her feelings of alienation from the society in which she lived. Unpopular in high school and unwilling to conform to the standards of dress and behavior deemed appropriate for girls her age, Joplin struck out on her own in search of new possibilities. She began her singing career performing Jimmie Rodgers-styled country songs in an Austin night club, but she also imitated Bessie Smith, the "Empress of the Blues." After moving to the west coast (an old Texas tradition) she wound up working as a secretary in San Francisco. An impromptu singing session at a party there led to the formation of the band Big Brother and the Holding Company, and their free concerts in Golden Gate Park made Joplin one of the focal points of the Haight-Ashbury counter-culture.

In every detail, Joplin personified the ideals of the counter-culture. Her untrained but powerful voice and her accidental "stardom" reinforced the belief that everyone could become an artist. Her emergence as a sex symbol elevated sensuality and emotion over conventional standards of beauty. Like Hendrix, her absorption in her art, indulgence in drugs and alcohol, and intense passion reflected the values of young people living for the moment and anticipating little future. But Hendrix and Joplin also shared a profound sense of the past, of the emancipatory cultures of early rock-and-roll music forged in urban industrial settings in their childhoods. Joplin's music relied on techniques originating in country music and blues, but honed and refined by the rock and roll of her youth—three line, twelve bar blues, falsettos, call and response, and bending notes for effect. For both artists and audiences, historical working-class music offered an appropriate grammar and vocabulary for the oppressions and alienations of a new cultural moment.

The hippie counter-culture confronted its own demise most dramatically in the deaths of Hendrix and Joplin. With the break-up of the Beatles, the murder of a participant in the 1969 Altamont Rock festival while the Rolling Stones played onstage, and the degeneration into drug-ravaged slums of hippie "liberated zones" like Haight-Ashbury and New York's East Village, it became clear even to its adherents that "the dream" was over. But that very recognition spread most powerfully through a popular song that placed hippie aspirations within the historical context of 1950s rock and roll—Don McLean's "American Pie." The nation's best-selling song during the winter of 1971–1972, "American Pie" located the death of the counter-culture within a historical cycle of death and rebirth, beginning with the plane crash that killed Buddy Holly and Ritchie Valens and ending with the death of Janis Joplin. McLean's song paid tribute to the erotic and life-affirming currents in rock music, drawing a direct connection between the teen-age passion of the 1950s and the cultural and political dissent of the 1960s. It interchanged references to musicians Bob Dylan, the Beatles, and the Rolling Stones with references to historical figures like the Kennedys and Martin Luther King. By citing a long history of struggle, the song attempted to cushion the blow of current failures and hold open the possibility of future victories.

Against the Wind, the 1970s and 1980s

Much of 1970s and 1980s rock and roll shows the traces of the impact of working-class culture on the industrial cities of the 1940s and 1950s. Bruce Springsteen's automobile metaphors and musical structures borrow freely from Chuck Berry, and Springsteen's characteristic sound—devoid of either high or low tones—echoes the "wall of sound" pioneered by Phil Spector's productions for the "girl groups" of the early 1960s. Springsteen's ties to the past are exemplified by his work as a co-producer with his friend Little Steven Van Zandt for 1960s star Gary Bonds's comeback album "Dedication" (1981). Buddy Holly's first work as a producer brought together country singer Waylon Jennings and rhythm and blues saxophone player King Curtis to do the Cajun song "Jole Blon"; in a gesture of recognition Springsteen and Van Zandt placed the same song on Bonds's album. Van Zandt's co-production of Artists Against Apartheid's "Sun City" album and video in 1985 (which featured Springsteen and a pantheon of rock-and-roll heroes), displayed the same ability to draw upon the rock-and-roll past to reinforce its capacity for mixing races and cultures in progressive unity in the present.

Yet for all his talents as a collaborator with Van Zandt, Springsteen's working-class past informs the present most profoundly on his own records. Whether making autobiographical references to the factory that took his father's time and labor, or defining the American condition through the working people of his "Nebraska" album, Springsteen contrasts the pains of alienated labor to the utopian aspirations for emancipation that have always occupied center stage within rock-and-roll performances. As he explains in "My Home Town," the roots of the malaise confronting men and women "born in the U.S.A." in the 1980s lie in the de-industrialization that has killed off so much of the heterogeneous culture of industrial urban communities.

From Bob Seger's self-conscious anthems about "that old time rock and roll" to the stylistic and lyrical tributes to Chuck Berry and Bo Diddley by Dave Edmunds and George Thorogood, rock and roll in the 1980s carries an extraordinary awareness of its own history. Bo Diddley toured with the Clash, appeared on a George Thorogood video, and found his famous Bo Diddley beat revived in hit records by Bow Wow Wow ("I Want Candy," 1982) and Joan Jett ("Bad Reputation," 1981). Brian Setzer of the Stray Cats pays tribute to Eddie Cochran in interviews, and members of The Look wear Buddy Holly shirts. Even Jim Morrison and the Doors have become favorites among young people who were born years after Morrison's death.

Values and beliefs rooted in working-class experiences set the standards of criticism and the parameters of debate about American life within popular music. Just as previous generations of middle-class listeners nurtured memories and values of working-class pasts, today's "middle class" turns to images from working-class life to express its own discontents as in Billy Joel's 1982 "Allentown" and John Cougar Mellancamp's 1987 "Empty Hands." The working class in the U.S. exists as an empirical fact in the lives of those trading their labor power for wages, but it also lives in the collective historical memory of the middle class. Oppositional thought denied expression by the monopolies who market culture survives in the subtle nuances of cultural moments too small for co-optation or censorship. The working class may not be the agency of emancipation envisioned by Karl Marx, but whatever form emancipation eventually takes, it will be that much easier because there is and has been an American working class. As a class, American workers are "older now, but still running against the wind," nurtured and sustained by a dialogue within popular music that enables them to remember the past and to imagine the future.

6

Cruising Around the Historical Bloc: Postmodernism and Popular Music in East Los Angeles

During his first visit to Los Angeles, Octavio Paz searched in vain for visible evidence of Mexican influence on that city's life and culture. The great Mexican writer found streets with Spanish names and subdivisions filled with Spanish Revival architecture, but to his surprise and dismay he perceived only a superficial Hispanic gloss on an essentially Anglo-American metropolis. Mexican culture seemed to have evaporated into little more than local color, even in a city that had belonged to Spain and Mexico long before it became part of the United States, a city where one-third of the population traced its lineage to Olmec, Maya, Toltec, Aztec, Spanish, and Mexican ancestors, and a city which had more Mexican residents than all but two of Mexico's own cities. Paz detected a "vague atmosphere" of Mexicanism in Los Angeles, manifesting itself through "delight in decorations, carelessness and pomp, negligence, passion and reserve." But he felt that this "ragged but beautiful" ghost of Mexican identity only rarely interacted with "the North American world based on precision and efficiency." Instead, this Mexicanism floated above the city, "never quite existing, never quite vanishing."[1]

As both the oldest and the newest immigrants to Los Angeles, Mexican-Americans have faced unique problems of cultural identity and assimilation. But the anguish of invisibility that Paz identified among them is all too familiar to minority ethnic communities around the globe. Everywhere, cultural domination by metropolitan elites eviscerates and obliterates traditional cultures rooted in centuries of shared experience. For ethnic minorities, failure to assimilate into dominant cultures can bring exclusion from vital economic and political resources, but successful assimilation can annihilate prized traditions and customs essential to individual and collective identity. Cultural institutions and the mass media alike depict dominant cultures as "natural" and "normal," while never representing the world from the vantage point of ethnic communities. Active discrimination and economic exploitation reinforce a sense of marginality among aggrieved peoples, but mass-media images rarely grant legitimacy to marginal perspectives. Traditional forms of cultural expression within ethnic communities lose their power to order and interpret experience, yet they persist as important icons of alienated identity. Surrounded by images that exclude them, included in images that seem to have no real social power, ethnic communities come to feel that they never quite exist and never quite vanish.

But the transformation of real historical traditions and cultures into superficial icons and images touches more than ethnic communities. A sharp division between life and culture provides an essential characteristic of life in all modern industrialized societies, affecting dominant as well as subordinated groups. As Walter Benjamin points out, the production and distribution of art under conditions of mechanical reproduction and commodity form lead to an alienated world in which cultural objects are received outside of the communities and traditions that initially gave them shape and meaning.[2] Created artifacts from diverse cultures blend together into a seeming contextless homogenized mass, encountered independently from the communities that gave birth to them. Mass communications and culture rely on an ever-expanding supply of free-floating symbols only loosely connected to social life. Experience and traditions seem to have no binding claims on the present. Ours is a world in which "all that is solid melts into air" as Marshall Berman asserts in a phrase appropriated from the *Communist Manifesto*.[3]

Members of dominant social groups might not feel quite the same anguish of invisibility that oppresses cultural minorities, but cultural identity for them has become no less an exercise in alienation. The seeming collapse of tradition and the tensions between cultural commodities and social life make mass cultural discourse a locus of confusion and conflict. A proliferation of composite cultural creations and marginal subcultures claim the same "authority" wielded by traditions rooted in centuries of common experience. The revered "master narratives" of the past—religion, liberal humanism, Marxism, psychoanalysis—survive in truncated form, influencing but not dominating social discourse. Instead, a multivocal and contradictory culture that delights in difference and disunity seems to be at the core of contemporary cultural consciousness. This "postmodern" culture allows the residues of many historical cultures to float above us, "ragged but beautiful," "never quite existing and never quite vanishing."[4]

Postmodern culture places ethnic minorities in an important role. Their exclusion from political power and cultural recognition has allowed aggrieved populations to cultivate sophisticated capacities for ambiguity, juxtaposition, and irony—all key qualities in the postmodern aesthetic. The imperatives of adapting to dominant cultures while not being allowed full entry into them leads to complex and creative cultural negotiations that foreground marginal and alienated states of consciousness. Unable to experience either simple assimilation or complete separation from dominant groups, ethnic cultures accustom themselves to a bifocality reflective of both the ways that they view themselves and the ways that they are viewed by others. In a world that constantly undermines the importance and influence of traditions, ethnic cultures remain tied to their pasts in order to explain and arbitrate the problems of the present. Because their marginality involves the pains of exclusion and exploitation, racial and ethnic cultures speak eloquently about the fissures and frictions of society. Because their experience demands bifocality, minority-group culture reflects the decentered and fragmented nature of contemporary human experience. Because their history identifies the sources of marginality, racial and ethnic cultures have an ongoing legitimate connection to the past that distinguishes them from more assimilated groups. Masters of irony in an ironic world, they often understand that their marginalized status makes them more appropriate spokespersons for society than mainstream groups unable to fathom or address the causes of their alienations.

Discussions about postmodern sensibilities in contemporary culture often revolve around trends and tendencies in painting, architecture, and literature, but they have even greater relevance to analyses of commercialized leisure. It is on the level of commodified mass culture that the most popular, and often the most profound, acts of cultural *bricolage* take place.[5] The destruction of established canons and the juxtaposition of seemingly inappropriate items characteristic of the self-conscious postmodernism in "high culture," have long been staples of commodified popular culture. With their facility for cultural fusion and their resistance to univocal master narratives, expressions of popular culture contain important lessons about the problems and promises of culture in a world in which "all that is solid melts into air."

The Mexican-American community of Los Angeles that so disappointed Octavio Paz provides an instructive example of how ethnic minority groups can fashion forms of cultural expression appropriate to postmodern realities. Paz's static and one-dimensional view of Mexican identity prevented him from seeing the rich culture of opposition embedded within the Los Angeles Chicano community. What seemed to him an ephemeral cloud "hovering and floating" above the city in actuality represented a complicated cultural strategy designed to preserve the resources of the past by adapting them to the needs of the present. In many areas of cultural production, but especially in popular music, organic intellectuals within Mexican-American Los Angeles pursued a strategy of self-presentation that brought their unique and distinctive cultural traditions into the mainstream of mass popular culture. Neither assimilationist nor separatist, they drew upon "families of resemblance" — similarities to the experiences and cultures of other groups—to fashion a "unity of disunity."[6] In that way, they sought to make alliances with other groups by cultivating the ways in which their particular experiences spoke with special authority about the ideas and alienations felt by others. They used the techniques and sensibilities of postmodernism to build a "historical bloc" of oppositional groups united in ideas and intentions, if not experience.[7]

Popular Music in Mexican-American Los Angeles

During the 1940s, defense spending and war mobilization changed the face of Los Angeles, stimulating a massive in-migration of whites, blacks, and Chicanos. Traditional residential segregation confined Afro-Americans to the south-central area, while limiting Chicanos largely to housing in downtown East Side neighborhoods.[8] Private bankers and government planners encouraged housing segregation by class and race, viewing ethnic heterogeneity in Los Angeles (as in other cities) as a defect of urban life rather than as one of its advantages. In this way vicious prejudice became written into federal loan policies and private commercial practices. For example, the Home Owners Loan Corporation City Survey File on Los Angeles for 1939 contained a confidential memorandum that argued against the feasibility of loans to Mexican-Americans because

> While many of the Mexican race are of high caliber and descended from the Spanish grandees who formerly owned all of the territory in Southern California, the large majority of Mexican peoples are a definite problem locally and their importation in the years gone by to work the agricultural crops has now been recognized as a mistake.[9]

Translated into public policy, that perception of Mexican-Americans meant that Chicano neighborhoods would not be eligible for housing loans, thereby ensuring residential segregation in the region. Federal appraisers rated the eligibility of each Los Angeles neighborhood for home loans, giving the highest rating to areas reserved for the exclusive use of white Christians, while assigning the lowest rating to black, Chicano, and mixed neighborhoods. The Federal Housing Authority gave its lowest possible rating to Boyle Heights in East Los Angeles because its mixture of Chicano, Jewish, and Eastern European residents convinced the appraisers that

> This is a "melting pot" area and is literally honeycombed with diverse and subversive racial elements. It is seriously doubted whether there is a single block in the area which does not contain detrimental racial elements and there are very few districts which are not hopelessly heterogeneous.[10]

Yet the opening of new shipyards and aircraft assembly plants combined with Los Angeles's severe housing shortage produced unprecedented inter-ethnic mixing in the city. Official segregation gave way bit by bit as Chicanos and European ethnics lived and worked together in Boyle Heights and Lincoln Park, while blacks and Chicanos lived in close proximity to each other in Watts and in the San Fernando Valley suburb of Pacoima.[11] On the factory floor, on public transportation, and on the streets of thriving commercial districts, diverse groups mixed with each other as never before. Wherever one traveled in the city's *barrios*, ghettos, and mixed neighborhoods, one could easily find the potential for inter-group conflicts and rivalries;

sometimes they took the form of actual racial and ethnic violence. But there also existed a vibrant street life built upon communication and cooperation in community organizations and in neighborhood life.

In this milieu, small entrepreneurs catering to the local market sensed a demand for cultural commodities that reflected the social life of the new urban environment. Before RCA's purchase of Elvis Presley's contract from Sun Records in 1955, the major studios ignored the music emanating from working-class neighborhoods, leaving the field to the more than four hundred independent labels that came into existence after the war. Existing outside corporate channels, the smaller firms in working-class areas produced records geared to local audiences, especially in minority communities. The invention of magnetic recording tape made it possible to enter the record business with relatively little capital, while concentrations of transplanted war workers provided a ready market for music based on country music and blues.[12] (See Chapter 5)

Recruiting performers from the communities they knew best, small-scale local record producers responded to trends in the streets. In addition, the proliferation of local radio stations in the postwar years offered exposure to new audiences. Juke box operators, furniture-store owners, and musicians responded to the consumer demand for a popular music that reflected the folk roots and multiracial ethos of the new urban streets. For example, a 1948 hit record by Los Angeles's Don Tosti Band titled "Pachuco Boogie" went on to sell more than two million copies, an extraordinary total for any Spanish-language record in the U.S., but especially for one that glorified one of the *barrio*'s more reviled subcultures—the Pachucos.[13]

In many ways, Pachucos embodied the defiance of conventional authority that came to symbolize the appeal of rock and roll. Pachucos were teen-aged gang members sporting zoot suits, ducktail haircuts, and distinctive tattoos; they had attracted public attention during the war years when newspaper stories blamed them for much of the youth crime in Los Angeles. Tensions peaked in June 1943 when hundreds of sailors invaded the East Los Angeles community to beat up Mexican-American youths who wore zoot suits. The police, prosecutors, and city council joined forces to praise this criminal attack, lauding the sailors for the efforts to "clean up" the city. But the racism manifest in the attacks caused many Mexican-Americans to start looking at the Pachucos as defenders of the community against outside encroachments and as symbols of Chicano victimization and marginality.[14]

The Don Tosti Band's "Pachuco Boogie" captured the spirit of that new-found admiration for street rebels. The song's lyrics employed *calo*, the street slang associated with Pachucos but considered vulgar by "respectable" Mexican-Americans. "Pachuco Boogie" blended Mexican speech and rhythms with Afro-American scat-singing and blues harmonies to form a provocative musical synthesis. Some Spanish-language radio stations refused to play the song, but Anglo disc jockeys programming black rhythm-and-blues shows aimed at white teen-agers put it on their playlists, to the delight of their listeners. Band member Raul Diaz remembers what it was like before that record became a hit, how Mexican-American musicians like himself often had to wear sombreros and tropical outfits to get work playing music during intermissions at motion-picture theaters. "We wanted to play Chicano music, not come on like some clowns," Diaz recalls, "but at the time the scene was dominated by people like Desi Arnaz and Xavier Cugat and the music was really bland."[15] The Don Tosti Band changed that when "Pachuco Boogie" sold more than two million copies. Itself a blend of Chicano, Anglo, and Afro-American musical forms, "Pachuco Boogie" garnered commercial success by uniting a diverse audience into a new synthesis—a "unity of disunity."[16]

"Pachuco Boogie" signaled the start of creative new links among previously divided groups. Anglo youths especially imitated the distinctive dress of Mexican-American "cholos" with their khaki pants and long-sleeved Pendleton shirts over sleeveless white undershirts, and "cholo" became a hip slang word with larger meanings. The word "cholo" probably derives from an Aztec word meaning servant, and it connotes someone with low status, usually a recent immigrant from a rural area. Cholos spoke a bilingual slang, displayed elaborate tattoos, and staked their claims to urban neighborhoods by covering walls with stylized graffiti. The studied disinterest and cultivated detachment affected by cholos echoed the oppositional postures of other postwar subcultures including bop musicians and beat poets. But in Los Angeles the cholo relationship to rock and roll made that subculture the most accessible model of "otherness" for middle-class white youths. When Anglo, black, or even Chicano youths embraced the cholo image, they flaunted their alienation by openly identifying with one of society's most despised groups.[17]

The ability of musicians to learn from other cultures played a key role in their success as rock-and-roll artists. For example, in 1952, black saxophonist Chuck Higgins had a hit recording with "Pachuko Hop"—a song he wrote as a tribute to the dancing, style, and slang of the Mexican-American youths he encountered while playing dances at East Los Angeles union halls.[18] White songwriter Jerry Leiber's widowed mother operated a grocery store near a black neighborhood in Baltimore in the early 1940s where he was first exposed to black music. The family moved to Los Angeles in 1945, and as a teen-ager he resumed his infatuation with the blues while working in a record store with a largely black clientele. A high-school classmate introduced Leiber to another middle-class white fan of black music, Mike Stoller, who had grown up on Long Island but had taken piano lessons in Harlem as an eleven-year-old student of the great jazz and blues pianist James P. Johnson. As a teen-ager, Stoller joined a Harlem "social club" before moving to Los Angeles with his family in 1949. "I learned the pachuco dances and joined a pachuco social club," Stoller later explained when asked how he got his start as a musician.[19] He played piano with the Blas Vasquez band which exposed him to Chicano appropriations of Afro-American and Euro-American forms and styles as well as to indigenous Mexican music. Within a year after joining the Vasquez band, Stoller began writing rhythm-and-blues songs for black vocal groups along with his writing partner Jerry Leiber. "We found ourselves writing for black artists," recalls Leiber, "because those were the voices and rhythms that we loved. By the Fall of 1950, when both Mike and I were in City College, we had black girlfriends and were into a black lifestyle."[20] Leiber and Stoller went on to write the original "Hound Dog" for Big Mama Thornton, and they fashioned dozens of best-selling songs for black artists that celebrated the speech, folklore, and subcultures of Afro-American city life.

Perhaps the artist who best exemplified the new cultural fusions engendered by Chicano rock-and-roll music was Johnny Otis. The son of a Greek immigrant grocer and shipyard worker from Northern California, Otis first came to Los Angeles in 1943 as the white drummer in a black band playing at the Club Alabam on Central Avenue in Watts. Otis had developed his interest in black music while growing up in a mixed but mostly black neighborhood in Berkeley. He accompanied his playmates to "sanctified" churches to listen to the gospel preachers, singers, and choirs, and they made a lasting impression on him. "This society says no white kid can stay in black culture," Otis observes, "but see, that culture had captured me. I loved it and it was richer and more fulfilling and more natural. I thought it was mine."[21] When a high-school teacher suggested that he spend less time with blacks and associate more with whites, Otis capped a long battle with his teachers and principals by dropping out of school in disgust. He became a drummer with Count Otis Matthews's West Oakland House Rockers and then went on the road to tour with a variety of Afro-American bands including Lloyd Hunter's Territory Jazz Band.

In Los Angeles, Otis worked with black musicians, married his high-school sweetheart, a black woman, and thought of himself as "black by persuasion." But part of the consciousness of the black community he joined there involved staking a claim for full participation in American life and culture, and that claim led to interactions with other groups and other cultures. "I got here in '43 and at that time the Avenue [Central] was just swinging. It was like a transplanted Harlem Renaissance," Otis remembers.[22] One night at the Lincoln Theater he saw the blues singer and piano player Charles Brown win a talent contest by playing "Clair de Lune." Otis recalls,

> He kind of apologized for what he played, but they loved him, they made him do an encore—"Rhapsody in Blue"—he just broke it up. And it was a good lesson for me, because in later years people would tell me that 'You can't take Big Mama Thornton to New York because she's too rough and bluesy, and you can't take Sally Blair to the Apollo because she's not bluesy enough,' well, bullshit on both counts. The people just liked it. If it's really strong and it has artistry, they like it.[23]

Otis began promoting rhythm-and-blues shows for mixed audiences, offering Chicano and white youths a chance to hear the music of the black community. He promoted and starred in weekly rhythm-and-blues shows at Angeles Hall on the East Side that demonstrated the powerful appeal of black music for Mexican-American audiences and which helped stimulate the growth of rock-and-roll music within the *barrio*.[24] Otis had rock-and-roll television programs on three Los

Angeles television stations in the early 1950s and promoted dances all over the city, despite harassment from local authorities upset about a music that crossed racial and class lines. "The cops would come and hassle the kids standing in line to get into the television show," Otis recalls. "They see black kids and Hispanic kids and Asian kids and they don't like it. They just didn't want to see that. If it were all Asian and Hispanic and black they wouldn't care, but there were whites there and they're mixing with the blacks and what not."[25] Despite the official harassment, the teen-agers kept coming out to Otis's shows, and despite rumors of gang violence and racial incidents about to happen Otis remembers "We never had any trouble, the people got along great."[26]

Exemplifying the fusion of small entrepreneur and musician that often brought rock and roll to the public, Otis started a small record label and recording studio in the mid-fifties featuring many of Los Angeles's leading rhythm-and-blues singers including L'il Julian Herrera, the city's first commercially successful Chicano rock and roller. Otis produced Herrera's 1956 local hit "Lonely, Lonely Nights," a classic do-wop ballad, and featured him in his stage shows as part of a special effort to attract Chicano audiences. As Otis tells it,

> L'il Julian came to me as a kid, a young Mexican-American guy and sang. He wasn't great, but he could sing and he was charming and it was nice and real. I put him on stage and the little Mexican girls loved him and our Chicano audience was a big part of our audience in those days. I put him in the band and then he lived in my house.[27]

Herrera's relationship with Johnny Otis illustrates the ways in which rock-and-roll music became a common ground for people from diverse backgrounds in Los Angeles in the early 1950s. After all, "Lonely, Lonely Nights" presented a Chicano's rendition of a black vocal style on a record produced by a white man who thought of himself as black. But Otis found out that the story of L'il Julian Herrera was even more complicated than he knew. One day a juvenile officer walked into Otis's record company in search of Ron Gregory, a run-away youth from the east. When the officer showed Otis a picture, he realized that Ron Gregory was L'il Julian Herrera. "He ran away from home, hitchhiked out here, and this Mexican lady in Boyle Heights takes him in and raises him as her son," Otis relates.[28] It turned out that Los Angeles's first Chicano rock-and-roll star was born a Hungarian Jew and became "a Chicano by persuasion," just as Johnny Otis had become "black by persuasion."[29]

The pinnacle of this brown-white-black mixing in rock-and-roll music in Los Angeles came with the enormous popularity of Ritchie Valens, East Los Angeles's best-selling and most significant rock-and-roll artist. Independent record producer Bob Keane discovered Valens when he noticed that the car-club cholos of East Los Angeles and of the San Fernando Valley responded to a band called the Silhouettes and their lead singer, Richard Valenzuela. Shortening (and Anglicizing) the youth's last name to Valens, Keane signed him to a contract and recorded the singer with the same back-up musicians that Keane used on sessions by the black gospel and rock singer Sam Cooke. These session musicians brought a wealth of musical experience to Valens's recordings—bass player Red Callendar had played with jazz great Art Tatum, and drummer Earl Palmer had recorded with rhythm-and-blues artists in New Orleans, including Roy Brown, Fats Domino, and Little Richard.[30] But Ritchie Valens did not have to learn his cultural pluralism in a studio; life in postwar Los Angeles prepared him well for the mixing of forms and styles that would come to characterize his recorded music.

More than any other artist, Valens brought the folk traditions of Mexican music to a mass audience via rock and roll, but his music also reflected an extraordinary blending of traditions and styles from other cultures. Valens's father, Steve, and his mother, Concepcion, met while both were employed at a munitions factory in Saugus, California, north of the city of San Fernando. He was born in 1941 in the San Fernando Valley suburb of Pacoima, where he learned music by listening to his relatives sing Mexican songs as they gathered at each others' homes in the evenings. At the age of five Valens made a toy guitar out of a cigar box and learned to fret it with the help of an uncle who taught him how to play his first song—the traditional Mexican *huapango* "La Bamba." In Pacoima, Valens met William Jones, a black musician who lived across the street from the youth's Aunt Ernestine. Jones taught Valens how to tune a guitar and play chords. After building a green and white electric guitar for himself in his junior-high-school wood-shop class, Valens began to experiment with the Afro-American rhythm and blues songs he heard on the radio. But he liked country music as well, idolizing Roy Rogers and

Gene Autry, and delighting his classmates in school with a parody of the theme song to the Walt Disney television program "Davy Crockett."[31] The very plurality of the industrial city excited Valens, he drew his friends from diverse communities. As classmate Manny Sandoval recalls, "They used to put Ritchie down, especially the Mexican kids. They used to call him *falso* and call me that, too, because we liked to be with everybody—Blacks, Mexicans, whites, whatever. So they [Chicanos] wouldn't come around that much to group into the music thing with us. It would be the Blacks, some of the whites, and a few Chicanos."[32] In 1957 he joined the Silhouettes, a mostly Chicano but multi-racial band put together by vibraphonist Gil Rocha that included Valens on guitar, William Jones's Afro-American sons Conrad and Bill on drums and woodwinds, Italian-Americans Dave Torreta and Sal Barragan on trumpet and alto saxophone, and Japanese-American Walter Takaki on tenor saxophone. Although primarily a rock-and-roll band, the Silhouettes' Chicano members were well schooled in traditional music; when the occasion called for it, they could break into Mexican *corridos* as easily as they played "Shake, Rattle, and Roll."[33] Valens became the featured vocalist with the band, and his tributes to the black rhythm-and-blues singer Little Richard motivated his admirers to start calling him "Little Ritchie."[34]

In the brief period between Valens's emergence on the best-selling record charts and his death in a plane crash early in 1959, he brought an extraordinary range of music before pop audiences. He borrowed from white rockabilly, black blues, and Mexican folk musicians because they all made up parts of his cultural environment in postwar Los Angeles. "La Bamba" and "Come On, Let's Go" featured variations on melodies and harmonies common to Mexican fiesta music, while "Ooh My Head" employed the boogie-woogie form and vocal mannerisms common to Afro-American music. One of Valens's unfinished records included an attempt to lay the rhythm popularized by blues guitarist Bo Diddley underneath the melody of "Malagueña," a song originally written by Cuban bandleader Ernesto Lecuona, but blended by Valens with the Mexican march "Espani Cani." Radio programs and phonograph records made Eddie Cochran's rockabilly and Bo Diddley's rhythm-and-blues songs an organic part of Valens's life, while the limited but nonetheless real cultural mixing in working-class neighborhoods enabled young people to explore the culture of their neighbors. Valens wrote his big hit song "Donna" about a failed romance with an Anglo classmate whose father ordered her to stop going out with "that Mexican," and he recorded a version of his favorite rhythm-and-blues song "Framed," which had originally been recorded by a Los Angeles rhythm-and-blues group, The Robins, but which had been written by Mike Stoller and Jerry Leiber.[35]

Valens's tragic death at age seventeen deprived the Los Angeles Chicano community of its biggest star, and it cut short the career of one of rock and roll's most eclectic synthesizers. But other artists carried on his propensity for blending the folk music of the *barrio* with the styles and forms circulated within popular music. In the late 1950s and early 1960s, groups including the Salas Brothers, Carlos Brothers, Rene and Ray, and the Romancers had regional and national hit songs that reflected the *barrio*'s dialogue with mainstream rock-and-roll music. Just as Ritchie Valens established himself as a commercial performer by playing rhythm-and-blues-styled versions of Anglo and Mexican songs for a mixed audience, later Chicano musicians played a mix of different kinds of music for a combination of audiences. In concerts at East Los Angeles College and at El Monte Legion Stadium, at dances held in youth centers and union halls, and in popular nightclubs like the Rhythm Room and Rainbow Gardens, Chicano rock and rollers learned to blend Mexican and rock music into a synthesis that won them admirers both inside and outside the *barrio*.[36]

In 1965 Frankie "Cannibal" Garcia and his group, the "Headhunters," brought Los Angeles Chicano rock music to new audiences when their "Land of a Thousand Dances" entered the national best-seller charts. Garcia got his start as a rock singer when the lead vocalist for the Royal Jesters (another East Los Angeles rock group) got sick, and the band recruited Garcia to take his place "because I sang in school with a mariachi band, doing traditional Mexican music."[37] Garcia later joined with some friends from the Ramona Gardens Housing Project to form Cannibal and the Headhunters, taking their name from Garcia's "street" (gang) name of "Cannibal" gained when he bit an opponent in a fight. One of their most effective songs in live performances had been Chris Kenner's "Land of a Thousand Dances," but at one show Garcia forgot the words at the beginning of the song and ad-libbed "na-na-na-nana" to the delight of the crowd. In the studio they retained Cannibal's accidental improvisation to give the record a captivating introduction. They also borrowed the double drum sound prominent in Stevie Wonder records to forge a synthesis that attracted the attention of audiences all over the country.

Yet however much they might influence popular culture, Chicano rock musicians could not be completely assimilated. Frankie "Cannibal" Garcia feels that his group's Chicano identity prevented them from attaining greater success after they reached the Billboard Top Forty with "Land of a Thousand Dances" in 1965. Garcia remembers, "They didn't know how to market us, for one. There were basically only black or white groups in the early 1960s, not even many mixed groups. The people didn't even know what we were half of the time; a lot of people thought we were Hawaiian or something. And with the name Cannibal and the Headhunters, most people just assumed we'd be black."[38]

Whether the audience knew what they were or not, Cannibal and the Headhunters found that *they* could not forget who they were. Remembering a tour through the southern states with the Rolling Stones, Garcia relates, "It was a shock to us to go somewhere and see restrooms that would say 'white only' or 'black only.' I'd say 'Where do *we* go? We would get kicked out of restaurants, no Latins allowed. There was a big billboard in Jacksonville, Florida that said 'No niggers, no spics, no Mexicans allowed.' I wrote home and said 'You know what Mom? There's this big marquee that says they don't like us here.' "[39]

Other Chicano musicians in the 1960s combined a fusion of popular and Mexican music with lyrics that evoked the complex pluralities of the city streets. Thee Midnighters scored a national hit in 1965 with "Whittier Boulevard," a song honoring the main traffic artery of the East Los Angeles *barrio*. Drawing inspiration from the energy and imagination of the car customizers and cruisers who claimed the boulevard as their own territory on weekend nights, Thee Midnighters presented the activities of the car-club cholos to the outside world, while at the same time elevating the self-image of the cruisers by inserting their subculture into the discourse of mainstream popular culture. As Thee Midnighters' lead singer Little Willie G (for Garcia) once explained, "A lot of people say you guys made Whittier Boulevard famous, but we just took the action off the boulevard and made it into a song."[40]

The car culture's quest for fun and good times expressed a desire for the good life of material success, but it also provided a means for satirizing and subverting ruling icons of consumer society. Just as Chicano car customizers "improved" upon the mass-produced vehicles from Detroit, Chicano rock songs like "Whittier Boulevard" celebrated Mexican-American appropriations of automobiles as part of a community ritual. By the late 1960s, that dialogue between the images of mass culture and the realities of *barrio* life increasingly took on an expressly political cast. At that time, changes in urban economics and politics threatened to destroy the social basis for the cultural pluralism of Los Angeles rock and roll by undermining the social and economic infrastructure of the central city. The cumulative effects of postwar highway and housing policies had subsidized suburban growth at the expense of the inner city, had exacerbated racial and class polarizations, and had encouraged residential segregation. For Chicanos, increased migration from Mexico, inadequate access to decent housing, and discrimination within a segmented labor market all combined to help create a new consciousness.[41]

The failures of 1960s social programs including the War on Poverty, the effects of the Vietnam War on poor and working-class youths, and the repressive policies of the Los Angeles Police Department all contributed to a growing political activism and cultural nationalism. On August 29, 1970, the Chicano community mobilized for a massive anti-war demonstration that expressed anger over many pent-up grievances and complaints. Taking their opposition to the war and their growing nationalism to the streets, demonstrators relied on their cultural traditions to give form to their protest activity. As one participant chronicled the start of that day's events,

> The boulevard was filled with *gente*, doing Latino chants and playing *musica* right in the streets. It started taking on the atmosphere of a carnival. Some even danced.[42]

This demonstration involved an attempt to reclaim city streets as a terrain for culture, politics, and celebration. But its aggressive festivity provoked a violent reaction from the authorities. Los Angeles police officers used force against the demonstrators; one officer shot and killed *Los Angeles Times* columnist Ruben Salazar. The Salazar killing outraged many people within the Mexican-American community and helped mobilize subsequent activism and demonstrations.[43]

The political ferment surrounding the 1970 demonstration found its way into Mexican-American rock-and-roll music in significant ways. Thee Midnighters (who had recorded "Whittier Boulevard") recorded a song titled "Chicano Power" in 1970, and the V.I.P.'s changed their name that same year to El Chicano. In the early 1970s, East Los Angeles musicians began to feature Latin musical forms and Spanish-language lyrics more prominently in their songs, and they attached themselves to a variety of community icons and subcultures. A series of outdoor music festivals, known popularly as "Chicano Woodstocks," showcased the community's musicians and provided an arena for displaying and celebrating diverse images of Chicano identity. The band Tierra emerged as a favorite of the "low rider" car customizers in the early 1970s, while Los Lobos got their start with an album recorded under the aegis of Cesar Chavez's United Farm Workers union. Mixing images from the past of pachucos and cholos with contemporary ones like low riders, these bands and their audiences placed current struggles in historical perspective, preserving a measure of continuity in a period of extraordinary change.[44]

Yet the music of East Los Angeles still had a significant influence on artists and audiences outside the *barrio*. In 1975, for example, a mostly Afro-American jazz/funk ensemble from Long Beach calling themselves War recorded "Low Rider," a tribute to Chicano car customizers, cruisers, and musicians.[45] One of the year's best-selling records, "Low Rider," expressed War's own experiences playing dances and concerts for Mexican-American audiences throughout southern California, but the song also reflected demographic trends in Los Angeles that encouraged black-Chicano cultural interaction. In 1970 more than 50,000 Hispanics lived in the traditionally black south-central area of Los Angeles; by 1980 that figure had doubled, with Chicanos making up 21% of the total population of the south-central area.[46] The clear Latin influence on the subject and style of "Low Rider" testifies to the importance of Chicano music to American popular music, even when Chicano artists themselves might not enjoy access to a mass audience.

Popular Music and Postmodernism

The rock-and-roll music created by Mexican-American musicians in

Los Angeles since World War II bears particular relevance to the issues of ethnicity, identity, and culture raised in Octavio Paz's lament. From the Don Tosti Band of the 1940s through Los Lobos in the 1980s, Los Angeles's Chicano musicians have made commercially successful records by blending the folk music of Mexico with the cultural fusions of the modern day *barrio*. [47] Their proclivities for mixing eclectic styles, for making references to their community and its history, and for acknowledging the diverse influences on their art display a conscious or intuitive postmodernism—delighting in difference, undermining univocal master narratives, and celebrating the decentered and polyglot nature of popular culture. In its most successful commercial forms, Chicano rock-and-roll music from Los Angeles transformed a specific ethnic culture rooted in common experiences into more than just a novelty to be appropriated by uncomprehending outsiders. Confronted with media monopolies and public sentiments blind to the unique circumstances of Mexican-Americans, Chicano musicians drew upon both residual and emergent elements in their community to win some measure of participation in the creation and dissemination of mass popular culture. Musical forms and social attitudes emanating from the isolation and marginality of *barrio* life took on new meaning when appropriated as "youth" music by consumers with little knowledge or concern about the ethnicity of the musicians.

In his superb work on ethnic autobiographies, anthropologist Michael M. J. Fischer identifies the core components of the postmodern sensibility as bifocality or reciprocity of perspectives, juxtaposition of multiple realities, intertextuality, inter-referentiality, and comparisons through families of resemblance.[48] Fischer's categories encompass the central practices of Los Angeles Mexican-American rock-and-roll musicians since World War II. Caught between the realities of life in their community and the hegemony of Anglo-capitalist culture, Chicano artists fashioned a bifocal music accessible from both inside and outside their community. They juxtaposed multiple realities, blending Mexican folk music with Afro-American rhythm and blues, playing English-language songs in a Mexican style for audiences filled with Spanish speakers, and answering requests for both Mexican and rock music with the same song—"La Bamba." They practiced particularly intricate forms of intertextuality by connecting their music to community subcultures and institutions ori-

ented around speech, dress, car customizing, art, theater, and politics. References to shared historical and cultural experiences
permeated Mexican-American rock-and-roll songs, but these references extended beyond the immediate Chicano community as songs
featured rockabilly and soul influences borrowed from white and
black working-class music. That inter-referentiality complemented
an equally adept facility for making comparisons through families of
resemblance. Chicano musicians and artists could incorporate white
rockabilly or black rhythm-and-blues music into their songs because
they recognized similarities in form and content that transcended
surface differences. Yet even while drawing upon families of resemblance, Mexican-American musicians in Los Angeles never lost sight
of the singular historical realities shaping them and their community.

The emergence of Los Lobos as a significant commercial rock-and-
roll band in the 1980s provides an illustration of the persistent bifocality, juxtaposition of multiple realities, intertextuality, inter-referentiality, and comparisons through families of resemblance in Los
Angeles Chicano music. Mixing Mexican *Norteno* accordions and
guitarrons with Afro-American and Anglo rockabilly drums and electric guitars, Los Lobos stand between Chicano culture and mass culture, playing to audiences in both camps. The five members of the
group first learned to play their instruments in response to the popularity of the Beatles, but they secured their first employment as musicians playing Mexican folk music for neighborhood gatherings. In
response to critics who charge that the band's forays into rock and
roll betray their roots in folk music, drummer Louis Perez replies,
"We always aspired to play to everybody, but there was no place to
expose it. We haven't gone back on the basic philosophy of this band,
which was to play cultural music. It's a music that's as much Mexican
culture as it is American, and that's what we are."[49]

Rock-and-roll audiences first discovered Los Lobos when they
served as the opening act for a U.S. tour by the punk/new wave band
the Clash. A white band from England playing new-wave music with
strong reggae and rhythm-and-blues influences, the Clash recognized the families of resemblance that tied their music to that of Los
Lobos, and sought to give the Chicano band greater commercial exposure. Subsequently, the Blasters, a Los Angeles Anglo band
steeped in rhythm and blues and rockabilly, arranged to have Los
Lobos open live shows for them. Conrad Lozano of Los Lobos ac-

knowledged his group's debt to the Blasters in a 1984 interview when he told a reporter, "Musically it gave us someone to look at and reinforced our commitment to our style. We met them and had a lot in common. We became friends and they liked our music so much that they had us open some gigs for them. That really allowed many more people to see and hear us."[50]

Anglo saxophonist Steve Berlin left the Blasters to join Los Lobos, a transition that seemed logical to him because of his own commitment to juxtaposing multiple musical realities. Born in Philadelphia and nurtured on that city's rhythm-and-blues music, Berlin introduced Los Lobos to some old rhythm-and-blues songs, while they taught him to play their traditional polkas and *corridos*. Describing his connections with Los Lobos and other artists on Los Angeles's Slash Records label, Berlin observes, "A lot of us have similar record collections, and a shared appreciation for people like Hank Williams and George Jones. The Del Fuegos' heroes are the Blasters' heroes and they're our heroes too. If you went to everybody's house, there would be the same bunch of records they consider important."[51]

When similar record collections enable Steve Berlin, a white musician influenced by black rhythm and blues, to join a Chicano rock band on the basis of a mutual affinity for country and western singers Hank Williams and George Jones, we have gone a long way toward a world in which "all that is solid melts into air." Cultures appear interchangeable and works of art seem divorced from real historical experience. But the fusions that characterize Chicano rock-and-roll music reflect more than the confusions and ambiguities of postmodern society. Their definitive contours come from the conscious choices made by organic intellectuals attempting to address the anguish of invisibility by bringing their own cultural traditions into the mainstream of mass culture. Mexican-American musicians could stay with traditional Chicano musical forms like *ranchera* or *cumbia* musics and find recognition and reward within their own community. Or they could master Anglo styles and assimilate into the mainstream without anyone being aware of their Chicano identity. But Los Angeles Chicano rock-and-roll artists have generally selected another path. They have tried to straddle the line between the two cultures, creating a fusion music that resonates with the chaos and costs of cultural collision. Their choices arbitrate particularly complex tensions emanating from ethnicity and oppression for Chicanos, while holding open to other groups a vision of cultural fusion based on families of resemblance and similarities of emotion and experience.

As members of an aggrieved community, and as artists involved in the generation and circulation of ideas reflecting the needs of that community, Mexican-American rock musicians from Los Angeles have functioned as what Antonio Gramsci referred to as "organic intellectuals."[52] Gramsci felt that dominant social groups wield power as much through ideological hegemony as through physical force, and he charged that traditional intellectuals reinforce social hierarchies by serving as "experts in legitimation."[53] But Gramsci pointed out that subordinated groups have their own intellectuals who attempt to pose a "counter-hegemony" by presenting images subversive of existing power relations. The elite try to "manage consent" by making domination appear natural, voluntary, and inevitable. Organic intellectuals, on the other hand, attempt to build a "historical bloc"—a coalition of oppositional groups united around counter-hegemonic ideas. The efforts by Chicano rock musicians in Los Angeles to enter the mainstream by linking up with other oppositional cultures reflect their struggle to assemble a "historical bloc" capable of challenging the ideological hegemony of Anglo cultural domination. In the struggle, they found that their primary weapons included bifocality, juxtaposition of multiple realities, intertextuality, inter-referentiality, and comparison through families of resemblance.

Juxtaposition of multiple realities in Chicano life allowed for juxtaposition of multiple realities in Mexican-American music. In a culture that drew sharp lines among black, white, and brown music and audiences, Chicano rock-and-roll artists worked to break down barriers. To a commercial marketing structure that imposed rigid categories on rock, popular, folk, and ethnic music, they offered songs that fit no simple description. The dominant culture and its popular culture industry often treated ethnicity as a discrete and finite entity, but Chicano musicians treated it as plastic and open-ended. For them, ethnicity seemed as much a dynamic construct as an inherited fact, as much a strategic response to the present as an immutable series of practices and beliefs derived from the past. Consequently, they brought a sense of play and whimsy to the arts of *bricolage*. Just as Ritchie Valens experimented with a Bo Diddley-style rhythm-and-blues bass line beneath the Latin guitar standard "La Malaguena," Los

Lobos brought the accordion and *guitarron* into use as rock-and-roll instruments.

The same forces that encourage Los Angeles's Chicano rock-and-roll musicians to roll back the boundaries of ethnic identity also compel them to incorporate ideas from nonmusical sources into their work. As organic intellectuals chronicling the cultural life of their community, they draw upon street slang, car customizing, clothing styles, and wall murals for inspiration and ideas, as well as upon more traditional cultural creations such as literature, plays, and poems. Their work is intertextual, constantly in dialogue with other forms of cultural expression, and most fully appreciated when located in context.

The commercially successful Chicano band Tierra got its start in the early 1970s as a favorite band of the low-rider subculture in Los Angeles. As anthropologist Brenda Bright demonstrates in her fine work on Mexican-American car customizers, low riders are themselves masters of postmodern cultural manipulation. They juxtapose seemingly inappropriate realities—fast cars designed to go slowly, "improvements" that flaunt their impracticality, like chandeliers instead of inside overhead lights. They encourage a bifocal perspective—they are made to be watched but only after adjustments have been made to provide ironic and playful commentary on prevailing standards of automobile design. They are intertextual—cars are named after songs or incidents in Mexican history, zoot-suited *pachucos* appear in car paintings. Low-rider "happenings" incorporate elements of popular fashion, dance, and music in a community ritual celebrating the utility and beauty of automobiles that the dominant culture would deem impractical, tasteless, and garish. Tierra incorporated low-rider intertextuality in its music, using fragments of *barrio* memories in song lyrics that celebrate zoot suits and rhythms that approximate the jitterbug dancing of the 1940s and 1950s. In a similar fashion Thee Midnighters wrote and recorded "Whittier Boulevard" in 1965 to celebrate the culture of car customizers and cruisers along East Los Angeles's main thoroughfare in the 1960s. In 1982 Ruben Guevara's "c/s" explored Chicano history through the "writing on the walls"—the distinctive graffiti of the *barrio*.[54]

Chicano musicians had to assume a bifocal perspective as a matter of self-respect. The dominant culture imposed an identity on them. Regardless of their characteristics as individuals, Anglo stereotypes

about Mexicano and their culture influenced the ways in which Chicanos were perceived outside the *barrio*, and they had to be aware of
the limits imposed on them by that cultural domination. But to accept the stereotypes would mean denying one's own vision. Prevented from defining themselves because of pervasive discrimination and prejudice, but unwilling to leave the work of definition to
others, they adopted a bifocal perspective that acknowledged but did
not accept the majority culture's images of Chicanos.

A conscious inter-referentiality accompanies the pervasive intertextuality of Los Angeles's Chicano rock-and-roll music. Even though
they seek success in commercial popular culture, these musicians
employ repeated references to individual and collective histories in
the manner of folk artists. Mexican-American rock-and-roll artists acknowledge their roots; Ritchie Valens hit the best-seller charts with
"La Bamba," a song that he learned from his family when he was five.
Los Lobos won a Grammy Award for folk music with a faithful rendition of "Anselma," a hundred-year-old Mexican song. But they also
connect the musical past to social and political history. "I grew up
listening to the folk groups and balladeers," Ruben Guevara explains
in tracing the origins of his music, but he plays little traditional music
himself. Instead, Guevara adapts the music of today to collective popular memory. He founded Zyanya Records in 1982 ("zyanya" is a
Mexican-Indian word meaning "always") to provide an outlet for
Chicano musicians and a forum for addressing the community's
youth. "The younger Chicanos who did not experience the Chicano
movement of the 60s and 70s lost a cultural awareness, and through
this music I would like to make them aware of social issues," Guevara insists. Groups on the Zyanya label including Con Safos, Los
Perros, and Califas use overtly political lyrics and a self-conscious
ethnic nationalism to address the problems of contemporary *barrio*
life. But even those groups that shun direct political or historical references in their lyrics still evoke the past through references to *pachucos, cholos*, zoot suits, and community heroes like Ritchie
Valens.[55] Willie Herron, a Chicano punk/rock musician, mural
painter, and poet, sees the fate of *barrio* musicians directly wrapped
up in the fate of the community itself. Explaining why Chicano rock-
and-roll music has failed to achieve greater commercial acceptance,
Herron points out, "We had setbacks all along—the death of Ritchie
Valens in '59 being one of the biggest. In the 70s the reasons became

154

more political—the Chicano moratorium [an anti-war demonstration that ended in a police riot], the death of Ruben Salazar [a newspaper columnist killed by police officers during the Chicano moratorium], many of the people in the Hispanic community just dropped out."[56]

Decisions by Chicano rock-and-roll musicians to blend cultural and political history echo the stance taken by artists in other media in their community. John Valdez, an artist who grew up in the Estrada Courts Housing Project in East Los Angeles, gained critical recognition in the 1980s for paintings that featured *pachucos* and other *barrio* symbols. "I like to show the Pachuco image," Valdez relates, "even if some Chicanos who are trying to assimilate think they left this in the past. It's still something that is very much with us." For Valdez, *pachuco* imagery retains meaning because it displays "the beauty of a people we have been told are not beautiful."[57] Similar tensions inform the writing of Mary Helen Ponce from East Los Angeles. In one of her short stories she recalls a childhood in which, "We really lived in two worlds. The secure *barrio* that comforted and accepted us, and the 'other,' the institutions such as the school that were out to acculturate us, sanitize us, Americanize us, and de-lice us at least once a year."[58] Ponce describes her feelings of solidarity with a classmate found to have lice in her hair, because Ponce resented the smug sense of superiority that enabled Anglo school officials to make Chicano children feel ashamed of their homes. The same bifocality that makes Ponce want to describe the world as divided in two, and that makes her side with the despised ethnic world, induces Willie Herron to claim that he formed his punk rock group Los Illegals "to talk about the experience of being a *cholo*, a low rider, of being in gangs, all of it."[59] The same stubborn inter-referentiality that leads John Valdez to celebrate the *pachuco*, compels Ruben Guevara to explain his song "c/s" with a motto—"The present day Pachuco refuses to die."[60] Inter-referentiality, intertextuality, juxtaposition of multiple realities, and bifocality characterize the music of Los Angeles's Chicano rock-and-roll musicians, and they explain much of its aesthetic. As part of mass popular culture that aesthetic appealed to people from other communities, building alliances on the basis of comparisons through families of resemblance. In Los Angeles, Anglo rock-and-roll musicians Frank Zappa and Captain Beefheart (Don Van Vliet) included references to *pachucos* in their 1970s albums, and Zappa invented a mythical Chicano band, Ruben and the Jets, to embody the pure spirit of rock and roll. He persuaded Ruben Guevara to form an actual group called Ruben and the Jets during a backstage conversation after Zappa had attended Guevara's cultural nationalist play, "Who Are the People?" Guevara's recollection of that meeting testifies to the power of families of resemblance; he recalled that he and Zappa "rapped from Bo Diddley to Beethoven. We found that we had the same musical roots."[61] Of course, neither Zappa nor Guevara made music that actually sounded very much like Beethoven's or Bo Diddley's, but the commodity culture of the postmodern world made them feel they were on common ground because they shared appreciation of those two musicians.

Families of resemblance also brought together suburban Los Angeles punk and new-wave audiences and artists with rock bands from East Los Angeles in the late 1970s and early 1980s. Chicano bands including the Brat, Odd Squad, and the Plugz blended the urgency and emotionalism of 1950s rock and roll (the Plugz even recorded a version of Ritchie Valens's "La Bamba") with lyrics speaking to the alienation and frustration of contemporary youth. Relatively affluent suburban teen-agers could identify with the music of a band like Los Illegals, not because they really knew what it was like to be a *cholo*, but because the real historical experiences of the Chicano community gave its artists a well-developed vocabulary for talking about alienation and oppression. Neither the punk-rock musicians nor their audiences were actually *cholos*, but the subjective act of identification with *cholismo* created a family of resemblance — a mutual desire to draw upon real historical experiences to proclaim distance from the dominant culture and its values.

The commercial popularity of Los Lobos in the 1980s provides another example of the capacity for Los Angeles's Chicano rock-and-roll musicians to form a historical bloc with other groups based on families of resemblance. Los Lobos proudly affirm their cultural heritage, but they reject separatism. They insist on acceptance as "legitimate contributors to contemporary music" without having to hide their ethnic identity. Aware of the ways in which they might be perceived as a novelty by a mass audience, they attempt to use their marginality to find families of resemblance connecting themselves to other groups. Drummer Louis Perez explains the group's philosophy by talking about the title song from their 1984 album, "How Will the Wolf Survive?" Perez recalls that he read a *National Geographic* article about wolves as an endangered species and that he compared their plight to those of people he knew. As he describes writing the song

> It started out being about the wolf and the next verse turned into a message of hope for the middle class. And the last verse is about how bands all over the country are trying to preserve something close to the heart of America. So yeah, it's about whether or not Los Lobos will survive. Not only us . . . [62]

Perez's lyrics talk about a wolf "running scared now forced to hide, in a land where he once stood with pride"—a clear reference to the Chicano people and to Los Lobos ("the wolves" in Spanish) themselves. The narrator predicts that the hunted creature will somehow find its way and concludes with a tribute to the "young hearts and minds" in bands whose "songs of passion" keep alive the wolf's hope for survival. For Perez, the world of rock-and-roll music does not obliterate local cultures by rendering them invisible; rather, it is an arena where diverse groups find common ground while still acknowledging important differences. The prefigurative counter-hegemony fashioned by Los Lobos has succeeded in winning the allegiance of musicians from other marginalized cultures. Their songs have been recorded by polka artist Frankie Yankovic as well as by country and western star Waylon Jennings. The southern "swamp rocker" Tony Joe White introduced Jennings to "Will the Wolf Survive." At first, Jennings could not make out all the lyrics in the song, but he loved the record's sound, so he decided to record it himself. He recalls,

> The funny thing is, we couldn't understand all the words on the record, and that often means the lyrics are bad and they are trying to cover them up. Still, I loved the feel of the record and we decided to record it—even without knowing what it said completely. When we got the words from the publisher, I was knocked out. The words were great. I think everyone can relate to that song.[63]

The Cajun accordion player and singer Jo-El Sonnier views Los Lobos as artists whose cultural struggles parallel his own. As he explains

> I've sold myself as French, as R&B, as country, and as rock. But I want to do it all if I can; I think we could open doors for this music. Look at what Los Lobos has done for ethnic music, and they got

signed without really changing. It can't just be that all people want is Madonna and punk music! All I've ever wanted to do is bring my music and my culture to the people. I have a message about the preservation of it. I feel like if I let my culture die, I die with it.[64]

Sonnier's strategy of using the plasticity of popular music as a means of preserving his ethnic culture echoes the efforts by Chicano musicians like Los Lobos to build a historical bloc; his acknowledgment of their importance as a model reveals a self-conscious understanding of the families of resemblance that they nurture and cultivate. With their bifocality, juxtaposition of multiple realities, intertextuality, inter-referentiality, and families of resemblance, Chicano rock-and-roll musicians from Los Angeles explore all the main axes of postmodern art. Jean-François Lyotard has celebrated this postmodern condition as a logical and healthy response to the totalitarian imperatives of technology and capital. Lyotard and other postmodernists see the proliferation of marginal subcultures and the confusing display of remnants from past eras in contemporary culture as a break with oppressive master narratives. To postmodernists, improvised cultural forms and free-floating signs and symbols appropriated out of context can open up a world of play and desire previously constrained by the tyranny of master narratives.[65]

Scholars uneasy about the open-ended implications of some postmodernist theory nonetheless concede its central point—that contemporary society entails a fragmentation and decentering that radically alters the nature and function of cultural creation and reception. Fredric Jameson attempts to steer Lyotard's discussion toward a re-emphasis on the importance of history and historical consciousness, arguing that a world view with no sense of the past or expectation for the future only degenerates into schizophrenia, trapping individuals within the bounds of their own immediate sense perceptions. Jameson maintains that the emancipatory possibilities in contemporary cultural forms come from a "political unconscious"—from "buried" master narratives that carry on the historical traditions of opposition sedimented within the collective experience and memory of aggrieved populations. In a similar vein, Jürgen Habermas argues that the plasticity of contemporary culture reveals a "legitimation crisis" brought on by the failure of capitalist society to fulfill the promises of Enlightenment and revolutionary traditions. Thus the decentered and fragmented culture of the contemporary world is not an end in itself for Habermas, but, rather, an indication of popular desire for an eventual consensus, for a practice that closes the ruptures and disruptions of capitalism.[66] Marshall Berman shares the sentiment voiced by Jameson and Habermas that modernity is "an incomplete project" rather than a totalitarian master narrative, and like them he champions the "unity of disunity" by which modern culture represents a collective struggle to feel at home in the world.[67]

What Jameson, Habermas, and Berman champion on the plane of criticism, Mexican-American rock-and-roll musicians have created in art. The marginality of Chicano rock-and-roll musicians has provided them with a constant source of inspiration and a constant spur toward innovation that gained them the attention of mainstream audiences. But this marginal sensibility amounts to more than novelty or personal eccentricity; it holds legitimacy and power as the product of a real historical community's struggle with oppression. The "buried" narratives in this music—narratives about group identity, oppositional subcultures, and a desire for unity—amount to more than a "political unconscious." As Chicano musicians demonstrate in their comments about their work, their music reflects a quite conscious cultural politics that seeks inclusion in the American mainstream by transforming it.

Almost forty years after Octavio Paz's visit to Los Angeles, Mexican-Americans in that city still suffer from the anguish of invisibility. Their numbers have increased, but discrimination and exploitation leave them under-represented and under-rewarded. The expanded reach and scope of the mass media over the past four decades has exacerbated the cultural crisis facing Mexican-Americans; rarely do they see their world presented sympathetically or even accurately in the communications media that reinforce and legitimate Anglo cultural hegemony. But the "vague atmosphere" of Mexicanism perceived by Paz persists in the present. In community subcultures and styles, in the prefigurative counter-hegemony of organic intellectuals, it continues to inform the struggles of the present with the perceptions and values of the past. Conscious of the fragmentation of the modern world, this constantly changing "Mexicanism" cultivates its own marginality even as it reaches out to other groups. It is not a buried master narrative, but, rather, a conscious cultural politics that survives by "floating and hovering," never quite existing and never quite vanishing. Invisibility has its psychic and political costs, but for

Chicano musicians in Los Angeles, it provides the ultimate camouflage for the difficult but necessary work of building a historical bloc.

Popular Film

7

No Way Out:
Dialogue and Negotiation
in Reel America

Commercial motion pictures generally do not claim to present historical truth. Even when films are set in the past, artists and audiences understand that the function of the movies is to entertain. Few would consider subjecting movies to the kinds of tests about evidence and logic that we routinely apply to printed historical narratives. Yet Hollywood pictures need to engage the attention and the emotion of individuals who live within historical time and who construct their identities, at least in part, in dialogue with the past. If film-makers have our permission to tell fanciful lies, we nonetheless insist that they make those lies moderately credible. We require "true" lies, depictions of the past and present that are comprehensible to us and that locate our own private stories within a larger collective narrative.

It may seem strange to assert an important connection between lived experience and film viewing. We have come to think of the movies as an "escape" from the world. Inside theaters, motion pictures occupy their own space and time, and even on home video they command a level of attention that distinguishes our reception of them from our viewing of television or our listening to popular music. Camera angles and film editing fragment vision and time as much in film as in as any other art, and the effective spectacles of cinema— its giant screen, lush colors, powerful soundtracks, and special effects—overwhelm us as no other medium does. In addition, film seems more resistant to popular influence than almost any other popular culture form, because the high capital costs required to enter the film industry discourage new entrants and vest control of film contents in an infinitesimal segment of society.

Yet motion pictures could not function as an "escape" if they were merely distraction. An escape must take us from one place to another, specifically from confinement or peril to a locus of freedom. If films show us a world too little like our own, they fail to address and neutralize our feelings of confinement and peril. If they show us a world too much like our own, they deprive us of the freedom to recast the past and present in keeping with the preferences of imagination and desire. Hollywood films highlight the tensions between confinement and peril, on the one hand, and freedom and imagination, on the other. They depict battles between necessity and desire, between inherited objective circumstances and subjective human will. In that respect they resemble historical narratives. Whether situated in the past, present, or future, commercial motion pictures invariably resonate with the value crises of the times in which they appear. Thus they are historical in the sense of being cultural artifacts and social-history evidence about the times in which they were made. But films are historical in another way as well: they reposition us for the future by reshaping our memories of the past.

An exceptional body of research by historians and film scholars in recent years has highlighted the historicity of the motion picture experience. Social historians Roy Rosenzweig and Kathy Peiss explain how the very existence of motion-picture theaters served to alter the consciousness of urban industrial workers in the late nineteenth and early twentieth centuries. In his study of Worcester, Massachusetts, Rosenzweig contends that a search for "free spaces"—capable of posing alternatives to the time-work discipline of the factory—led workers to saloons, parks, and picnic grounds before they found refuge in the motion-picture theater. Peiss shows how early commercial cinema helped unmarried working women in New York break the constraints of family, ethnicity, and class that tied them to a restricted "women's world," giving them new access to public space and new control over personal relationships.[1] Similarly, Lary May explains how both the content of motion pictures and the process of watching them taught audiences in the 1920s ways to break with the Victorian past and to embrace the leisure-oriented hedonism of the emerging consumer commodity-oriented society. In addition, recent detailed studies of motion-picture content and its relationship to specific time periods by Dana Polan (1940s), Peter Biskind (1950s), and Michael Ryan and Douglas Kellner (1967-1987) have clearly established the importance of film as evidence about social and cultural history.[2] Social historians Rosenzweig, Peiss, and May locate the process of viewing motion pictures within larger historical contexts, while film critics Polan, Biskind, Ryan, and Kellner concentrate on the texts of films themselves for general trends and tendencies in the periods they have elected to examine. But their fine work leaves one important aspect of the relationship between films and history under-examined—the congruence between the "escape" mechanisms of movies and the necessary practices of historical thinking. Hollywood films may get all the details wrong, they may perpetuate misinformation and ignorance about everything from the frontier to the family, yet they still might encourage ways of asking and answering questions conducive to historical investigation.

However, when we look for broad categories capable of creating coherence out of the many kinds of stories told by Hollywood in the years since World War II, the five main themes that emerge do not seem sensitive to issues of change over time. These themes—the family in jeopardy, agonies of empire, corruption at the top, personal autonomy, and what literary critic Nina Baym (in another context) calls "melodramas of beset manhood"—encompass an extraordinary number of Hollywood productions during this period. The groupings may seem more structural than historical, evidence of recurrent myths reworking the same ground over and over. But what changes over time in these representations is often more important than what stays the same.

Two Hollywood films from 1946 illumine the complex contradictions of the historical context in which they were made. Robert Montgomery's *Ride the Pink Horse* and Edward Dmytryk's *Till The End of Time* addressed the anxieties of postwar America by emphasizing antagonistic aspects of collective memory. *Ride the Pink Horse* spoke to the accumulated anger and bitterness produced by wartime suffering and sacrifice, while *Till The End of Time* played upon the satisfactions of solidarity, upon the mutuality and sense of connection to others attendant to the war effort. The two films reveal widely divergent possibilities within the same historical moment, and the differences between them underscore the uncertain relation between objective social conditions and subjective popular perceptions.

Ride the Pink Horse frames the postwar experience from the perspective of "Gagan," a returning veteran whose lack of a first name

reflects the anonymity of his social standing. The film opens with Gagan stepping off an interstate bus that had brought him to Taos, New
Mexico during festival time, but he has not come to celebrate. Gagan
wants "to finish a job," to exact revenge on a former war profiteer
responsible for the murder of Gagan's wartime pal "Shorty." Everything about Gagan emphasizes his marginality. Unable to get a seat
on the bus, he had been forced to stand for most of the trip. He made
no room reservation and cannot get into any of the hotels booked to
capacity for the festival crowd. There is no place for him on the bus
or in the hotels of Taos; he is a returning veteran who feels crowded
out of the society that he left behind when he went to war.

As Gagan walks the streets, his determination to avenge the past
sets him apart from the fiesta crowds who are absorbed in their celebration at the moment. His alienations stem from his memories of
the war. He feels that he and Shorty endured unbearable hardships
with no real reward, while people like the war profiteer got all the
benefits without doing any of the sacrificing. Yet Gagan's anger does
not quite take the form of class consciousness: his resentments are
personal, not systemic, and his experiences have made him suspicious of all people, not just war profiteers. These anti-social feelings
come out in racist contempt for the Chicanos in Taos as easily as in
resentment of the rich. When Pila, a young Indian girl, tries to help
him "because he looks in danger," he accuses her of soliciting him
for prostitution. When an elderly Chicano man lets Gagan sleep under the protective cover of the little carousel he runs, Gagan initially
dismisses the man's offers of help with condescending racial epithets.

Gagan discovers that he is not alone in pursuit of his prey. An FBI
agent has been following him and warns Gagan that private revenge
may endanger the government's case against the murderer. But Gagan wants no alliance with the government, bitterly reminding the
agent that the last "errand" he ran for Uncle Sam (the war) got him
nothing but made the profiteer wealthy. But the profiteer is too
strong for Gagan to handle alone. After a series of beatings that he
survives only because the Indian girl and the Mexican-American man
help him, Gagan corners his enemy and reluctantly turns him over to
the FBI. In a final twist, the carousel operator reminds Gagan that he
should express his gratitude to Pila. They encounter her by accident,
but as Gagan fumbles with his words, unable to acknowledge his
debt to a woman and an Indian, she informs him that no thanks are

necessary. Pila then turns to her friends and recounts for them, in Spanish, the entire story, obviously placing herself and her own heroism at the center. We realize that she has her own story to tell and that Gagan's narrative is only part of it.

Till The End of Time also focuses on a returning veteran, middle-class Cliff Harper. The war years have helped Harper mature; he is no longer the callow college youth who went to war. But he feels that the war has robbed him of time and direction, and he finds it hard to reconnect with the world he left behind. His old clothes no longer fit, his parents do not acknowledge that the dreadful things he has seen have changed him, and he feels no desire to get a job or resume his education. Unlike Gagan, Harper feels a nostalgia for the war, horrible as it was. The war gave him purposeful work, it revealed the sheltered nature of his previous experiences, and it bonded him closely to his fellow soldiers from diverse class, ethnic, and regional backgrounds. Harper and his friends miss the camaraderie of military life, their failure to fit into civilian life stems from a critique of its individualism and materialism.

Harper solves his problems with the help of a woman. Pat Ruscomb lost her husband in combat during the war, but she has made a new life for herself as a worker in a defense plant. She dates Cliff, but feels impatient with his lack of direction and purpose. It becomes clear that Cliff will have to display some responsibility and maturity to secure a relationship with Pat as well as to solve his own problems. But in this film, individual action is not enough—institutional and collective solutions must be found. While *Ride the Pink Horse* demonstrates a distrust of all institutions and authority figures as pawns of the elite, *Till The End of Time* presents business, army, and government as the salvation of the common man. From the lengthy "mustering out" Marine Corps ceremony to the careful counseling of the Veterans Administration to the kindly guidance of a factory foreman (certainly the most understanding foreman in the history of American industry) the big institutions in *Till The End of Time* are looking out for the little man. As one would expect from this benign picture of socialization, the film's characters solve their many problems in one heroic effort when they join together to beat up neo-Fascists harassing one of their buddies in a bar. They discover that they can translate wartime collectivity and solidarity to their civilian lives, and they resolve to face the future together.

On the surface, *Ride the Pink Horse* and *Till The End of Time* seem to represent diametrically opposite viewpoints. With its cynicism about wealth and power, its identification of corporate greed as the source of all evil, and its acceptance of broadened perspectives on ethnicity, gender, and class, *Ride the Pink Horse* seems to embody a cultural direction that we can term "democratic culture." Contrastingly, the middle-class perspective and the glorification of authority and collectivity in *Till The End of Time* marks it as emblematic of what we can call "corporate culture." But democratic culture and corporate culture, rather than being polar opposites, sometimes are in complicated dialectical relationships. Both *Ride the Pink Horse* and *Till The End of Time* address residual popular memories of the war, they also re-enact it. Gagan becomes a soldier fighting one more battle, but this time he identifies the "right" enemy—the war profiteer—and the "right" allies—an impoverished elderly Mexican-American, a young Native American Indian girl, and, more hesitantly, an agent of the government. Similarly, the wartime buddies in *Till The End of Time* suffer from their new status as "rugged individuals," until they join together to take violent action against the fascist threat once again. While the two films differ about the interests of authority vs. the interests of individuals, for Hollywood productions they both give extraordinary moral power to women, to workers, and to non-WASP characters. The ultimate meaning of the war may remain contested, but some of its attendant social consequences seem deeply embedded in the discursive world of these films.

The ironic personal histories of the creators of *Ride the Pink Horse* and *Till The End of Time* underscore the films' identities as products of their historical moment. Robert Montgomery, who made the more radical and anti-establishment film of the two, went on to become President Eisenhower's television coach after appearing as a friendly witness before the House Un-American Activities Committee. Edward Dmytryk, whose film expressed supreme faith in the government, became one of the "Hollywood Ten," the film artists called before the HUAC for suspected communist affiliations and sent to jail for refusing to testify as the committee required. Alone among the ten, Dmytryk renounced his former political ideas when he got out of prison. In 1954 he directed *The Caine Mutiny*, a film which exposed the "dangers" posed by people who question and belittle authority, and which argued that even paranoid and incompetent authority had to be obeyed and supported. There are many reasons for the evolution of Montgomery's and Dmytryk's views. One might even argue that the films contained contradictions that made the later political transformations consistent with earlier tendencies. But it also seems clear that the visions projected in *Ride the Pink Horse* and *Till The End of Time* reflected a social discourse about the past and present that set boundaries for the individual artists. That discourse, and its contradictions, illumines the ways in which Hollywood motion pictures can be important artifacts for historical research.

For example, both *Picnic* (1955) and *Kramer vs. Kramer* (1979) depict the family in jeopardy. But in *Picnic*, female dependence on men—mandated by unequal economic opportunities and by the power of the male gaze—leaves women vulnerable to the irresponsibility of individual males. In *Kramer vs. Kramer*, female independence and entry into the job market threatens the family and forces the man to take on new domestic burdens. The connections between these films and their historical contexts are far from simple: we know too much about the 1950s and the 1970s to to be convinced that *Picnic* and *Kramer vs. Kramer* reflect a direct linear progression or regression, that feminism influenced films of the 1950s more than films of the 1970s, or that the 1970s were a less progressive decade for women than were the 1950s. But what are we to make of the contradictions that these films expose? On the one hand, *Kramer vs. Kramer* shows none of the sympathy for women's confinement that resonates so powerfully in *Picnic*. On the other hand, *Picnic* cannot even suggest some of the possibilities for female autonomy that are accepted as a matter of course in *Kramer vs. Kramer*, even when the latter film argues that things have gone too far.

Each of these films responds to tensions exposed by the social moment of its creation, but each also enters a dialogue already in progress, repositioning the audience in regard to dominant myths. *Picnic* responds to arguments evident in preceding anti-feminist (*Our Very Own* 1950, *I Want You* 1951) and proto-feminist films (*Adam's Rib* 1949, *The Marrying Kind* 1952) as well as to the social contradictions that spawned them. Similarly, *Kramer vs. Kramer* makes its statements about the family in a context that included both conservative critiques (*An Unmarried Woman* 1978) and feminist critiques (*Girlfriends* 1978) of patriarchy and male privilege. Each of these films contains inscribed preferred readings: their conclusions

Imply one true source of conflict and one viable method of resolution. Yet those endings do not fully resolve the contradictions they raise. To engage our interests as viewers they need to make us fight against ourselves, to see opposite interpretations as plausible and desirable, making any closure somewhat unsatisfying. Both *Picnic* and *Kramer vs. Kramer* end by asserting that one can have both marriage and independence, obligations and freedom. Yet the emotional impact of the preceding narratives undercuts those closures; we know that the family might be in jeopardy again tomorrow, no matter how hopeful we find the happy endings of the films.

The complex and contradictory arbitrations of social tensions in *Picnic* and *Kramer vs. Kramer* preclude some kinds of historical conclusions. We cannot argue from this limited evidence that the history of the family has one clear trajectory from patriarchy to feminism or vice versa. But we can see that change over time depends on arguments, actions, and ideologies that are constantly being constructed and reconstructed even in periods of seeming stasis. In addition, we can learn that arguments have to change with circumstances, that generalized myths draw their social power from the ways in which they are articulated or disarticulated in any given social circumstance. Finally, diachronic narratives depend on revisionism. Present problems force us to redesign our psychic and intellectual maps of the past.

Similar historical processes underlie two films that combine "melodramas of beset manhood" with the "agonies of empire," *The Man Who Shot Liberty Valance* (1962) and *An Officer and a Gentleman* (1983). In both films men learn to make themselves strong enough to act in a brutal world, and their victories are not merely personal. In these films the "manly" capacity for violence wins the approval of women and makes possible the survival of the nation. In *The Man Who Shot Liberty Valance*, young Ransom Stoddard suffers from an idealistic devotion to law and the social contract that makes him seem too weak to combat the evil deeds of outlaw Liberty Valance. Only when rugged frontiersman Tom Doniphon arms Stoddard with some of Valance's brutality does the young man emerge victorious. He destroys Valance, makes the west safe for civilization, and acquires the respect he needs to win Doniphon's girl away from him. By contrast, in *An Officer and a Gentleman*, Zack Mayo's problem is the opposite of Stoddard's: he is too anti-authoritarian and anti-social to accept discipline and become a successful soldier. But just as Stoddard had Doniphon to guide him, the intervention of Drill Instructor Foley channels Mayo's rage and capacity for brutality into a form that enables him to become a credit to society—an officer and a gentleman. In both films, the young men initially see their tutors as enemies, while Doniphon and Foley display open contempt for the men they eventually transform. In each case, the voices of experience (Doniphon and Foley) triumph by transferring some of their own brutality to the novices to make them more like the enemies they must combat. For both tutors, the process entails an ultimate sacrifice—they must allow their charges to surpass them and receive the glory that should properly belong to them.

In *The Man Who Shot Liberty Valance*, both Doniphon and Stoddard wind up disgraced. Doniphon "helps" Stoddard by hiding in the dark and shooting Liberty Valance in the back when the outlaw and Stoddard appear to be dueling each other. On the surface this act enables Doniphon to get rid of Liberty Valance, and, therefore, a threat to civilization while making Stoddard a hero. But Doniphon has stooped to Valance's level; he cannot enjoy the fruits of civilization because he has violated its codes. Even worse, Doniphon could kill Valance only because he was so much like him. Valance's death and the triumph of civilization make Doniphon useless; he is not needed to deal with Valance any longer, nor can he fit into the civilized world. Stoddard becomes a hero because of Doniphon's act, but a false hero. He knows that he did not, in fact, shoot Liberty Valance, and the triumphs of civilization rest neither on his own beloved legal code or on Doniphon's code of honor. Instead, the moral basis of civilization rests upon the very barbarism it supplants. Stoddard "wins": he marries Doniphon's girl and becomes a senator, but his marriage is childless and his place in history has been secured by what he knows to be a lie. The inscribed reading of *The Man Who Shot Liberty Valance* implies that corruption is inevitable and maybe even necessary, but neither the "manhood" of Ransom Stoddard nor the "triumph" of civilization hold any real glory or merit.

In contrast with *The Man Who Shot Liberty Valance* and its serious self-reflection and criticism, *An Officer and a Gentleman* presents its closures as unproblematic. The sadistic brutality of Sgt. Foley and his power to humiliate Mayo put into play the main oppositions of the film: on the one side, an angry, white, working-class male who hates authority and commitment, on the other side, a military bureaucracy that makes him dependent upon a group of fellow officer candidates whom he hates, under the command of a black sergeant who seems determined to prevent his advancement. The inscribed reading of the plot encourages the audience to identify with Mayo's anger and resentments, and to share his sense of self-empowerment through aggression. To succeed, he must take on the identity of Sgt. Foley, channeling his brutality within the disciplined confines of the military. Just as Ransom Stoddard and Tom Doniphon "save" civilization by becoming like their enemy Liberty Valance, Mayo emerges as a hero to his fellow officers and girlfriend when he becomes like Foley.

The similarities between *The Man Who Shot Liberty Valance* and *An Officer and a Gentleman* suggest some underlying structural unities endemic to "melodramas of beset manhood" and the agonies of empire in Hollywood films. But important differences between the two films illumine significant historical traces as well. Made at a time when both U.S. military hegemony and patriarchal authority within the nuclear family appeared stronger than ever before, *The Man Who Shot Liberty Valance* betrayed serious doubts about the efficacy and legitimacy of these hierarchies. *An Officer and a Gentleman*, on the other hand, emerged after the American defeat in Vietnam and the Iranian hostage crisis, and after more than a decade of feminist criticism of patriarchy. *An Officer and a Gentleman* reaffirmed values that seemed to many to have been discredited and abandoned, while *The Man Who Shot Liberty Valance* questioned dominant values — or apparently dominant values. The inverse relationship between these films and their historical contexts illustrates the point made so effectively by Kellner and Ryan about a lag between historical experience and cultural expression. To Kellner and Ryan, Hollywood films often express the pent-up frustrations of an era, not reflecting dominant views as much as prefiguring the next swing of the pendulum.[3]

Just as *Picnic* could anticipate feminist critiques of female dependency during an era of seeming patriarchal hegemony, *Kramer vs. Kramer* anticipated the popularity of New Right anti-feminism by airing the resentments percolating against ascendant feminism. *Picnic* asked its audiences to question the legacy of the recent past, to reassess the 1950s gender roles that had reversed some of the gains made by women in the 1940s. *Kramer vs. Kramer* didn't celebrate the successes of ascendant feminism in creating opportunities for women, but, rather, blamed these women for broken homes and unhappy children. *Kramer vs. Kramer* ignores the historical and social fact that in our society men abandon women and children routinely; ideologically the film succeeded in putting the onus for broken families on women and on feminism. In the same way, a seemingly conservative film like *The Man Who Shot Liberty Valance* contained all the doubts about national legends and patriarchy that would soon emerge in 1960s social movements, while *An Officer and A Gentleman*, apparently liberal in its showing people from different races and classes becoming a unified group, actually played out the narcissistic grandiosity essential to the patriarchal family and the militaristic state.

This contrast between the criticisms of patriarchy and nationalism in *Picnic* and *The Man Who Shot Liberty Valance* and the antifeminism and authoritarian nationalism of *Kramer vs. Kramer* and *An Officer and a Gentlemen* of course is not to suggest that the 1950s and 1960s were more liberal than the 1970s and 1980s. It shows, rather, how films can be dissonant with their own time, asking and answering historical questions that might push discourse and political behavior in another direction.

Sometimes reversals in a genre can be directly emblematic of the context in which a film is made, as in two films organized around "corruption at the top," *The President's Analyst* (1967) and *Rambo* (1985). Consistent with its 1960s surroundings, *The President's Analyst* depicts a psychiatrist, Dr. Sidney Stone, chosen as therapist for the president of the United States. At first he is in awe of power, dazzled by his patient and the enormous responsibilities he wields. But exposure to the centers of power makes Stone a target for a tug of war between the FBI and the CIA, between the secret operatives of friendly and hostile nations. He comes to see them all as interchangeable, committed to power rather than to values or ideology. When his inquiries eventually lead him to the conspiratorial force behind all of the pointless chicanery he has witnessed, the psychiatrist discovers it to be corporate capitalism — in the form of the telephone company. Although satirical and light-hearted in its barbs, *The President's Analyst* expresses a cynical distrust of corporate and national power which it contrasts with the good instincts of ordinary citizens who for the most part would do fine if they were just left alone.

Rambo also discovers malefactors in high places, but their identity and the putative solutions to their wrongdoing are distinctly different. For John Rambo, the conspirators are Washington bureaucrats whose incompetence "lost" the War in Vietnam despite the gallant efforts of soldiers like Rambo. Even after the war they attempt to sabotage his efforts to rescue U.S. prisoners left behind in order to neutralize the war as a political issue. Rambo uses physical bravery and rather unbelievable fire power to escape their "no-win" philosophy and to kill and maim the Vietnamese enemies responsible for his memories of suffering.

Both *The President's Analyst* and *Rambo* use individualism as the focal point for historical revisionism. Iconoclast and rebel Sidney Stone battles the FBI and the CIA, understands the working relationship and mutual respect manifest between KGB and CIA operatives, takes refuge with hippies and other social outcasts while fleeing from a middle-class suburban family, and eventually takes up arms against the "real enemy," corporate monopoly capitalism. In contrast, working-class John Rambo gives the appearance of 1960s rebellion (he has long hair and eats natural foods), but finds his enemy in the government bureaucracy and his solution in a "rescue mission" that serves as a surrogate replay of the war in Vietnam. *The President's Analyst* questioned the entire legacy of the cold war at a time when Americans were being asked to fight in Vietnam; *Rambo* sought to control the historical verdict on Vietnam by arguing for renewed war in a time of peace. In the 1960s film, individual distrust of government served liberal ends; by the 1980s that same sentiment had become the foundation for an ultra-conservative critique.

Two motion pictures about personal autonomy evidence a similar reversal in themes. In *Rebel Without a Cause* (1955) teen-ager Jim Stark resists the conformist pressures of his affluent suburban community. His parents live for appearances. They tell him to choose his friends carefully and to be seen with the right crowd, but he is more concerned with proving himself to a gang of delinquents when they tease him about being "chicken." The world of his parents suffocates Jim. His domineering grandmother, hen-pecked father, and embittered mother provide him with inadequate adult role models. The surveillance at school is even more intense. Peer pressure drives him to participate in a dangerous and foolish automobile race simply because he would lose face by declining a challenge. Home and school worlds converge when Jim's opponent dies in the race. In the pivotal scene in the film, he tells his parents he wants to inform the police about his involvement in the race, but in typical 1950s fashion they tell him not to get involved. "You can't be idealistic all the time," his father tells him. But Jim insists that a human life has been taken, that he has responsibility for it, and that he cannot choose to turn his back on that responsibility to society. Through a complicated series of circumstances, his nonconformity enables him to form an egalitarian relationship with a girlfriend, a relationship that becomes a model even to the adults around him. Although Jim's sense of responsibility ultimately cannot save the life of a young friend who idolizes him, Stark's decision to connect his life to others eventually puts nonconformity to the service of social advancement.

Director Nicholas Ray once commented about Jim in his *Rebel Without a Cause* saying a hero is not someone who is better than you; a hero is someone just like you who for a little while does something better than you.[4] That kind of egalitarian populism provided the informative moral power behind *Rebel Without a Cause*; the film championed nonconformity as a way of unleashing the nobility and heroism of the ordinary person. A different notion of nonconformity was presented in *Amadeus* (1984), a notion that reflected the neoconservatism of the 1980s. The Wolfgang Amadeus Mozart in *Amadeus* rebels because he believes that he really is better than other people: he is a genius who produces great art without labor, while they are mediocrities who conspire against his superior talents. Mozart's nonconformity is vicious, anti-social, and contemptuous of others, but the film implies that it is all validated by his music. Whereas society seemed oppressive in *Rebel Without a Cause* because its materialism and conformity constrained the potential of an ordinary citizen, in *Amadeus* society's oppressions served the common people by cheating the exceptional ones. As was the case with *Rambo* and *The President's Analyst*, anti-authoritarian individualism in the 1980s served the purposes of hierarchy and conservatism in *Amadeus* whereas it had been a feature of liberalism in *Rebel Without a Cause*.

Yet it would not be accurate to say that liberalism captured the concept of individualism in the 1950s and conservatism captured it in the 1980s. Instead, both liberalism and conservatism have jockeyed for position throughout the postwar era by appropriating overt and latent structures of feeling capable of legitimating and sustaining their positions. No fixed inventory of character traits marks a film as belonging to corporate culture or to democratic culture; rather, it is the way character traits are put in place in any given historical moment. Furthermore, effective ideological argument often anticipates hostile reactions, if only to co-opt them. For example, the 1941 film *Sergeant York* succeeds as pro-war interventionist propaganda largely because it presents the pacifist position so movingly, then disposes with it so effectively. Director Dorothy Arzner's *Craig's Wife* (1937) advances a persuasive feminist critique of marriage as an institution by misdirecting audience resentments against the heroine and then showing us how the built-in power relations of patriarchal marriage turned her into the person we have come to dislike. Sometimes these oppositions appear so compelling that we do not know which side to choose. Film scholar Peter Biskind argues that *Rebel Without a Cause* works to reconcile a rebel to the nuclear family, teasing us with the possibilities of opposition but eventually disciplining the hero into submission. Yet other critics offer a directly opposite interpretation: they argue that Jim Stark's position wins out, that the family and society change because of his actions rather than vice versa. Effective presentation of both options widens the potential audience for a film, but it leaves questions about any film's ideological and political effectiveness. In the case of *Rebel Without a Cause*, reception may depend upon the historical consciousness of viewers—whether they read the rise of suburbia as an advance for American society or as a moral and social disaster.

The contradictory readings inscribed in most Hollywood motion pictures may seem like craven opportunism, examples of how commercial culture compromises the moral authority of art. For commercial and ideological reasons, producers do want to "have it both ways," and they do not want to polarize the audience unduly. But this two-sided nature of ideology in films also illumines the innately dialogic nature of political discourse itself. Part of persuading others involves understanding their points of view. Constructing alliances around unifying ideals and images necessitates concessions and compromise, and a recognition of what we might call a "unity of opposites." Only someone frightened by the temptations of democratic culture would submit to the repressions of corporate culture. Only someone capable of submitting to the oppressions of corporate culture would endure the risks of fighting for a democratic culture.

These polar positions do not represent fixed dramatic forms, or even fixed segments of society. They reflect battles that take place inside each of us as we negotiate our relationships to other people, past and present.

In their studies of "black rage," psychiatrists William Grier and Price Cobbs identify a peculiar phenomenon among Afro-American males that they term "tears without emotion." They observe a tendency among black men to break into tears while watching popular-culture representations of celebration. The sight of a halfback exulting after scoring a touchdown or an actress bowing to the applause of an adoring audience might start tears streaming down the cheeks of a black male viewer. Grier and Cobbs attribute these "tears without emotion" to an unlocking of repressed hopes. These men cry for "all that might have been," for all the desires and ideals crushed by historical power relations, for all the celebrations they will never have.[5] Popular culture often works very much as these "tears without emotion" do. It resists univocal interpretations and inscribed ideological closures because of the hurts of history. The deep emotional investment with the fictions of popular culture amounts to more than brain-washing or a stupefied numbness engendered by the power of the media apparatus. Rather, it stems from the gap between lived experiences and human hopes in a world with too many broken promises and too many unrealized dreams.

8

The New York Intellectuals: Samuel Fuller and Edgar Ulmer

In his trenchant analysis of the gangster film, Robert Warshow noted that "a dark city of the imagination" pervades the crime genre. In his view, the city menaced the American imagination because it represented a psychic landscape on which desires for upward mobility turned into cut-throat competition, a place where rugged individualism expressed itself through brutalization and humiliation of others. By contrast, traditions of American pastoralism represented the frontier and the farm as places of freedom, opportunity, and mutuality.

Anyone familiar with American history might object that the frontier and the plantation have been sites of extraordinary brutality and sadism, while the city has been the place where compromise and mutual accommodation enabled diverse populations to live together. But the pastoral myth does not rest on historical facts and cannot be refuted by evidence. In addition, historical understanding in America has become so entwined with the pastoral myth that a historical critique of pastoralism seems a contradiction in terms. For the frontier and the farm seem innately historical; they seem to be places where a future is still possible and where individual narratives of success can unite the past and present. The city, on the other hand, seems to be the place where the freight train of history jumped the track. The city enjoys the latest technologies and conveniences, but its very collectivity seems to rebuke the tradition of individual narratives that Americans have come to understand as history.

The city became a cultural and intellectual problem in the nineteenth century, at the very moment when anxieties about history

179

emerged as the constitutive problem of modern society. As Laura Mulvey writes

> Over and over again, the mysterious, fascinating and frightening image of the city recurs throughout the nineteenth century. It represents an outside to the rule of order. To the individual swallowed up in the crowd, to the law in the refuge given to the criminal, to morality faced with a profusion of bars and prostitutes, the city at night epitomises chaos and uncertainty.[1]

Chaos and uncertainty were the problems history was expected to solve. The serious dislocations and distortions of industrialization disoriented individuals from their pasts and led to what E. J. Hobsbawm calls "the invention of tradition." Much of the public imagery and ceremony celebrating "history" in the nineteenth century had in fact been invented and fabricated in the present simply to ease anxieties about disconnection from the past. In this context, historical narratives tended to stress the inevitability of progress, the heroism of isolated individuals, and the narrative closures that brought reassurance or fatalism to people suffering amid chaos and uncertainty.

Thus the city became an enemy of history, or at least of historical narratives. Its energies and pluralities suggested many stories not just one. Its injustices and exploitations called into question the inevitability (or even the reality) of progress. Finally, the real city of mutuality and accommodation rebuked both the dark city of the imagination and the unrealistically bright countryside of pastoralism. As Warshow's critique suggests, dominant culture continued to contrast the dark city with the bright frontier, but in the art of organic intellectuals the city and its relationship to history became a focal point for a plethora of oppositional narratives.

Two film-makers exemplify the recovery of the city as a terrain for a new kind of historical thinking. Samuel Fuller and Edgar Ulmer are not the kind of people usually included in discussions about "New York intellectuals," but their love for that city and their recognition of the possibilities within it mark them as profound contributors to debates about the city and history. Operating on the fringes of the film industry, they were far removed from the world of traditional intellectuals and the institutions that support them. But as artists committed to their communities and to the still unrealized potential within them, they served as organic intellectuals, as agents of agitation and education for hopes that had not yet taken organized political identity. Because they were engaged in making low-budget products for a commercial medium, they often found themselves constrained by the tools at their disposal. Both the form and content of their professional work resonated with a sensationalism and an intentional vulgarity that deflected critical attention from the reflective, contemplative, and critical core of their films. But life as organic intellectuals also gave them access to the rough energy of the city, to the democratic pluralism of its communities, and there they found a vision capable of critiquing the seemingly unquestioned myths of their day.

Samuel Fuller: A Post-Industrial Prophet

Samuel Fuller is very much a New Yorker and very much an intellectual. His childhood in the city and his experiences as a copy boy and crime reporter for its tabloid newspapers gave determinate shape to the artistic and social vision that permeates all of his professional work. Many of Fuller's books and films use New York for local color and dramatic tensions, but they also use the complexities and contradictions of the twentieth-century metropolis as a stimulus for a unique kind of intellectual work. For Fuller, the textures of urban experience challenge the preoccupations of traditional intellectuals by privileging human interaction and inter-subjectivity over abstract standards of refinement and performance.

Critics have rarely appreciated the complexity and integrity of Samuel Fuller's world view. In fairness it must be conceded that he has made it difficult for them. A director who gives a goofy smile and waves to the camera while wearing a silly hat and gaudy flower-print shirt as Fuller did during the closing credits of *Dead Pigeon on Beethoven Street* is not likely to be revered as a serious artist. Nor is an auteur who insists on writing, directing, and producing films about mental illness (*Shock Corridor*), child molesting (*The Naked Kiss*), safecracking, teen-age drug addiction and school-girl prostitution (*Underworld U.S.A.*) likely to be understood as a sensitive interpreter of the moral dilemmas of modern life. And someone who celebrates violence as enthusiastically as Fuller did in his description of a scene from *Pickup on South Street* ("I liked the idea of Widmark pulling Kiley down by the ankles, and that the heavy's chin hits every step. Dat-dat-dat-dat dat. It's musical.") can hardly expect intellectu als to look to him for moral guidance. Given these choices on Full- er's part, it is not surprising that even his admirers have frequently qualified their praise by describing him as "an intelligent primitive," a "master of shock realism," and "the maker of a few brilliant movies and a few more awful ones."[2]

Yet part of Fuller's flamboyant quirkiness comes from his serious- ness as an interpreter of urban life. The low budgets that sometimes make his feature films look like glorified home movies also enabled Fuller to make films free from interference by producers and studio executives. As he once explained, for most of the seventeen "B" pic- tures he made between 1948 and 1963 "the budget was so little that they [producers and financial backers] never gave a damn about my premise, my content, and that's what interested me."[3] Despite their lurid and melodramatic content, most Fuller films raise serious is- sues in serious ways. "Every film must have a message," Fuller de- clares. "Maybe I'm too didactic. If so, too bad. That's just the way I write. Even if people don't agree with me, I like to make them think a bit. I'd like them to learn something. I'm not what you would strictly call an educator, but all the same I think the cinema must be used in this way."[4]

Those critics who have been able to look beyond Fuller's excesses and eccentricities have discovered profound meaning in his work. Frank McConnell hails Fuller's film *Pickup on South Street* for its sen- sitive representation of the crises in American popular mythology and American political aesthetics generated by anti-communism in the McCarthy era.[5] Luc Moullet praises Fuller for the ways in which his films challenge the unrealistic glamour of Hollywood conven- tions, choosing instead to explore life at the margins of society by raising difficult issues and presenting unpleasant images.[6] Jim Ho- berman celebrates Fuller's "shock realism," locating the film-maker within a tradition of urban-influenced artists that include the cartoon- ist Chester Gould and the photographer Weegee.[7] As these critics discern, Fuller has more to offer us than his questionable taste and his uneven professional history. Yet his ideas about culture, ideology, and society are more significant than even his most sympathetic crit- ics have thus far acknowledged. McConnell's emphasis on Fuller's historical location, Moullet's understanding of Fuller's aesthetics, and Hoberman's appreciation of Fuller's ties to the city all present part of the picture. But it is necessary to integrate these three frames of analysis into one unified totality to grasp the full import of Fuller's artistic and social vision.

In all of his films, but especially those set in New York City (*Pickup on South Street, Park Row,* and *Underworld U.S.A.*), Fuller uses urban life as a vehicle for examining key questions about culture and ideology in the modern world. In his films and books, he shuns the noble and the heroic to concentrate on the ordinary and the mundane. He distrusts institutions and ideologies, but displays great faith in the instincts and intuitions of ordinary people. Working in a cinematic tradition generally dominated by simple binary oppositions, Fuller depicts his protagonists as disturbingly similar to the enemies they go out to confront.

The cultural positions articulated within Samuel Fuller's films should be easily understood by intellectuals in the 1980s; indeed they resonate with the concerns of much contemporary cultural criticism. The "new social history" of the past decade has used the everyday life experiences of ordinary people as a basis for generalizations about entire societies, past and present. Poststructuralists have challenged the dominance of "master narratives" and the legitimacy of cultural institutions in order to illumine and savor localized practices of subjectivity and resistance. My purpose in this presentation will be to examine how Fuller's engagement with late industrial New York City enabled him to formulate these distinctly postmodern principles in an era of seemingly unchallenged and ascendant modernism.

In formulating his artistic vision, Fuller drew upon his personal history and upon the history of the society in which he lived. His focus on the underside of urban life was partially autobiography and partially social commentary. Fuller spent his earliest years in Worcester, Massachusetts, but his mother brought the family to New York when his father died in 1922. Fuller attended elementary school in Manhattan and explored the city's complex urban textures selling papers on street corners after school. Fascinated by tabloid newspapers, he dropped out of high school to secure employment as a copy boy for the *Daily Graphic*, and soon found himself running errands for William Randolph Hearst's prize columnist Arthur Brisbane. While still a teen-ager, Fuller worked his way onto the crime beat, and he soon familiarized himself with the lives of gamblers, street hustlers, thieves, and pickpockets in the underworld of his beloved city. He found himself horrified by the brutality, aggression, and systematic corruption of the city, but at the same time attracted to the peculiar moral codes and social loyalties that he encountered on the streets of poverty-stricken ethnic neighborhoods. In the city he found the worst manifestations of selfishness and competition, but he also discovered there a sense of community and mutuality that enabled people to survive in a hostile environment.

Fuller worked as a crime and waterfront reporter for the *San Diego Sun* in the 1930s. He published four novels between 1935 and 1944, including one about a criminal sentenced to execution in the electric chair and one about the newspaper industry. Fuller started work as a screen writer in Hollywood in 1937, where scripts like *Federal Man-Hunt, Gangs of New York, Bowery Boy, Power of the Press*, and *Gangs of the Waterfront* reflected his interests in crime and urban life. During World War II, Fuller served with distinction as an infantryman in Europe, and after his return from the war began to produce, direct, and write his own films.

Critics have often observed that every Fuller film is a "war" film, focused on violent conflict, the solidarity of comrades in arms, and the unfair burdens placed on individuals who find themselves caught up in other people's battles. Certainly, Fuller's wartime experiences left a lasting impression on him, and his films resonate with the lessons he learned in combat. But every Fuller film is also an "urban" film, even his westerns and war movies. His motion pictures characteristically explore the difficulties of uniting diverse populations and reconciling competing interests. They examine the tensions generated by ethnic rivalries, and they investigate the dangers of unbridled individualism in an interdependent world. No matter what their setting or ostensible genre, his films again and again return to the core tensions of the urban communities that Fuller encountered in his years as a journalist for tabloid newspapers.

Just as they did for him as a reporter, murders initiate the action in many Fuller films, drawing him out into some kind of city on a quest for information and understanding. In *The Steel Helmet*, a 1951 film about the Korean War, the massacre of the rest of his company leads Sgt. Zack into a "city" composed of misfits and undesirables from other units. The dramatic tension within *The Steel Helmet* comes from efforts by this multi-racial group of stragglers to get along with one another in order to successfully resist assaults by their common enemy. The shooting of a stripper in *Crimson Kimono* leads two Los Angeles detectives (one Japanese-American and one Anglo) into the mysterious world of that city's "Little Tokyo," which in turn makes them examine the ways in which their ethnicity has shaped their identities and their relations with each other. *Crimson Kimono* uses the city of Los Angeles as a "supporting character" much as John Ford used the wide-open spaces of the Monument Valley to symbolize pastoral freedom. Aerial views of the city stress its density, but as the camera focuses on individuals the viewer begins to make sense out of the chaos. Young Tolly Devlin in *Underworld, U.S.A.* sees a group of thugs beat his father to death on New Year's Eve, and he embarks on a life of crime to avenge that slaying. The murder of a mental patient attracts the attention of an ambitious reporter in *Shock Corridor* and leads him into another kind of city—a mental hospital where the main hall corridor is called "the street." In *Dead Pigeon on Beethoven Street*, the murder of a private detective's partner brings him out into the streets of Bonn, Germany and into alliances with unreliable and dishonest accomplices.

Yet while Fuller's city suffers from violence and disorder, it also contains important sources of sociability and mutual aid. Ultimately, the city educates and eventually offers salvation to Fuller's protagonists. In his films, the people on the margins of urban life, especially women excluded from the centers of power, give the city its moral capacity. From the derelict bag lady in *Pickup on South Street* to the alcoholic artist in *Crimson Kimono* to the café owner in *Underworld, U.S.A.*, unmarried, aging, androgynous female characters offer moral instruction to confused male "heros." These women exude moral authority without being mothers or grandmothers or wives; they act on the world even though they hold no positions of authority within it. But Fuller does not need to divorce women from sexuality in order to take them seriously. A series of sensuous young women engaged in amorous relationships also play key roles in his films. A prostitute in *Pickup on South Street* risks death to help the pickpocket hero who clearly does not deserve her loyalty, while another prostitute in *Underworld U.S.A.* testifies against the mob to help her gangster boyfriend. A stripper in *Crimson Kimono* displays intellectual curiosity about another culture when she tries to incorporate an authentic Japanese dance into her act, and another stripper in *Shock*

Corridor provides the only voice of reason in the film which she argues that her journalist boyfriend's unbridled ambition is dangerous because it isolates him from meaningful connection to other people. These women represent the residue of the urban past. They function as part of mutual-aid networks (Sandy is not related to Tolly in *Underworld U.S.A.* but raises him in her home when his parents cannot), as conduits of working-class solidarity (Moe protects Skip from the police in *Pickup on South Street* and takes a bullet in the heart rather than sell his address to the communists even though she needs the money), and as moral witnesses testifying to the necessity of forming meaningful attachments to people rather than to ideas or possessions (Mac tells Charlie she doesn't want to be called "a pearl" in *Crimson Kimono* because she prefers anything made by man to something made by an oyster). Fuller trusts these women because they have their feet on the ground—figuratively, in the sense that they make rational and practical choices without being beguiled by money, position, or power, but literally as well, in the sense that their feet touch the pavement of city streets and their choices are grounded in the moral imperatives of their sphere of the city.

Jim Hoberman correctly identifies Fuller's ruling aesthetic as the product of "sensibilities so keyed to the routine textures of urban life that they hardly seem to be sensibilities at all."[8] He compares Fuller's cinematic New York to the 1940s photography of Weegee, but the film maker's work also bears a striking resemblance to those other great New York photographers, Helen Leavitt and Berenice Abbott. As Max Kozloff points out, Leavitt saw the city as "a jumble of diverse sensations," not as a unified set of images signaling the triumph of progress. Her photographs of the 1940s counterposed a "humbling, problematic, and apparently deflating modernity" to the self-congratulatory appeals to "history" in public art.[9] Abbott studied with the Parisian photographer Atget in the 1920s, and absorbed her mentor's notion of depicting "history" through the everyday activities of ordinary people.[10] In her 1939 collection, *Changing New York*, Abbott concentrated on city streets and small businesses, on the neglected corners of New York life. Her depiction of New York displayed little enthusiasm for "progress," neglecting the city's great skyscrapers and famous landmarks to lovingly detail activities and enterprises that might be exhausted or obsolete. For Abbott, images of the waterfront formed the core icons of urban life in New York, images that underscored the city's economic dependence upon the movement of products and people, but which also emphasized the interdependence of Manhattan Island's inhabitants.[11] Fuller's depictions of urban life echo Abbott's sensibilities in significant ways. For example, in *Pickup on South Street* we encounter New York City from the perspectives of the major characters—a pickpocket, a prostitute, and a professional informer. Much of the film's action takes place in slum apartments, on the subway, under the Brooklyn Bridge, and in the pickpocket's dwelling which is constructed on pylons above the East River. In *Underworld U.S.A.*, Fuller acknowledges the existence of another New York—one which boasts modern skyscrapers and "hip" coffee houses. But we soon learn that the skyscrapers conceal the business activities of a crime syndicate responsible for gambling, prostitution, and racketeering, while the coffee houses are fronts for drug pushers. Like Abbott and Weegee, Fuller distrusts big institutions, but finds redeeming value in the immediate, local, and personal networks created by even the shadiest characters in the city.

Yet while Fuller's urban films of the 1950s and 1960s resonated with the sensibilities pioneered by Weegee and Abbott, they also responded to fundamentally changed historical circumstances. Abbott's photographs from the 1930s, and Leavitt's and Weegee's pictures of street life in the 1940s portrayed the fears and tensions of New York City life during the Depression and World War II. It is not difficult to understand Abbott's perception of New York as an aging and exhausted city during a decade when economic hardships precluded the construction of new buildings or the renovation of old ones. Her skepticism about large institutions and her curiosity about small-scale communities (and the people in them) echoed the dominant cultural preoccupations of her time.[12] Similarly, Weegee's emphasis on urban violence and instability reflected the frenzied pace of urban life during the war years as well as the threat posed to traditional values by violent behavior on all sides during that conflict. In that respect, Weegee's photography reflected the dominant cultural aesthetic of the 1940s, an aesthetic pervading many forms of popular culture from film noir to crime fiction.[13] But Samuel Fuller presented his dark vision of New York City during a decade of prosperity and growth, in an era of urban renewal and upward mobility. Instead of reinforcing the dominant cultural vision of the 1950s and 1960s, Fuller challenged it. He swam against the current by expressing both

his fondness for the gritty residues of the urban past and his skepticism about the promises of the urban future.

Fuller championed the dying industrial city at a time when surbur-
banization and superhighways emerged as the putative cure to "urban blight." He focused his cameras on aging inner-city neighborhoods at a time when popular magazines and commercial network
television glorified the residential suburb. He continued to make
films in black and white at a time when most producers and directors
insisted on using color. Yet Fuller was no stubborn reactionary,
clinging to an idyllic past. In his westerns and historical films, Fuller
goes to great lengths to show that the triumphs of "civilization" in the
past rested on the same kinds of barbarism that plague humanity in
the present. For Fuller, the past offered no escape from the difficult
realities of the present. But rather enduring remnants of the past
seemed to him a repository of moral guidance for understanding and
acting within the historical present.

In his extraordinary critique of *Pickup on South Street*, Frank Mc-
Connell argues for the historicity of Fuller's work, demonstrating the
degree to which the film-maker responded to the imperatives of
post-World War II America. McConnell argues that the repressions
and paranoia attendant to cold war anti-communism provided the
crucial historical subtext for the issues aired in Fuller's film. In
Pickup on South Street a pickpocket accidentally intercepts the deliv-
ery of microfilmed defense secrets to Russian spies. At first he resists
pressures from his old enemies—police officers and the FBI—to
turn over the film and help them track down the spies, but eventually
comes to the aid of the authorities, albeit for personal rather than for
political or patriotic reasons. McConnell argues that the convoluted
nature of the film's plot helps it succeed in articulating the full complexities and contradictions of American anti-communism. He notes
that the film eschews the binary oppositions characteristic of the "spy
thriller," instead infusing the "spy thriller" genre with the sensibilities of "film noir" where the lines between good and evil are often
indistinct. In McConnell's view, Fuller's genius in this film rests on
the film-maker's understanding that anti-communism functioned in
part as a means of channeling uneasiness about life in America into
hatred of an outside enemy that could be blamed for the very qualities Americans most feared in themselves. As McConnell explains,
"Our fear of the alien political machine, in other words, was in many

ways a psychological projection of postwar fears of the economic machine, the Detroit which had beat the Germans but could provide only Levittowns for the families of the victors."[14] For McConnell, *Pickup on South Street* uses the outward devices of a spy thriller to cloak its real message—the elevation of personal responsibility and desire over the commands of ideologies and authorities.

McConnell is quite correct in his identification of McCarthyism as a relevant historical subtext for *Pickup on South Street*. Just as he does in *The Steel Helmet* (1951) and *China Gate* (1957), Fuller views the American struggle against communism in *Pickup on South Street* as pre-eminently a confrontation with itself. Fuller recognized a serious threat to individual citizens by government mobilization for World War II and by postwar anti-communism. Even while affirming pride in his own tour of combat duty, to this day Fuller refuses to call World War II a just war. After conceding the necessity to act against Hitler, Fuller once told an interviewer: "But even for such a reason, and I personally feel it was the right reason and the right move we made against [Hitler], it was wrong because the bottom line of living is that it is wrong to kill a human. It is abnormal, it is immoral."[15] Similarly, Fuller directed the full force of his cynicism and sarcasm against anti-communism in another interview in which he said: "One day I'd like to make a film on McCarthy the great Witch Hunter or Martin Dies, and on that shifty Parnell Thomas, and show them as they were: racketeers sleeping with the flag for a toga and ripping off a nation for loot and position."[16]

Yet while making a plausible and persuasive case for a political/historical reading of *Pickup on South Street*, McConnell neglects the distinctly urban character of the film and the urban sociology of its creator. Postwar disillusionment and the cold war provided one historical frame for Fuller, but urban history also figured prominently in shaping both the content and the form of *Pickup on South Street* and his other urban films. Fuller once bragged, "I did a film, *Pickup on South Street* set in New York but I shot it all in Los Angeles and the backlot at 20th Century Fox. *The New York Times* gave it an immense review: said it was tremendous and how for the first time in a long time a Hollywood movie had captured the spirit of New York, the smell of the metropolis."[17] Urban life itself provides the core dramatic tensions confronting Fuller's urban heros, and their quests end only when they find ways to draw upon the resources of the city for solutions to their problems. But it is not just any city that commands Fuller's attentions in these films; he directly addresses the urban crisis of the 1950s and 1960s by locating his films in the forgotten corners of exhausted industrial cities.

A sense of living in a "post" period pervades Fuller's urban imagery. Skip McCoy in *Pickup on South Street* literally lives on the margins of the city in a lean-to fabricated on top of a pier in the East River, connected to others by only a tiny wooden bridge. His "home" was built to sell bait to fishermen, and the word "bait" on the outside reinforces Skip's marginality—he is a way for police officers to trap "bigger fish." The person who cares most about him, an elderly female derelict, talks constantly of her fear of being buried in an unmarked pauper's grave and, consequently, sells his name to the police in order to buy herself a burial plot. In *The Crimson Kimono* Fuller presents Los Angeles's "Little Tokyo" as a no longer vital neighborhood, a place where young Nisei disown their heritage. The person with the most knowledge about the community is a forlorn and isolated figure, the sole remaining worshiper at the sole remaining Shinto shrine. Tolly Devlin in *Underworld U.S.A.* moves through the modern city blind to both its dangers and its rewards because he remains rooted in the past through his desire to avenge the murder of his father which he witnessed as a child. In *Shock Corridor*, the mental hospital's "street" numbers among its inhabitants three men unable to escape the tragic consequences of their pasts. Even the community inside the Buddhist Temple in *The Steel Helmet* consists of undisciplined and battered survivors from diverse units who remain divided by class and racial hatreds even when under attack by the enemy.

The seedy corners of the exhausted industrial city trap Fuller's characters in the past, leaving them to sift through the rubble of blasted hopes and unfulfilled aspirations. History has not been kind to them, and their dilapidated dwelling places and their worn clothing symbolize the stigma of their connection to the past. Moe, in *Pickup on South Street*, is living just to die, hoping to earn enough money to be buried in a cemetery. The scene that introduces her murder begins at a construction site, the modern powers of urban renewal mean death for the marginal inhabitants of the city. But Fuller invests his street people with a certain moral power, a certain dignity. As he explains,

I am only concerned that these people, whom I call "Gutter People," have their own code of honor. Even though I may not agree with them, they have a code that interests me. I met quite a few when I was a reporter. I found out that their way of thinking and living, ironically enough, had more solidity, as far as the unity of their camaraderie, than the saintly people. They are thieves, pimps, and whores, and are very "low" people, but they stick together in a way that the churches would like to have people in their congregations unite, though they never do. They do not secretly try to outlive each other or live on lies—and we do.[18]

Once Fuller begins contrasting the shabby remnants of the urban past with the relentless processes of the urban present, he finds that the appearance of decay masks the enduring moral resources at the margins of the city, while the pretense of progress obscures the festering corruption at the center.

In *Pickup on South Street*, the police and the FBI use the same tactics as the communists, while the Russian spies themselves look like successful businessmen. Organized crime and an anti-crime strike force in *Underworld U.S.A.* occupy similar looking buildings and function through similar chains of command. Fuller presumes that his audience will share the dominant culture's uncritical faith in progress and modernity. He plays to these prejudices with his evocations of the ugliness of the urban underworld at the beginning of his New York City motion pictures, but by the end of the films, Fuller inverts the icons of morality to expose ugliness at the center and beauty at the margins. Implicit in that process is a revisionist interpretation of urban history, one that questions the assumptions of more than one hundred years of urban development. Rather than celebrating the world being created by the forces of progress, Fuller looks back wistfully to the world being lost because it provides a profound critique of the present. Nowhere is this process more evident than in his critique of the atomized nuclear family of the 1950s in *Underworld U.S.A.*

This is one of the few Fuller films in which blood ties to relatives meaningfully affect the identity of the characters. Released in 1961 at a time when the postwar baby boom, the growth of single-family, detached suburban housing, and the saturation of the market for commercial network television all contributed to a largely uncritical celebration of the family in popular discourse, *Underworld U.S.A.*

presents the glorification of families as a cruel hoax. In the film, a crime syndicate that sells drugs to teen-agers and recruits schoolgirls for prostitution wins awards from the Chamber of Commerce for youth work because it admits underprivileged children to its swimming pool in the summer. A hit man for the mob tells how much he enjoys serving as a lifeguard for the children at that pool, then calmly drives his car over a little girl because her father gave information about the syndicate to the police. The police chief himself takes bribes and allows the syndicate free rein in their corruption of youth because he wants to protect his own wife and daughter from retaliation by the gangsters. The lead character in the film embarks on a life of crime to avenge his father's murder. After killing two of the syndicate's "soldiers" as part of his revenge, he asks to join the syndicate, explaining that he killed their henchmen out of loyalty to his father. "I wish I had a son that felt that way about me," says the mob boss tenderly. Throughout the film, the concept of family appears as an empty slogan, an invocation of natural and noble sanction for vile and violent ends. Like other abstractions and grand narratives—from patriotism to progress—family represents an empty promise to Fuller. But he takes quite seriously the mutuality and affection imputed to family ties. His investigations of life in the late industrial city coalesce around a quest for networks and associations that can genuinely provide to people what progress and modernity only promise them.

Fuller's solutions to the problems posed by modernity come directly from the enduring practices of the urban past. Unlike urban reformers who promise to "clean up the mess" and ensure an orderly reorganization of city life, Fuller revels in the diversity and difference of the industrial city. He accepts the inevitability of conflict and expresses skepticism about the chances for grandiose reforms. But he does insist on an active subjectivity and a recognition of the needs of others. In many small ways, his characters save themselves by helping others; they acquire an ability to live with contradictions by rooting themselves in concrete ties to the people around them. As Fuller explained in one interview, "Listen, we're living in a world where you have to belong to something, even if you're a loner."[19]

Yet that something to which Fuller wants us to belong is not an institution, a political movement, or an ideology. His blueprint does not come from any projected utopia purporting to represent universal truth. Rather, he seeks to draw upon the resources of the past to solve the problems of the present. He finds his model in a world that actually exists, but which is fast disappearing. The late industrial city with its deep divisions, its incorrigible characters, and its disturbing disorder nonetheless contains an enduring relevance for Fuller. In it, he finds an appreciation of difference, a delight in diversity, and an obligation to engage oneself in the problems of others. The late industrial city provides Fuller with a vision which is both political and artistic, a vision encapsulated in one of his formulaic proclamations,

> You cannot force people to love one another, to think in the same way. You cannot make them, and I'm delighted. I love confusion, I love conflict. I love argument.[20]

Fuller's artistic choices flow naturally from his politics. His uneasiness about the oppressions of modernist rationality lead him to value interruption, incongruity, and difference. Luc Moullet writes, "In Fuller we see everything that other directors deliberately excise from their films: disorder, filth, the unexplainable, the stubbly chin, and a kind of fascinating ugliness in a man's face."[21] This is not personal perversity or unintentional artlessness on Fuller's part. The inclusion of what has generally been excluded provides an essential part of his intellectual perspective. Rather than rubbing our noses in the dirt of everyday life, Fuller seeks to make us suspicious of the "prettiness" of the Hollywood and Madison Avenue images that dominate our lives and to rediscover the unconventional beauty that we might find all around us. It is not enough for Fuller to make this argument merely on the level of dialogue and plot; like all good artists, he helps us experience for ourselves the sensibilities that his art and politics seek to advance.

By drawing on his own experiences with the city, Samuel Fuller formulated a critique of modernity in his urban films that anticipated subsequent arguments by cultural critics of many political perspectives. Precisely because he remained so rooted in the modern industrial city and its contradictions, he created a body of work with tremendous import for our postmodern postindustrial present. In his films we find a way of savoring the legacies of the past without resorting to reactionary self-deception, and we find as well a means of actively contesting the present and the future without succumbing to the allure of grand narratives that account for everything but the lives of ordinary people like ourselves. Fuller's cultural practice might not fit into our conventional definitions of intellectual work, but perhaps that only underscores the necessity of changing those definitions to fit our current circumstances.

Beyond a Boundary: Edgar G. Ulmer

In the face of low budgets, hurried production schedules, and inferior supporting personnel, Edgar Ulmer made films stunning in their simplicity and awesome in their aspiration. In a medium that involves visual, aural, and narrative elements as a matter of course, Ulmer's films stand out for their ability to make us see, hear, and think about the world in new ways. Behind his aesthetic commitments lies a powerful social vision insisting that loneliness and alienation are neither necessary nor inevitable.

Samuel Fuller once told an interviewer that anyone could make a great film with millions of dollars, great actors, and a strong dramatic premise, but that real talent lay in making a work of art out of more limited resources. Most film-makers simply coast on the strengths of their medium, but directors like Fuller and Ulmer plumb the depths of cinema to come up with something new. It is the integrity of their inquiry as much as the ingenuity of their answers that touches us when we watch their films. Like all of the best cultural creators, they concentrate on process rather than on conclusions. They explore the ambiguities of life instead of reducing complicated experiences to simple formulas.

To contemporary film-viewers accustomed to elaborate special effects, sophisticated camera work, and extensive editing, Ulmer's films may appear appallingly unsophisticated and primitive. He made 128 films, many in less than six days, most with budgets that permitted no wasted footage and allowed no opportunities for alternate takes. In fact, what little critical reputation Ulmer currently enjoys comes in large part from tongue-in-cheek cultists who see his films as subjects for "camp" humor. One critic described *Detour*, probably Ulmer's greatest film, as "an exercise in sustained perversity." Another gave an annual award to the best low-budget film capturing the aesthetic of Edgar Ulmer, whom he portrayed as "the most tattered *auteur* ever to emerge from the Hollywood underground"

and whose work he described as defined by "gratuitous artistic for-
titude in the face of infinitesimal budgets, utter disregard for prevailing standards of good taste, complete commercial failure, and instant
critical obscurity."[22]

Ulmer's own sense of humor encourages a sense of playfulness in
his audience; we can never be sure that he is not putting us on. In
Detour, a musician gets a $10 tip, but calls it "a piece of paper with
germs crawling on it," and a dying woman's cough in the same film
invites jokes about *Camille*. In *Bluebeard*, Ulmer responds to the
limitations of a small budget by staging a musical production number
performed by puppets "lip-synching" to a record. He uses low-key
lighting, smoke pots, and dream sequences to create moods and effects that directors with larger budgets establish through scenery, editing, and dialogue in more deliberate, and perhaps more believable,
fashion.

There is nothing wrong with our sharing in this fun—indeed, one
suspects that Ulmer would be flattered to see the minute attention
paid to his money-saving schemes. But it would be quite foolish to
assume that Ulmer took those steps unknowingly or to believe that in
making his tough little films he tried to make *Gone With The Wind*
and failed. Ulmer chose to make small films on low budgets because
they gave him an opportunity to explore ideas and techniques that
would not have been tolerated by the big studios. His entire life history in theater and films testifies to a self-conscious struggle to pursue artistic and social truths at the risk of commercial failure. That the
finished products appear more laughable than laudable to some critics tells us more about the distorted values of our culture than about
the unworthiness of Ulmer as an artist. For by any fair standard of
evaluation, Ulmer's films display the consummate skill of a master
craftsman absorbed in a personal (albeit somewhat odd) agenda.

Born in Vienna in 1904, Ulmer studied architecture in preparation
for employment as a set director in Max Reinhardt's famous Josef-
stadt Theater. Like other film directors who came to cinema from architecture study (Nicholas Ray and Orson Welles), Ulmer maintained
a commitment to complex visual imagery throughout his career. His
minimalist but carefully designed sets exude atmosphere, and he
uses pictures to convey what other directors might have to belabor
through complications of plot and dialogue. Ulmer came to the
United States in 1923 to work on the set of the play "The Miracle,"

and while there he started designing sets for Universal Studios. The
great director F. W. Murnau, a colleague from theater productions in
Berlin, introduced Ulmer to Hollywood and used his sets in early si-
lent films including *Tabu* and *Sunrise*.

Returning to Europe in 1929, Ulmer gained his first experience as
a film director collaborating with Robert Siodmak on *Menschen Am
Sonntag* (People on Sunday). Less than an hour long, the film employs a documentary style in its fictional treatment of a typical Sunday
in the lives of five people. In its effort to peer into the everyday lives
of ordinary people, *Menschen Am Sonntag* prefigured the concerns
that would dominate most of Ulmer's later work, just as it also influenced the subsequent cinematic efforts of Siodmak and of scriptwri-
ters Billy Wilder and Fred Zinneman.

With the release of *Menschen Am Sonntag*, Ulmer moved back to
the United States. He worked as an art director at MGM Studios and
directed films there for overseas release. At the same time, he pursued a career in music, teaching music history and designing opera
sets in Philadelphia. Ulmer's life-long love of music assumed an important role in his films as well. In many of them he played out his
childhood dream of becoming an orchestra conductor through innovative uses of music as part of the cinema experience. Ulmer used
a classical music score in *The Black Cat* in 1934, possibly the first
such use of classical music by Hollywood. In *Detour*, the lead character plays the piano. The villain in *Bluebeard* acts out his sinister
desires by putting on puppet shows with operatic themes. *Carnegie
Hall* revolves around a woman who works as a janitor in that concert
hall to assist her son's musical education. It would be difficult to
identify a film director more interested in music than Ulmer; the entire corpus of his work engages in serious and profound exploration
of the relationship between life and art, and he consistently selects
musicians, actors, and painters as protagonists.

After making *Mr. Broadway* in 1932 (a film starring Ed Sullivan),
Ulmer's second American film provoked controversy because of its
theme—the treatment of venereal disease. Sponsored by the American Social Hygiene Association and advised by health-care professionals, *Damaged Lives* used a fictive scenario about a young couple
seeking treatment for syphilis to relay correct clinical information in
an effective manner. But it touched on too delicate a subject for its
time (1933) and encountered fierce opposition from censors who

tried to stop its distribution. After a successful battle with the New York State Board of Censors, the film won high praise for both its social and cinematic accomplishments. Ulmer made the film in eight days; it earned $1.4 million in box-office revenues.

One year later, Ulmer made *The Black Cat* with Boris Karloff and Bela Lugosi. Produced by Carl Laemmle for Universal Pictures, it remains the one Ulmer film remembered by the casual moviegoer, probably Ulmer's greatest commercial success. Ostensibly based on an Edgar Allen Poe story, it features a conflict between old adversaries in a strange castle built on a World War I battlefield. Ulmer took advantage of Laemmle's absence from the studio to experiment with sets, camera movement, and music. But even though the producer hated the final version of the film, Laemmle had to respect its box-office appeal. *The Black Cat* rode the crest of popular interest in previous horror films like *Frankenstein*, but it succeeded on its own largely because of the performances Ulmer elicited from its stars. Ulmer thought of *The Black Cat* as a satire about the stupidity of war, but audiences more likely came away from it with memories of the rich characterizations by Karloff and Lugosi, which they repeated over and over again in subsequent pictures. Ulmer enjoyed particularly fine rapport with Karloff, who amused the director and crew by habitually staring into the camera upon entering a scene and intoning "Here comes the heavy . . . ," although, of course, they always had to reshoot those scenes.[23]

Ulmer's skill with actors in *The Black Cat* revealed a talent that characterized his entire directing career. We might not know to this day that Hedy Lamarr could act were it not for her riveting performance under Ulmer's direction in *The Strange Woman*. John Carradine created one of the most memorable characterizations of his career in *Bluebeard*, as did Arthur Kennedy in *The Naked Dawn*. For a film-maker whose reputation rests on *mise en scène* and visual effects, Ulmer succeeded magnificently with the actors under his direction. That skill would serve him well in the mid-1930s when he began making motion pictures outside of Hollywood, largely with amateur casts from diverse ethnic communities.

After a brief stint directing westerns under the name John Warner, Ulmer left Hollywood to make films with amateurs. A trade union of Ukranian window-washers hired him to make *Natalka Poltavka* in 1936, a self-financed film celebrating the culture and language of their homeland. Ulmer threw himself into the project with enthusi asm, even though he personally knew nothing about Ukranian culture. He believed that cinema as a medium had a responsibility to educate and communicate, that it belonged as much to people striving to define their ethnic identity as it did to investors seeking profits from whatever product Hollywood could convince the public to buy. Volunteer carpenters built the sets for *Natalka Poltavka*, and Ukranian cultural groups from Canada provided singers and dancers who worked under the tutelage of the famous Ukranian dancer Avromenkov, who also served as the film's producer. The picture opened at the Roosevelt Theater in New York City on Christmas Day 1936 with strong patronage from Ukranian-Americans. *The New York Times* film reviewer praised the picture's music and dancing, lauded its amateur cast, and gave special mention to the fine camera work and dance sequences designed by Edgar Ulmer.[24]

Success with *Natalka Poltavka* led to a series of Yiddish films beginning with *Green Fields* in 1937. Drawing on the stories of S. J. Abramowitz and the plays of Peretz Hirschbein, Ulmer's Yiddish films featured the talents of the Jewish Art Theater and other New York ensembles. Although Ulmer had been born a Jew, he had no formal religious training and no cultural familiarity with Yiddish literature, theater, or speech. But thanks to the sensitive tutelage of Peretz Hirschbein, who asked Ulmer to make these films, Ulmer's pictures beautifully reflected the subtle nuances of Yiddish culture, especially its delicate balance between humorous satire and serious ethical commentary.

Green Fields, The Singing Blacksmith (1938), and *The Light Ahead* (1939) featured wonderful performances by Michael Goldstein, Helen Beverly, Izidore Casher, David Opatashu, and a very young Herschel Bernardi. Financed by community organizations including the International Ladies Garment Workers Union, these films dramatized life in eastern European *shtetls* in the nineteenth century for 1930s audiences made up of immigrants and their children. Traditional themes from literature and folklore reminded American Jewish audiences of their roots and helped preserve ties to their European cultural heritage. In *Green Fields*, a bashful young man leaves the serenity of religious studies and encounters a farmer with an interest in learning and the farmer's daughter who may or may not have an interest in marriage. *The Singing Blacksmith* recruited its cast from the Jewish Art Theater and relates a David Pinski tale of a poverty-stricken apprentice blacksmith who gives himself over to the pleasures of wine, women, and song until the prospect of marriage presents him with a conflict of desires and loyalties.

Ulmer received critical and commercial acclaim for his Yiddish films. *Green Fields* won an award as the "Best Foreign Picture" of 1938, and it earned Ulmer an offer from Darryl Zanuck to make pictures in Hollywood with Shirley Temple. But Ulmer declined that opportunity, because, as he confided later to an interviewer, "I did not want to be ground up in the Hollywood hash machine."[25] In fact, he prided himself on having become the kind of film-maker whom the Hollywood establishment would not hire. Instead, he directed his energy toward making additional ethnic films, including the beautiful *The Light Ahead*.

Of all his Yiddish motion pictures, *The Light Ahead* best demonstrates Ulmer's extraordinary skill at combining personal problems with social circumstances. The film details the slow evolution of a love affair between a blind girl and a crippled youth in a poor Polish village in the 1880s. When a cholera epidemic strikes, the villagers squabble over whom to blame for provoking the wrath of God. To placate evil spirits, they concoct a "good deed" and arrange for a marriage between the blind girl and the crippled boy. Faced with an outside calamity, the villagers respond selfishly, trying to ingratiate themselves with heaven by patronizing the outcasts they have scorned in the past. Yet for all their hypocrisy, the villagers inadvertently bring happiness to the young couple. Released in 1939 as the Nazi war machine advanced its conquest of Europe, *The Light Ahead* presented its knowing audiences with a parable about the horrifying tragedy confronting European Jewry at that very moment. The past and present of the Jewish people became linked in this motion picture, with its ruminations about the dangerous weaknesses and enduring strengths of the Jewish community in the face of outside enemies. Rooted in a collective past and present, *The Light Ahead* enabled its audience to address fears about the future that empowered it for the difficult tasks ahead.

Ever curious about the ethnic mosaic of American culture, Ulmer also made two films in 1938 about Afro-American life and culture, *Let My People Live* and *Moon over Harlem*. Financed by the Department of the Interior and filmed at Tuskeegee Institute, *Let My People Live* used a dramatic story as the vehicle for delivering an educational message about the dangers of tuberculosis. Starring Rex Ingram, *Let My People Live* won a prize at the 1939 New York World's Fair. A black producer saw *Let My People Live* and asked Ulmer to join him in making a motion picture about the Harlem underworld. Ulmer entered production of the film with the script already completed and the main actors already cast, but he soon found they could afford no full reels of film, only short ends left over from other productions. He had to stop and reload the cameras whenever they ran out of film, sometimes in as little as one hundred feet. Ulmer hired extras off the streets of Harlem and directed the all-black cast and crew with skill and efficiency. Consequently, for all its quick cuts and cheap sets, *Moon over Harlem* comes across as an effective film, representative of political trends and social conditions in the community that gave it determinate shape. It broke the monopoly of light-skinned actors in Afro-American films, and its complicated story line included an attempt by Harlem gangsters to free their community from domination by the white mob.

Ulmer spent the first years of World War II making educational films for the Ford Motor Company, as well as for the Health Education division of the Department of the Interior. He returned to fiction films with the low-budget Producers Releasing Corporation in 1943, where he made some of the films for which he is best known and most reviled—*Girls in Chains, Isle of Forgotten Sins*, and *Jive Junction*. But operating with the low budgets and concomitant artistic freedom offered at PRC, Ulmer created some fine moments in small films, and he did much to shape the genre with which he would be most closely identified—film noir.

Identified as a genre by admiring French film-makers and critics including François Truffaut, André Bazin, and Luc Moullet, "film noir" refers to the dark, claustrophobic, and paranoid films made in the U.S. during the 1940s and 1950s. Ulmer's old colleague from Berlin, Robert Siodmak, had a hand in shaping the genre, but it was Ulmer as much as any other film-maker who provided its characteristic techniques. He used low-key lighting to emphasize shadows that made it difficult to distinguish friend from foe. Tightly framed shots of people in doorways and windows accentuated the psychological traps and social constraints ensnaring the characters. Most typically relating stories about isolated male heroes adrift in a hostile world, film noir played out anxieties about alienation and persecution in the years after the second World War.

Bluebeard and *Strange Illusion* employ film noir techniques, but *Detour* remains the quintessential expression of the genre. In less than one hour, its fatalistic narrative draws the viewer into a world of overpowering hopelessness shaped by the random blows of fate. Its hero bitterly recounts the story of his attempt to hitch-hike to the west coast to be reunited with his girlfriend, only to run into detours that draw him first into the appearance, and then into the actuality of murder. His innocent intentions and actions cannot save him from the fact that everyone would likely think him guilty of one murder; his panic over his appearance of guilt then leads him to accidentally commit a second. Fate, he tells us, can stick out its foot and trip any one of us at any time.

Like many of Ulmer's other films, *Detour* calls upon all of Ulmer's resources as a master of minimalism. He shot the film in six days and was forced to rely on a few stock sets for background. Most Hollywood film-makers of that time shot twenty to fifty feet of film for every foot used, but low budgets forced Ulmer to shoot *Detour* with a ratio of one and a half to one. Yet those technical limitations forced him to make more imaginative use of lighting, music, and camera angles to fashion an absorbing and convincing film.

In their incisive critiques, Tania Modleski and Dana Polan have demonstrated how *Detour* signals a radical break with dominant narratives. Ulmer had always been a rebel, but even films like *The Black Cat* or *Damaged Lives* or *Natalka Poltavka* had been content to argue that films should include the excluded, that their glorifications of war should be balanced by accounts of its destructiveness, that their focus on glamour should be balanced by insights into illness, and that their univocal story of white Anglo-Saxon America should be balanced with narratives about other ethnic and racial groups. But in *Detour*, Ulmer identified an emptiness in the heart of America, and it caused him to question his previous optimism about history, cities, and culture itself.

Polan notes how the image of a detour appeared prominently in '40s films as an appropriate metaphor for individuals whose lives and hopes had been interrupted (or shattered) by the war. In *Detour*, Ulmer shows us a world out of control, as Polan writes, "where coffee cups are visually enormous, where the opening of a car door can kill, where temporal progression dilates and becomes a nightmare of coincidence and alogical repetition."[26] This sense of rupture pervades the film's narrative, as hero Al Roberts's very American journey to Hollywood in search of his girl leads him to the shabbiest recesses of inner-city Los Angeles. Modleski shows how Ulmer's disillusionment with the heroic narratives of culture extends to a disillusionment with the very terms and conditions of social activity itself. Modleski sees the unsettling confusion of *Detour* (all plans go awry) as an expression of both a refusal by the hero to make an oedipal break and his refusal to remain at the pre-oedipal stage. Beginning with Al's meeting with Sue at the "Break of Dawn Club" (an appropriate name in a film exploring a return to origins), Al acts like a child abandoned by his mother. Instead of following the normal narrative trajectory from outlaw to husband and father, Al slides from being Sue's fiance into a series of identities that disconnect him completely from identity and responsibility. In Modleski's view, it is no accident that the villain in *Detour* is a woman whose insatiable greed "forces" Roberts into his retreat from identity.[27]

Detour reveals a dark side of human experience, one rarely portrayed in Hollywood films. The bitter resentments of lead character Al Roberts, and the predatory viciousness of Vera, the woman whom he accidentally kills, make us uneasy because they convey a tone rarely hinted at on screen, but all too present in life. In a culture where happiness preoccupies mass-media representations and where all popular art appears to have enlisted in the army of positive thinking, the existential despair of *Detour* stands out with stunning clarity. Yet, it is a despair with a social context. The amoral, frightening universe faced by Al Roberts is the world of postwar America in Ulmer's view. Film noir techniques pervaded the movies of the postwar era because they spoke to popular fears about the demoralizing influences of war and the proliferation of conflicts that followed it. Coming from Edgar Ulmer, the man who celebrated the joyful creativity and energizing diversity of prewar America, the radical pessimism of *Detour* bears powerful witness to the latent consequences of World War II.

In a series of minor masterpieces, Ulmer further developed his critical vision of postwar America. *The Strange Woman* (1946) shows the ruinous consequences of a beautiful woman's lust for power and wealth. Its most memorable scene presents a frontier preacher delivering a lengthy jeremiad against the vanity and destructiveness of materialism. Similar themes inform Ulmer's 1948 film *Ruthless*, secretly scripted by blacklisted writer Alvah Bessie. In that picture, an ambitious young man rises to the top of the business world by betraying friends, victimizing everyone in his path. Ulmer depicts capitalism as innately exploitive, a system in which one can make gains only at the expense of others. In the climactic final scene, two rival millionaires grapple for a gun at the edge of pier. They tumble into the water and thrash about fruitlessly until they both drown in a deadly stalemate. Observing how the lead character's greed brought this end upon himself, a woman who had appeared to be falling under his spell comments, "He wasn't just a man, he was a way of life."[28]

Although best known for his 1940s films, Ulmer went on to make significant motion pictures in succeeding decades. His science-fiction films especially revolved around social issues. In *The Man from Planet X* (1951), an explorer from a dying planet visits earth to assess its suitability as a resettlement center for his own people. An American pilot travels into the future in *Beyond the Time Barrier* (1960), and a mad scientist uses his powers for criminal purposes on his path to worldwide domination in *The Amazing Transparent Man* (1960). The fantasies of science fiction offered Ulmer the opportunity in the 1950s and 1960s to raise some of the same questions about society that informed his psychological dramas of the 1940s and his examinations of ethnic cultures in the 1930s. He produced significant works in other genres as well. *Naked Dawn* (1955) explored corruption in rural Mexico in a taut drama that won the Venice Film Festival award for best picture and served as the inspiration for Truffaut's *Jules and Jim*. In *Murder Is My Beat* (1955) Ulmer updated some film noir elements to present a complex study of delusion and paranoia, while he displayed a fine gift for comedy in *St. Benny the Dip* (1951) and *Babes in Bagdad* (1952).

In 1965 Ulmer made *The Cavern*, a war picture about six men and one woman trapped in an Italian cave during World War II. That would be his last picture. He spent the years until his death in 1971 battling the effects of a series of serious strokes. He received belated critical recognition for his work from film-makers Jean-Luc Goddard, François Truffaut, and Peter Bogdanovich as well as from sympathetic film critics Myron Meisel and John Belton. In the years since

his death, the prescience of Edgar Ulmer's vision and the emancipatory implications of his world view have begun to take hold among
audiences and artists alike.

To what can we attribute the growing reputation of Ulmer's films?
One answer lies in the way that the compulsive cheerleading of the
mass-culture industry wears thin as Americans confront the disappointments of deindustrialization and the agonies of imperial decline. An artist like Ulmer who detailed impotence, rage, and claus-
trophobia has much to say about our world. While cynical and
pessimistic about authority figures and elites, Ulmer's films explore
the realities of ordinary people in a compassionate, yet critical manner. Unlike John Ford's films, Ulmer's heroes do not rise above the
masses. They like everybody else are trapped in mass insanity. In
contrast to Alfred Hitchcock's films, the obsessions of Ulmer's villains
contain a melancholy allure rather than an abhorrent terror. Unlike
Frank Capra's characters, Ulmer's suffer the burdens of societal corruption without recourse to easy individualistic solutions. By remaining on the margins of the film industry, and by focusing on the social
and psychological frontiers of American culture, Ulmer left a legacy
of pictures that seem to penetrate the internal logic of everyday life.
He respected film audiences and felt he could entertain and educate
them at the same time. He made serious and significant statements
about life and art under the most preposterous pretexts in an intensely commercial and notoriously unreflective medium.

How can we explain why a refined and cultured European artist
would choose to make low-budget films about a homicidal puppeteer (*Bluebeard*), a deranged architect (*The Black Cat*), and a paranoid night-club pianist (*Detour*)? Why does an associate of F. W. Murnau and Max Reinhardt choose to make "B" movies shot in six days
on topics ranging from venereal disease to time travel? Why would a
perfectionist trained in set design and legitimate theater turn his
back on the major studios and choose to make motion pictures dependent upon the uncertain financing and amateur acting of ethnic
Americans during the hard years of the Great Depression?

Ulmer hinted at the answer to these questions in an interview with
Peter Bogdanovich during which he confided, "I really am looking
for absolution for all the things I had to do for money's sake."[29] In
most of Ulmer's films, art and money are bitter enemies; for him,
money corrupts all it touches, and it forces everything to conform to

its needs. Ulmer's real sympathies lie with artists—the piano player whose music expresses his passion for his lover, the puppeteer who plays out obsessive fantasies in his shows, and even the deranged architect who builds his dream house on a former battlefield. These men at least have real feelings and passions. They may be tragic, but their tragedies come from real struggles between their own aesthetic visions and the mercenary logic of the outside world.

Ulmer's disdain for materialism helps explain his fascination with ethnic subcultures. In the music of *Natalka Poltavka* and *Moon over Harlem* he found a cultural creativity and eloquence of articulation unrepresented in commercial popular music. The Ukranian-Americans and Afro-Americans in those films had organic cultures tied to everyday life experiences. Their art celebrated and interpreted life, it brought them closer together as a group. They created art collectively, drawing upon common traditions to be shared with a knowing audience. In contrast, film-makers in Hollywood sought the lowest common denominator of mass taste to fulfill their profit-making responsibilities to the monopolists who employed them. Hollywood directors censored the contents of their pictures, they surrendered control over editing decisions to producers, and they participated in pandering to whatever weaknesses might motivate film-goers to part with the price of admission. Instead of using their powerful medium to expand experience and break down barriers, Hollywood film-makers created artificial commodities designed to overwhelm and paralyze viewers rather than to connect them to other peoples and cultures.

Edgar Ulmer had an alternative vision. In ethnic films and "B" movies, he found small spaces for representations of life that could not be co-opted by the culture industry. He found that he could work in those small spaces and carve away niches of independence that allowed him more artistic integrity than he would have had in the heart of the industry. Precisely because the "B" film did not appear to be serious art, it escaped the censorship imposed on other films. Of course, the section of Hollywood's "poverty row" in which Ulmer worked had its own set of limitations—low production values, frantic shooting schedules, bad scripts, and preposterous plots. But all in all, the "cheap" film allowed auteurs like Ulmer a freedom for artistic exploration and social dialogue unavailable at the major studios.

Perhaps the most enduring contribution to cinema by Edgar Ulmer lies in the breakthroughs made possible by his film aesthetics. His long takes, inventive uses of music, and "noir" sensibilities now form a basic vocabulary for film artists and audiences alike. In the long take, film time approximates real time, and scenes seem to have a life of their own. The extended dialogue in *The Black Cat, Detour*, and *Ruthless* provides emblematic examples of this technique, one of Ulmer's favorite devices for disguising the limitations of his budgets. Musical backgrounds provide another important element in Ulmer's aesthetic. Whether relying on the beautiful scores of Erdody, the folk music of his ethnic films, or classical musical selections, Ulmer's choices about melody and rhythm expand his arsenal of devices for determining mood and pace in his films. The sardonic use of an idyllic love song, "I Can't Believe You're in Love with Me," throughout the most bitter moments in *Detour* provides an unnerving musical/social counterpoint, setting an example for later uses of the same technique, like Carl Foreman's "Merry Little Christmas" in *The Victors* and Woody Allen's "You Make Me Feel So Young" in *The Front*. But even more than the long take and inventive uses of music, it is the "noir sensibility" that endures as Ulmer's lasting contribution to cinematic language.

"Noir" sensibilities pervade the aura of persecution that consumes Ulmer's lead characters, but those thematic elements depend to a great degree upon technical manipulations. Ulmer uses lighting to suggest a dark world with danger lurking in the shadows. The inner world of psychological torment finds external expression in the cramped quarters of rooms without windows, closed automobiles, and underground caves and passageways. The conflicts that initiate his dramas pit the frailties of ordinary people against frightening and evil external realities threatening to overwhelm them.

In *Ruthless* and *Strange Illusion*, the good people triumph; in *Detour* and *Bluebeard* evil wins. But in all of Ulmer's films, the outcomes are uncertain and the prospects for tragedy ever present. By comparison with almost any other film-maker, his is a dark vision. But not by comparison with history. After Auschwitz and Afghanistan, after Saigon and San Salvador, can we afford to dismiss a film-maker who insists that the world is a frightening and threatening place, who worries about the alienated individuals in mass society, and who fears that the emancipatory potential of art may be obliterated by the machinations of materialism? The ugliness in Edgar Ulmer's films reflects the pain and horror of history. We do not act honorably if we condemn him for showing us a world that we know exists. By directly addressing the dark sides of life, Ulmer reminds us that other people see the evils around us and still dream of something better.

In the end, it may all be futile. It just may be that it is not darkest before dawn. Rather, as David Wagner puts it, it is darkest just before real, real, real dark. But in the art of Edgar Ulmer we find the hopes of one artist who tried to buck the tide, who tried to assert his independence from money worship and its attendant moral corruption. His little films with their low production values and silly titles may seem like unusual vehicles for conveying profound thoughts, but his messages have much to teach us.

In *The Black Cat*, one of Ulmer's characters explains to a young husband that his wife's sleep-walking has been caused by a variety of medical, psychological, and mystical factors, that in fact she has become a conduit for the intangible forces of evil around her. The husband snorts that this explanation sounds to him like "superstitious baloney." Like the young husband, we may find Ulmer's allegations about society and its evils to be just so much superstitious baloney. But we would do well to remember the film's next line, and to offer it to all who scoff at Ulmer's seemingly paranoid vision of society. The older man leans forward and says to the young husband, "Superstitious perhaps. Baloney, perhaps not. There are many things under the sun."

Popular Narrative

9

History, Myth, and Counter-Memory: Narrative and Desire in Popular Novels

I will tell you something about stories,
[he said]

They aren't just entertainment.
Don't be fooled.
They are all we have, you see,
all we have to fight off
illness and death.

Leslie Marmon Silko[1]

In the opening paragraph of *Their Eyes Were Watching God*, the novelist Zora Neale Hurston draws a distinction between men and women. According to Hurston, men watch the far horizon where ships at a distance carry their wishes on board. Some men, whose ships come in with the tide, see their dreams realized. Others, whose ships stay out at sea, find their dreams "mocked to death by Time." But women's lives, in Hurston's view, proceed by another process. "Now, women," she writes, "forget all those things they don't want to remember and remember everything they don't want to forget. The dream is the truth. Then they act and do things accordingly."[2]

The world of men in Hurston's account is a world of objectivity and action. It is the world of history, of events and of progress. The world of women, as she describes it, is contrastingly a world of subjectivity and sentiment. It is a world of myth, of stories, and of cycles. Men confront their dreams as entities outside themselves, as stories with clear resolutions knowable to all. Women experience their dreams as created constructs, as stories subject to revision under the pressures of conflict between desire and opportunity.

Literary critic Barbara Johnson detects a clear pattern in Hurston's imagery. The progression from "every man" to "men," and from "women" into a story about one woman signals to Johnson a refusal of totality, an insistence that every individual story belies a generalization. Yet Johnson also recognizes the ways in which individual stories take on added meaning to the extent that they symbolize generalizable experiences. "The task of the writer, then," Johnson argues, "would seem to be to narrate both the appeal and the injustice of universalization."[3] Real social experiences and injustices divide men and women; stories that elide that division compound injustice by rendering it invisible. Yet socially created divisions appear natural and inevitable unless we can tell stories that illustrate the possibility of overcoming unjust divisions. Thus, the point of Hurston's distinction between men and women was not so much to promote invidious comparisons between the genders as it was to foreground a strategy of story-telling appropriate to her experience as an Afro-American woman. Women and blacks, as subjugated groups, often find themselves relegated to the margins of the narratives fashioned by members of dominant groups. Excluded from a legitimate share of public power and victimized by male privilege in private life, women learn from both historical and fictional narratives that only men may look out to sea for their dreams. Similarly, Afro-Americans know all too well that historical narratives relating stories of "human" progress all too often conceal the inhuman oppressions of race and class upon which the triumphs of "civilization" rest. Women, Afro-Americans, and other groups relegated to the margins of dominant discourse learn that the "truths" of society obscure unconscionable lies, while the lies of myth and folklore offer opportunities for voicing long suppressed truths.

But myth and folklore are not enough. It is the oppressions of history—of gender, of race, and of class—that make aggrieved populations suspicious of dominant narratives. The radical subjectivity that Hurston describes, where the dream is the truth and where people act and do things accordingly, can only provide momentary refuge from the consequences of history. Story-telling that leaves history to the oppressor, that imagines a world of desire detached from the world of necessity, cannot challenge the hegemony of dominant discourse. But story-telling that combines subjectivity and objectivity, that employs the insights and passions of myth and folklore in the service of revising history, can be a powerful tool of contestation. Zora Neal Hurston advanced just such a strategy of story-telling in *Their Eyes Were Watching God*, and subsequent writers from marginalized communities have frequently followed her lead. Seizing upon the adaptive strategies of story-tellers from diverse oral traditions, these writers have advanced a consistent body of principles about communication and action in their battles against dominant narratives. These principles have privileged empathy over individualism, emotion over analysis, and effects over intentions. Their efforts to transcend the boundaries of dominant narratives have led them beyond history and myth to explore the sometimes dangerous terrain of counter-memory.

Counter-memory is a way of remembering and forgetting that starts with the local, the immediate, and the personal. Unlike historical narratives that begin with the totality of human existence and then locate specific actions and events within that totality, counter-memory starts with the particular and the specific and then builds outward toward a total story. Counter-memory looks to the past for the hidden histories excluded from dominant narratives. But unlike myths that seek to detach events and actions from the fabric of any larger history, counter-memory forces revision of existing histories by supplying new perspectives about the past. Counter-memory embodies aspects of myth and aspects of history, but it retains an enduring suspicion of both categories. Counter-memory focuses on localized experiences with oppression, using them to reframe and refocus dominant narratives purporting to represent universal experience.

My definition of counter-memory differs sharply from that used by Michel Foucault. In his view, counter-memory "must record the singularity of events outside of any monotonous finality." It must "cultivate the details and accidents that accompany every beginning," and it must describe "the endlessly repeated play of dominations."[4] Foucault's perspective offers an important critique of dominant ideology about myth and history, and it contains a healthy suspicion of totalizing narratives. Like Jean-François Lyotard, Foucault worries that historical writing tends to celebrate the oppressions of the past and present as necessary and inevitable. In addition, he fears that teleo-

logical thinking demands closure, that it requires disciplining the un-
certainties of the present to conform to some *a priori* vision of the
future. Yet in a world where dialogue, curiosity, and conflict create
webs of interdependency, no single story can be understood except
in relation to other stories. A "monotonous finality" could do violence to the "singularity of events," but refusal of all totality could just
as easily obscure real connections, causes, and relationships —
atomizing common experiences into accidents and endlessly repeated play. We may never succeed in creating a truly total story inclusive of the plurality of experiences on our planet, but the pursuit
of such totality is essential. Only by recognizing the collective legacy
of accumulated human actions and ideas can we judge the claims to
truth and justice of any one story. We may never succeed in finding
out all that has happened in history, but events matter and describing
them as accurately as possible (although never with certain finality)
can, at the very least, show us whose foot has been on whose neck.

Ever since the nineteenth century, the novel has been a crucial vehicle for intellectual exploration of the tensions between the past
and present. The novel tends to question the appearances of everyday life, it presents conflicts between individual values and social reality, while reliance on speech and dialogue open it to traces of influences by many sectors of society. Counter-memory's delicate
negotiation between local, immediate, and personal experiences and
global, indirect, and social realities can be illustrated in five popular
novels written since World War II by authors from marginalized
communities. *Song of Solomon* by the Afro-American female writer
Toni Morrison, *Losing Battles* by the southern, white female writer
Eudora Welty, *Ceremony* by the Native American Indian female
writer Leslie Marmon Silko, *No-No Boy* by the Japanese-American
male writer John Okada, and *Bless Me Ultima* by the Chicano male
writer Rudolfo Anaya all evidence the sense of counter-memory invoked in Hurston's introduction to *Their Eyes Were Watching God*.

These books speak to the needs of oppressed groups grappling
with the hegemony of dominant narratives, but they also address the
general contradictions and confusions of our time with unrivaled
clarity and coherence. In the contemporary world, the bifocal and
ironic sensibilities of marginalized groups take on new meaning because of their power in expressing the increasingly decentered and
fragmented consciousness characteristic of the current era. The de-

clining legitimacy of grand ideologies in both capitalist and communist countries, the role of the mass media in transcending time and space to fragment experience, and the loss of intimacy and identity engendered by bureaucratic mass societies have all contributed to a sense of alienation and displacement that in prior times primarily affected groups on the margins of society. But in our time, sensibilities nourished in the oral traditions of oppositional ethnic and racial communities, in the spheres of activity dominated by women, and in the subcultures of working-class life contain extraordinary significance. Thus, in recuperating strategies of story-telling from the past, Morrison, Welty, Silko, Okada, and Anaya not only tell the stories of particular oppressions, but they identify as well a use of the past that speaks to present day intellectual concerns with time, history, subjectivity, and fragmentation.

Beyond History and Myth

Contemporary novelists from marginalized cultures grapple with issues of consequence to everyone when they address the tensions between grand historical narratives and lived experience. Jean-François Lyotard identifies "an incredulity toward meta-narratives" as the operative principle of intellectual life in the world today. That incredulity poses particularly serious challenges to the legitimacy of both history and myth.[5] History is nothing if not a master narrative, a grand story that includes everyone whether they know it or not. Historians believe that time and chronology have meaning, that knowledge of the past enables people to place their "common sense" impressions of the world in a larger and truer context. As social historian Warren Susman explains in a formulaic statement

> It is history that can more reasonably explain the origin, the nature, and the function of various institutions and their interaction. Further, history seems able to point the direction in which a dynamic society is moving. It brings order out of the disordered array that is the consequence of change itself. As a result, history is often used as the basis for a philosophy that while explaining the past offers also a way to change the future.[6]

Susman realizes that his description undercuts any claim for history as trans-subjective or universal. For it is only in Western industrialized societies since the Enlightenment that this concept of history as an instrument of progress has taken root. Traditional societies often blur the distinction between the past and present, emphasizing the cyclical and repetitive aspects of human experience rather than its linear or teleological dimensions. On the other hand, what Susman calls "contract" societies—a short-hand term for Western capitalist countries—produce historical narratives that posit active and atomized individuals detachable from tradition, family identity, and ascribed roles.[7] Susman assumes that contract societies are superior to traditional ones; therefore he sees the decline of historical narratives in the West as a blow to progress and a barrier against positive future change. Yet Susman fails to acknowledge that the declining legitimacy of Western historical narratives is not just a reversion to a pre-modern consciousness; rather, it reflects an emerging critique of the inadequacies of contract societies and of the kinds of consciousness they nurture.

Unlike Susman, Hayden White, especially in his early writings on history, applauds the declining legitimacy of historical narratives. In White's view, history is an insidious fiction, a fabricated text passing for reality. White argues that historians impose a linear narrative on what is essentially a plural and nonlinear experience. He takes issue with formulations like Susman's that present history as a means of solving problems. To the contrary, White sees the thrall of history as a major barrier against action on immediate problems because the master narrative of history makes individual and local consciousness so insignificant. In addition, he sees in historical narratives a totalizing tendency, a compulsion to judge all actions by a single standard that in White's view can only encourage the powerful to impose their own self-interest on others in the name of "humanity."[8]

Yet for all its sensitivity to the totalitarian effects of historical narratives, White's critique does little to fashion a true and useful means of accounting for the accumulated legacy of human actions from the past that historical narratives generally encompass. The logical alternative to history is myth, a form of story-telling that goes beyond verifiable evidence to providing unifying symbols and rituals that enable people to interpret common experiences. Although often associated with pre-industrial peoples, myths flourish in modern societies as well, as even Warren Susman reluctantly concedes. In many ways, myths supersede history in contemporary popular consciousness.

Will Wright offers a useful explanation for this enduring power of myth in his exegesis of the Hollywood western film as one form of modern myth. Wright argues that

> For us the past is history; it is necessarily different from the present. ... But for this very reason, history is not enough: it can explain the present in terms of the past, but it cannot provide an indication of how to act in the present based on the past, since by definition the past is categorically different from the present. Myths use the past to tell us how to act in the present.[9]

Thus Wright reverses Susman's argument about utility and problem solving, claiming that it is myth rather than history which enables us to act in the present. But Wright also acknowledges the conservative nature of this kind of mythology. Because myth emphasizes the eternal and the cyclical, it speaks more to reconciliation with existing power realities than to challenges against them. Myth provides legitimation for the world as it is; it reconciles people to the disparity between their desires and their opportunities. Roland Barthes contends that myth functions primarily as a means for rendering "natural" and consequently inevitable that which is social and subject to revision. In this way, myth can explain the past and order the present, but it does so only by accepting the inevitability of the status quo.[10] History, on the other hand, involves a search for hidden truths and a look beyond surface appearances. History explores how things came to be, and it inevitably confronts all the roads not taken and all the blasted hopes of the past. It enables us to judge competing myths by a single standard, that of factual investigation into the accumulated consequences of past actions. If myth enables us to live with our pain by naturalizing it, history encourages us to ease our pain by understanding it intellectually and analytically.

In an age of incredulity toward meta-narratives, neither myth nor history can adequately order or explain experience. History's connection to contract societies with their instrumental and utilitarian philosophies prevents it from fully airing the continuities of human striving masked by narratives of progress. But mythical constructs with their emphasis on repetition and cycles tend to account for rupture, conflict, and change inadequately. The sense of change over time employed in the five novels that form the object of this study is neither historical nor mythical. Rather, they draw upon oral tradi-

tions and historical experiences to fashion the time of counter
memory. They challenge traditional Western historical narratives,
but not out of an unwillingness to solve problems or a denial of the
connections that bind all human beings together. On the contrary,
they seek to expand the scope of history by reconnecting with experiences and emotions rendered invisible by the ideology of individualism and by the privileging of power common to historical stories
as they are told within contract societies.

The Burden of History

In *The Song of Solomon*, Toni Morrison takes aim at the nature of
historical evidence by means of a story about the giving of names.
Her protagonist suffers from the embarrassing name "Macon Dead
III." When the young man inquires how his grandfather acquired
such an unflattering appellation, his father explains that it came from
a drunken white man representing the U.S. government. The father
relates

> He asked Papa where he was born. Papa said Macon. Then he asked
> him who his father was, Papa said, "He's dead." Asked him who
> owned him, Papa said "I'm free." Well, the Yankee wrote it all down,
> but in the wrong spaces. Had him born in Dunfrie, wherever the hell
> that is, and in the space for his name the fool wrote "Dead" comma
> Macon.[11]

In this instance, the written tradition of historical evidence obscures
total confusion by turning it into a seemingly immutable fact, while
the oral tradition of myth explains what really happened. Of course,
Macon has no particular reason to trust his father's version of the
story which comes from an oral tradition with a fanciful sense of invention of its own. But his contemporary experiences as an Afro-
American encourage Macon Dead III to distrust authority and the
written word on which it relies, while vital information about his
identity comes to him through the oral tradition throughout the
novel.

In *Song of Solomon*, people and objects have meaning only as they
bridge the past and the present. Milkman Dead has access to his father's money and property, but they only deepen his anomie by hid-

ing knowledge of his history. Only when Milkman embarks on a quest to find out the truth about the past can he live effectively in the present. By deciphering what critic Susan Willis calls "the twin texts of history: song and genealogy," Milkman manages to "unlearn" both false family narratives and malicious untruths of history. He discovers an Afro-American history that predates slavery and in it, a capacity to flee from oppression by recognizing it as such.

Traditional historical evidence also emerges as unreliable in Eudora Welty's *Losing Battles*. Faced with Enlightenment rationality as personified in the local school teacher and the local judge, a rural Mississippi family clings to the subjectivity of their oral tradition. When the judge tries to read them a letter, they protest the primacy he gives to the written word. "I can't understand it when he reads it to us," one of them complains. "Can't he just tell it?"[12] Similarly, the family constructs a young woman's identity out of speculation and memory in defiance of the "evidence" presented to them by the judge. He complains that they cannot possibly know her true identity because there are no birth certificates or marriage licenses to confirm the family's claim. He ridicules their interpretation of a scrawled message on a postcard which they interpret as evidence of her patrimony. The judge says, "But a postcard isn't the same evidence as a license to marry, or a marriage certificate; and even that — ," but one of the relatives interrupts him, saying "It's better! There's a whole lot more . . . in that postcard if you know how to read it."[13]

The argument in *Losing Battles* is less about the nature of evidence than it is about the necessity of interpreting it. Welty presents both oral and written sources as valid and invalid; each has strengths and weaknesses. Problems arise when individuals privilege one kind of evidence over the other, when they refuse to interpret information actively and creatively. Thus the rural family immerses itself in lies and rationalizations because their desires conflict with the known facts of linear history. But, on the other hand, the school teacher and the judge devote themselves so thoroughly to the primacy of written evidence that they cut themselves off from other people and their desires.

Welty encapsulates the battle between linear history and nonlinear myth in a conversation among members of the family circle concerning the teacher, Miss Julia Mortimer. In that exchange, Gloria Short tells Jack that the teacher wanted "everything brought out in the wide open, to see and be known. She wanted people to spread out their minds and their hearts to other people so they could be read like books." Jack Renfro says that Miss Mortimer must have been wise like Solomon, but Gloria replies "No, people don't want to be read like books."[14] For to be read like books is to acquire a static and impersonal identity.

The kind of history that gives each individual a separate and autonomous story that can be validated in marriage licenses and birth certificates is a history that denies intersubjectivity—the ways in which people shape and transform each other through collectively authored stories. Yet Welty insists that nonlinear histories preserved through oral traditions also distort and demean the human condition. The myths and mappings of the Beacham family produce a localized tyranny of misunderstanding and misreading. Political allegiances become matters of kinship. Individuals become defined by their places in family narratives rather than by what they actually do and think. Life and death issues of survival become clouded by paralyzing myths rooted in ignorance and deliberate misreadings of evidence. As Jennifer Randisi shows in her extraordinary critique of Welty, there is no winner in the battle between myth and history in *Losing Battles*. But there is something to be gleaned from the strengths of each form and something to be salvaged from the clash between them. That something, a blend of myth and history, belongs to the category of counter-memory.

A similar conflict between myth and history provides the operative tension in Native American Indian author Leslie Marmon Silko's *Ceremony*. In her story, a half-breed part Laguna Pueblo Indian works through his alienation from linear history and the scientific Enlightenment world view behind it. Much of Tayo's personal pain comes from experiences that we might consider historical—combat during World War II, captivity as a prisoner of war, incarceration in a mental hospital after his service as he attempts to accept the death of his brother in battle and to readjust to civilian life. His identity as a Native American forces Tayo to confront one other monstrous historical crime—the conquest and settlement of his native land by Americans of European ancestry.

Tayo's cultural clash with Anglo society revolves around questions of citizenship, property, and self-respect, but he experiences the con-

flict most directly as a battle about *which* stories are to be believed—
the mystical, mythical, and spiritual stories that order experience
along empathetic lines, or the linear, scientific, and historical "facts"
that keep the world divided. Tayo remembers being told that anything could be accomplished if one knew the stories from the past—
"If a person wanted to get to the moon, there was a way; it all depended on whether you knew the story of how others before you
had gone. He had believed in the stories for a long time, until the
teachers at the Indian School taught him not to believe."[15] By teaching him not to believe in superstition, the school authorities take
away Tayo's belief that his problems can be solved; they tell him that
the stories of the past must yield to the hegemony of historical and
scientific facts. In the world of the school, as well as in the world of
the army and the mental hospital, Tayo encounters the forces of division: dividing the past from the present, animals from people, people from the land, and people from one another. As he recalls when
thinking about school,

> The science books explained the causes and effects. But old
> Grandma always used to say, "Back in time immemorial, things were
> different, the animals could talk to human beings and many magical
> things still happened." He never lost the feeling he had in his chest
> when she spoke those words, as she did each time she told them the
> stories; and he still felt it was true, despite all they had taught him in
> school—that long ago things had been different.[16]

Yet while linear history and scientific thought provide barriers to
true understanding for Tayo, they are not irrelevant to his search for
truth and empowerment. The consequences of history cannot be ignored; the conquest of the Southwest, the war with Japan, and the
enduring racism of postwar America offer specific historical oppressions in need of historical understanding. To retreat into a localized
world of magic and tradition offers no solution to Tayo, because that
retreat would not explain or even address the root causes of his pain.
In addition, even the Indian "ceremonies" he tries have lost much of
their power because they have not been changed to fit new circumstances. Only a medicine man outside his own tribe can lead him to
the truth, a truth which involves a critical stance toward both Indian
myth and Anglo-European history. As Tayo realizes, "The liars had

fooled everyone, white people and Indians alike, as long as people believed the lies, they would never be able to see what had been done to them or what they were doing to each other."[17]

Only by combining myth and history can Tayo create a useful synthesis for understanding and action. The very forces of science and rationality responsible for division in his world also provide the possibility for ending division. Tayo understands that science has created a peculiar kind of unity in the modern world, because everyone is united in fear of a nuclear holocaust. The ancient minerals of his native New Mexico provide the elements for the epitome of scientific rationality, the atom bomb. Yet in creating a device with sufficient destructive power to destroy the whole world, the scientists have also restored ancient unities. Silko explains Tayo's perception of these unities by telling us

> There was no end to it; it knew no boundaries; and he had arrived at the point of convergence where the fate of all living things, and even the earth had been laid. From the jungles of his dreaming he recognized why the Japanese voices had merged with Laguna voices, with Josiah's voice and Rocky's voice: the lines of cultures and worlds were drawn in flat dark lines on fine light sand, converging in the middle of witchery's final ceremonial sand painting. From that time on, human beings were one clan again, united by the fate the destroyers planned for all of them, for all living things; united by a circle of death that devoured people in cities twelve thousand miles away, victims who had never seen the delicate colors of the rocks which boiled up their slaughter.[18]

The horrible power of the atomic bomb undermines the legitimacy of Enlightenment rationality, enabling Tayo to understand his own history for the first time. Because his story has been ostracized from or trivialized within the master narratives, he understands the evils of exclusion and trivialization as basic flaws in the system of Western thought. Yet rather than accepting or celebrating his marginality through a "delight in difference" as the postmodernists might advise, he struggles for a unity capable of overcoming centuries of division. In the mental hospital the white doctors try to cure Tayo by urging him to accept divisions, to adjust to his differences. But he comes to the realization that "medicine didn't work that way" and instead insists that "his cure could be found only in something great and inclusive of everything."[19]

A history that built its synthesis from the plural and diverse experiences of people like Tayo would be that "something great and inclusive of everything." Tayo's desire to understand both his personal crises and the oppression of his people through the interaction of grand and small narratives embodies the essence of counter-memory. His way of thinking recaptures the totalizing imperatives of historical thought, but grounds them in the plurality of particular oppressions. Counter-memory in this sense is not a denial of history, only a rejection of its false priorities and hierarchical divisions. In the modern world, marginal and excluded people like Tayo take on particularly important roles in reclaiming historical thought because their experiences make them uniquely sensitive to the diversities upon which a new unity might be built.

Marginalized and excluded groups also understand the shortcomings of the categories and labels employed within dominant narratives. Just as Macon Dead could not trust the name he had been given by the historical record in *Song of Solomon*, Tayo cannot accept the narrow range of identities open to him as a Native American Indian stereotyped and defined by the conquerors of his people. Barbara Christian points out that Afro-American female writers like herself must see beyond existing categories because their lives are more complex than the available descriptions and definitions applied to them. Christian writes, "Our expression of our lives cannot be narrowly conceived, for we cannot change our condition through a single minded banner."[20] Learning the truths of history for marginalized groups demands a complex negotiation between the legacy of historical events that affect everyone and the partial and limited accounts of those events that make up the historical record as authored by dominant groups. But women writers and authors from other aggrieved populations often have specific resources for managing that negotiation. "Such complexity," Christian contends, "is not confusion. It is that feeling awareness which June Jordan expresses in her 'Declaration,' the interconnectedness of supposed opposites, of mental knowledge and feeling knowledge, of the self and of the other."[21]

The sense of counter-memory that informs the work of women writers like Hurston, Morrison, Welty, and Silko also pervades the writings of male authors from ethnic communities. Japanese-American writer John Okada and Chicano novelist Rudolfo Anaya provide particularly strong presentations of counter memory as a means of reclaiming historical thinking from contexts created by dominant narratives. In their writings, a complex search for identity includes explorations into history that require more information than the written record can supply. For Okada as a Japanese-American and Anaya as a Mexican-American, ethnicity is a story filled with ambiguities and contradictions, not a static fact. To be an ethnic American for these authors is to be involved in a delicate set of relationships among multiple identities, to sort through the many competing stories that make up any one individual's story.

In Okada's *No-No Boy*, a son of Japanese immigrants finds himself torn between two cultures. The outbreak of war between the U.S. and Japan presents Ichiro Yamada with difficult choices, and underscores his uncertain relationship to both countries. The American government sends him and his family to an internment camp, where his mother prays for Japan to win the war. In an exercise of filial piety, Ichiro defers to his mother's wishes and refuses the army's offer to release him from the camp if he will accept service in the military. Thus he is a "No-No Boy," one who refuses to serve in the army. But still, he cannot accept his mother's view of Japan as a sacred homeland. Ichiro believes himself to be an American, even when his ethnicity and his own actions prevent him from being accepted as one.

The consequences of historical events—migrations from Asia to North America, war between America and Japan, and the anti-Japanese racism of the war and postwar years—combine to pose difficult questions of personal identity for Ichiro. Where does he fit into these quarrels not of his own making? He cannot attribute his problems simply to Japanese ancestry; he knows that his refusal to serve in the military brings him scorn from many other Japanese-Americans. Yet he knows that his people face suffering no matter what their choices. Like Tayo's brother Rocky in *Ceremony*, all the Japanese-Americans in *No-No Boy* who volunteer for army service are destroyed. Ichiro's friend Bob Kumasaka goes into the army and gets killed in combat. His friend Kenji serves gallantly only to die of war wounds on his return home. Kenji even tells Ichiro that refusing induction was the right choice, but Ichiro wishes in some ways that he could change places with Kenji. The reality for all of them is that there are no uniformly good choices, because they are all subject to forces beyond their control. But like Tayo in *Ceremony*, Ichiro survives only when he realizes that his pain and his marginality help him acquire wisdom about the nature of American identity.

Okada presents some kind of larger unity as the solution to the pain of marginality and division. But he does not call for assimilation into the dominant society or for an acceptance of dominant historical narratives. Rather, he demands that society and history acknowledge the truths found in experiences deemed marginal. Ichiro Yamada sees that the monolithic appearance of America is a lie; his own exclusion is merely symptomatic of all who have been left out. At one point Ichiro asks

> Where is that place they talk of and paint nice pictures of and describe in all the homey magazines? Where is that place with the clean white cottages surrounding the new, red-brick church with the clean white steeple, where the families all have two children, one boy and one girl, and a shiny new car in the garage and a dog and a cat and life is like living in the land of the happily ever after.

He the answers his own question with a suggestion,

> Maybe the answer is that there is no in. Maybe the whole damned country is pushing and shoving and screaming to get into someplace that doesn't exist, because they don't know that the outside would be the inside if only they would stop all this pushing and shoving and screaming, and they haven't got enough sense to realize that.[22]

But acting upon that answer proves more difficult than Ichiro anticipates. By the end of the novel he remains convinced that "the margins are at the center" as Derrida might put it, but that it is dangerous to pretend that the established center no longer exists. Ichiro seeks to reconstruct the center, to build a new consensus based on the utility and wisdom of marginalized perspectives. Using his own history of exclusion as a guide, he begins to understand other excluded individuals and groups. He cannot accept the "history" that relegates him to marginal status, but neither can he escape its consequences. Instead, Ichiro mixes his subjective understandings of his own oppression with objective evidence about the pain suffered by others. In this way, memories are not barriers to understanding; rather, they make it possible for Ichiro to understand his immediate experience and to move beyond it.

Like Okada, Rudolfo Anaya tells a story about ethnic American counter-memory in his novel *Bless Me Ultima*. Anaya's Antonio Marez confronts the same kinds of competing stories that confound the identity of the protagonists in *Ceremony* and *No-No Boy*. Antonio is Mexican and American, Catholic and pagan, Indian and Spaniard, promising student to his teachers and potential priest to his mother. The narratives surrounding Antonio's life force him to choose between languages, flags, religions, philosophies, and histories. Antonio's journey toward self-awareness revolves around his growing recognition that these choices are false, that he cannot give up any of them. Instead, he learns to step in and out of identities in order to fabricate a multi-layered consciousness reflective of his true history as the product of many cultures.

Given the sensitivity to these issues of multiple identity among female novelists, it seems particularly significant that a male author like Anaya chooses to embody wisdom in Ultima, the oldest female character in the book and the person who teaches Antonio that the highest truths involve connections to others. Ultima sees the unity of opposites and reconciles magic and science, paganism and Catholicism, and even men and women. Unlike Antonio's mother and father who want him to obliterate contradictions by choosing one side or the other, Ultima teaches Antonio to embrace contradictions, to use the divisions created by history without succumbing to their oppressions.

Yet Ultima also encourages Antonio to fashion a new synthesis by drawing on the past. As Antonio relates

> Ultima told me the stories and legends of my ancestors. From her I learned the glory and the tragedy of the history of my people, and I came to understand that history stirred in my blood.[23]

But like Tayo and Ichiro, Antonio cannot find the answer in difference and division. Ultima comes to him in a dream and explains, "You have been seeing only parts, . . . and not looking beyond into the great cycle that binds us all."[24] It is in looking at the great cycle that binds us all that counter-memory surpasses history and myth, that it transcends the false closures of linear history and the destructive ruptures and divisions of myth to create an active memory which draws upon the pluralities of the past and present to illumine the opportunities of the future.

Counter-Memory and History

Thus counter-memory is not a rejection of history, but a reconstitution of it. As Barbara Christian says on behalf of black women writers,

> It is the resonance of history that lets us know we are here. Memory not only reproduces the past, it gives us guides by which to evaluate the present, and helps to create the future, which is an illusionary concept unless we know that yesterday we saw the present as the future. It is not surprising then that contemporary Afro-American women writers have spent so much energy on reclaiming their history, so disrupted and ignored by both black and white scholarship.[25]

The truths of history that mean so much to Afro-American women also compel the attentions of white Southern women, Native American Indian women, and men from marginalized ethnic communities. By dwelling on difference and disunity, by playing myth against history, writers like Morrison, Welty, Silko, Okada, and Anaya have pointed the way toward a new synthesis, one that offers dignity interchangeably to all peoples without first forcing them into an imaginary identity constructed from a top-down perspective on human experience.

In his extraordinary book on modernism and postmodernism, *All That Is Solid Melts Into Air*, Marshall Berman argues

> Modern environments and experiences cut across all boundaries of geography and ethnicity, of class and nationality, of religion and ideology; in this sense modernity can be said to unite all mankind. But it is a paradoxical unity, a unity of disunity: it pours us all into a maelstrom of perpetual disintegration and renewal, of struggle and contradiction, of ambiguity and anguish. To be modern is to be part of a universe in which, as Marx said, "all that is solid melts into air."[26]

Cultural conservatives like Christopher Lasch bemoan the declining authority of traditional history in the modern world; they see the rise of counter-memory as a threat to knowledge and order, as a kind of contamination originating among the underclass and spreading to the rest of the population. As Lasch writes, "The poor have always had to live for the present, but now a desperate concern for personal survival, sometimes disguised as hedonism, engulfs the middle class as well. Today everyone lives in a dangerous world from which there is little escape."[27] Lasch's fear is that the middle and upper classes have sunk to the intellectual and cultural levels traditionally reserved for the poor and exploited. There is some truth in his assessment, but his pejorative description of the poor and their cultures prevents him from seeing the positive things they have to offer to displaced elites. The modern world described by Berman and Lasch does place a priority on the consciousness and perspectives developed over centuries by oppressed groups. They are the people who have had to develop dual and triple consciousnesses, who have had to live with the consequences of history, and who have had to find their identities in stories that never mentioned them. Out of necessity they have learned about both the pain and pleasure of division. But rather than impoverishing knowledge about the past as Lasch fears, the traditions of counter-memory provide for the first time an accounting of some of the complexities of collective experience.

By combining linear history and orally transmitted popular history, counter-memory combines the best of both modes. If counter-memory lacks the traditional truth tests of evidence basic to linear histories, it also subjects itself to an even more rigorous test—the standard of collective memory and desire. For these narratives to succeed, they must resonate with the experiences and feelings of their audiences. For them to succeed completely, they must address the part of audience memory in touch with real historical oppressions and memories. Authors take great risks when they draw upon oral traditions; they surrender some of their individual control over the text to the contours and demands of collective memory. But that very surrender of authority brings them closer to truth. As anthropologist James Clifford asks, "If we are condemned to tell stories we cannot control, may we not, at least, tell stories we believe to be true?"[28]

Women's Time and Counter-Memory

When Zora Neale Hurston wrote about men finding their dreams mocked to death by Time (using the upper case), she implied that women confront another kind of time. Julia Kristeva in her essay "Women's Time" offers a contemporary reformulation of the uses of time propounded by Hurston. Kristeva asserts that women find themselves torn between two kinds of time—cursive time and monumental time. Cursive time, the time of linear history, is important to women because it is there that sexism and discrimination become inscribed in state policies. In Kristeva's view, the first stage of the women's movement battled for inclusion in cursive time by demanding public political action against juridical and economic discrimination. Monumental time, the time of life cycles and private rituals, is important to women because it is there that private and personal spheres of autonomy are carved away within the constraints of male hegemony. Kristeva sees the second stage of the women's movement as oriented toward monumental time through demands for recognition of "the specificity of female psychology and its symbolic realizations" and through its efforts to "give a language to the intrasubjective and corporeal experiences left mute by culture in the past."[29] Thus Kristeva argues that women must understand both the time of men and the time of women, a parallel to the efforts by novelists using counter-memory to understand both the linear history of contract societies and the oral traditions of aggrieved populations.

But this dual consciousness is not enough. Left separate, these two spheres cancel each other out. Exclusive focus on cursive time obscures the resources and institutions nurtured by ritual and myth. Exclusive focus on monumental time obscures the institutional and structural forces of oppression that constrain local subjectivities. What Kristeva calls "women's time" is also the time of other oppressed and marginalized groups. It is the essence of counter-memory. Counter-memory understands the limits of historical time, but still tries to act within it. Counter-memory celebrates the subversive visions and stubborn *jouissance* of monumental time while still insisting on relating local oppositional practices to macro-social causes and consequences.

Literature plays a special role in the articulation of counter-memory. As public texts touching audiences with historical memories, popular novels have some responsibility for historical accuracy in order to be perceived as credible. At the very least, they cannot disregard collective historical memory. On the other hand, as works of art and imagination, they are not bound by the constraints of public records and verifiable evidence as would be the case for historical scholarship. They belong to a realm between myth and history, and they present a world view that mediates between the two. It is literature that brings out the hidden resources of collective historical memory. As Kristeva asks

> Is it because, faced with social norms, literature reveals a certain knowledge and sometimes the truth itself about an otherwise repressed, nocturnal, secret, and unconscious universe? Because it thus redoubles the social contract by exposing the unsaid, the uncanny? And because it makes a game, a space of fantasy and pleasure, out of the abstract, and frustrating order of social signs, the world of everyday communication?[30]

Kristeva's implied answer to her own rhetorical questions is an affirmative one, and her insights apply not only to popular literature but to the entire concept of popular culture.

In what sense are the novels by Morrison, Welty, Silko, Okada, and Anaya "popular?" They each appear in mass-market paperback editions, although Okada's and Anaya's are published by small presses. None of them have been commercially successful enough to make the top of the best-seller lists, and all have received critical acclaim from scholars and critics. Yet they do not fall into the realm of "high" culture; they do not attempt to live up to the codes of transcendent truth, of embodying the best and highest that civilization might imagine, as was true of elite culture in the nineteenth century. These novels, like so much else in popular culture, seem to lie in a sphere with no name. They are not folklore or disposable mass commercial art, but neither are they works clamoring for admission to the rarified canon of great art. In that sense, they are like their protagonists; composed of multiple and contradictory identities, hailed and classified by categories with real social power but which also obscure their own intentions and aims.

Traditional categories of classification cannot encompass the structure and aims of novels employing counter-memory, just as they cannot encompass other forms of popular culture from the romance novel to the rock-and-roll song to the "B" movie. All these forms share aspects of counter-memory; they can be considered "popular" not because of the sheer numbers of people who consume them, but, rather, because of certain sensibilities that occupy a central place within them. They all draw upon oral traditions, vernacular speech, and a focus on the immediate and ordinary concerns of everyday life.

Most important, they tap sources of collective popular memory to identify the repressed and suppressed traditions of resistance to oppression. While originating in local, particular, and specific experiences, they use modern means of communication to reach out to other groups and individuals with similar, though perhaps not identical oppressions and aspirations.

Cultural conservatives who bemoan the loss of historical consciousness in the modern world seriously misread the texts of popular culture. Certainly, dominant historical narratives have lost much of their legitimacy. But within the interstices of popular culture, a rich collective counter-memory carries on the tasks of historical thinking in new and significant ways.

Fredric Jameson understands the presence of this sedimented historical tradition when he argues that all works of popular culture have utopian dimensions that enable them to critique contemporary power relations. But even Jameson relegates the historical work of popular culture to a "political unconscious," an uncomprehending desire to give concrete form to the absent cause that might make sense out of the incoherence of a world without believable historical narratives. But the "empty chair" that Jameson believes to be waiting for a future history and politics is already occupied. The qualities that Kristeva attributes solely to literature exist within many forms of popular culture. They contain many limitations, shortcomings, and contradictions. But in their focus on counter-memory, they draw upon an oppositional cultural practice deeply rooted in art, in history, and in popular collective consciousness. In the midst of division and disunity, they dare to imagine a world in which everyone's wishes may come in with the tide.

10

Mardi Gras Indians: Carnival and Counter-Narrative in Black New Orleans

"It cannot be easy to move from oppression and its mythologies to resistance in history; a detour through a no-man's land or threshold area of counter-myth and symbolisation is necessary."

Laura Mulvey[1]

More than fifty years ago, alarmed by the rise of commercial culture and the attendant eclipse of literature and folklore, the great cultural critic Walter Benjamin envisioned a world without stories. Benjamin complained that in such a world, "It is as if something that seemed inalienable to us, the securest of our possessions, were taken from us; the ability to exchange experiences." Certainly, subsequent events have more than justified Benjamin's pessimism.[2] Social and economic changes have undermined the ascribed roles and inherited customs historically responsible for most story-telling traditions. A commodified mass-culture industry covers the globe, replacing traditional narratives with mass-produced spectacles, while the "ability to exchange experiences" often degenerates into the necessity to consume the same cultural commodities.

Yet story-telling persists, even inside the apparatuses of commerical mass culture. Indeed, commerical culture expressly depends upon the residues of local popular narratives for its determinate forms and themes. Blues and reggae music form the unacknowledged subtext of most contemporary popular music. Suppressed ethnic, class, and gender rage undergirds much of the comedy displayed on motion-picture screens around the world, while vernacular art and popular oral traditions provide the raw materials for much of mass culture's visual and aural stimuli.[3] Outside of popular culture, personal and collective memories of region, race, class, gender, and ethnicity continue to provide the raw materials for shared stories. But the pervasiveness of popular narrative forms and themes is not just a matter of the sedimented residue of historical communities and cultures. Mass society and commercial culture provoke a new popular narrative response, one that draws upon both old and new forms of cultural creation. By circulating the stories of particular communities and cultures to a mass audience, the culture industry invites comparison, interpretation, and elaboration. Culture consumers find profound meaning in stories fashioned outside their own communities, and they inevitably re-examine their own traditions in light of what they discover about other cultures.

Sensitive and sympathetic cultural critics have vested great hopes in the enduring emancipatory potential of popular narratives. In his extraordinary review essay, "Western Marxism and Folklore," José Limon argues that popular self-generating cultural expressions and performances can challenge the hegemony of the dominant commercial culture by presenting cultural creations as having an organic "use" value, rather than just a commercial "exchange" value. Limon quotes with approval Michel de Certeau's contentions that these kinds of cultural performances contain political meaning, and that they exist not just in the fading memories of marginalized groups, but "in the strongholds of the contemporary economy."[4] Fredric Jameson's germinal article "Reification and Utopia in Mass Culture" insists that all popular-culture texts contain a radical utopian kernel that contrasts the indignities of the present social order with the possibilities for happiness conjured up by collective and individual imagination.[5] Similarly, in his persuasive discussion of "Folklore and Fakelore," William Fox contends that even with a decline in identification with the traditional sources of popular narratives — region, occupation, race, ethnicity, and religion — contemporary society offers new possibilities for sources of identity, possibilities likely to produce stories underscoring the tensions between lived experience and the self-congratulatory propaganda for the status quo that is generated from within the culture industry.[6]

The Mardi Gras Indians of New Orleans offer an important illustration of the persistence of popular narratives in the modern world, providing a useful case study about the emancipatory potential of grass-roots cultural creation. Every Mardi Gras day, "tribes" of anywhere from fifteen to thirty working-class, black males dress as Plains Indians and take to the streets of New Orleans. They parade through black neighborhoods, displaying their costumes and flags, singing and chanting in a specialized argot, while treating themselves to the hospitality offered in neighborhood bars and private homes. The Indians work all year designing and sewing their costumes, but generally they show them in public only on Mardi Gras Day and St.Joseph's Day. Organized into a rigid status hierarchy of official positions (spy boy, flag boy, wild man, third chief, second chief, big chief, and council chief), the tribes celebrate their own worthiness in chants and songs, while remaining vigilant for competing tribes who might challenge them with aggressive word play to compare costumes, dances, or singing and rhyming ability.[7] Although tribe members must be chosen directly by the group leader, the organizations represent entire neighborhoods. They practice all year in neighborhood bars, and they draw a group of neighborhood residents into the streets behind them as a "second line" of supportive singers and dancers.[8]

On the surface, the core practices of the Mardi Gras Indians resemble quite conventional behaviors by other groups. Under the aegis of carnival, they form secret societies, wear flamboyant costumes, speak a specialized language, and celebrate a fictive past. Carnival revelers all around the world engage in the same practices to release tension from the repressions and frustrations of everyday life. But what distinguishes the Mardi Gras Indians is their use of conventional forms for unconventional purposes. Drawing upon dominant icons and images, they invert them and subvert them. What for other groups might be a symbolic and temporary release from deep-seated repressions functions very differently for the Indian tribes. Rather than merely expressing utopian desires, the Indian spectacle gives coded expression to values and beliefs that operate every day in the lives of black workers in New Orleans. Although it takes place in response to the rituals and timetables of European carnival traditions, the Indian spectacle is not primarily European. It presents visual and narrative references to Native American Indians, but it bears little resemblance to genuine Indian celebrations and ceremonies. It draws its determinate modes of expression from African culture and philosophy, but it is not a purely African ritual. Instead, it projects a cultural indeterminacy, picking and choosing from many traditions to

fashion performances and narratives suitable for arbitrating an en
traordinarily complex identity.

The working-class blacks who create the Mardi Gras Indian tribes
collectively author an important narrative about their own past,
present, and future. Drawing upon the tools available to them—
music, costumes, speech, and dance—they fashion a fictive identity
that gives voice to their deepest values and beliefs. They replicate
many traditional folk practices such as the aggressive festivity of carnival, the ritualistic observance of holidays, and the celebration of a
heroic lineage. They tap literary and oral traditions of story-telling
through song lyrics, chants, word games, and names. But their collective narrative goes beyond literature and folklore. It draws upon a
myriad of contradictory images and icons to fashion a syncretic unity.
In the aesthetics of their performance, the Mardi Gras Indians balance the competing claims of commerical culture and folk culture, of
America and Africa, of resistance and accommodation, and of spon-
taneity and calculation. Their art stems less from ancient story-telling
traditions or aesthetic intentions than from the necessity imposed
upon them by oppressive social conditions. Their utopian projec-
tions originate less from abstract images of an ideal future than from
a determination to read the lessons of solidarity and struggle from
the past and present into the future. If the practices of story-telling,
and the qualities of criticism and creativity embedded with them, are
to survive in the modern world, it will likely be through the multi-
dimensional practices of artists and individuals like the Mardi Gras
Indians.

The Mardi Gras Indian narrative does not always take the form of
pure narrative—of a sequence of events taking place over time in a
cause-and-effect relationship—but its central recurring theme is a
story of heroic warriors resisting domination. The Indians tell about
past Mardi Gras days when challenges from other groups forced
them to bring to the surface the bravery and solidarity they must re-
press in everyday life. Song lyrics, chants, and costumes celebrate
brave tribes who "won't kneel, won't bow, and don't know how."[9]
This Indian imagery draws upon many sources. In slavery times, Indian communities offered blacks a potential alternative to a society in
which to be black was to be a slave and to be white was to be free. In
New Orleans, black slaves mingled with Indians in local markets, and
interactions between Native American Indians and blacks gave many

Louisiana blacks a historical claim to a joint Indian and Afro-American heritage. In addition, more than twenty black spiritualist churches in New Orleans venerate the Native American Indian Chief Black Hawk as a martyr, in keeping with the teachings of Leith Anderson, a half Mohawk woman who preached the doctrine of "spirit returning." But the evidence tying the Mardi Gras Indians to direct Indian ancestry is slight.[10] New Orleans "tribes" wear the headresses and costumes of Plains Indians, not of Southeastern Indians, and with the exception of some styles of bead work, few of their practices replicate the crafts of local Native American Indian tribes. South American and Caribbean carnival traditions feature Indians prominently, and some of the New Orleans chants more closely resemble French and Spanish carnival phrases than they do any known Native American Indian tongue.[11] As one Mardi Gras Indian told a researcher

> We're not real Indians, we just masquerade as Indians really, and we just give our tribe a name, and different positions and things like that. But as for real Indians, like you'd have to go to Arizona or Texas or something like that to talk to a real Indian, and on a reservation or something like that, but he wouldn't tell you the things I'm telling you because what we're doing is just something that we copies behind the Indians really.[12]

In fact, the touring "Wild West" shows of Buffalo Bill Cody and other late nineteenth-century popular culture entrepreneurs were probably the real impetus for the creation of these mock Indian tribes. Carnival parades in New Orleans began in 1827, but blacks did not generally dress up as Indians until Becate Batiste formed the Creole Wild West tribe in the early 1880s.[13] Donning headdresses and face paint enabled Afro-Americans to circumvent the local laws that made it illegal for blacks to wear masks, but the Indian imagery held important symbolic meaning for them as well. One former Chief of the Golden Blades tribe suggests that *both* blood ties and consumer tastes played a role in the formation of an early Indian tribe, telling a reporter, "In 1895, Robert Sam Tillman got the idea to mask Injun by seeing a Wild West show that came through N'Awlins. Brother Tillman came from Indians himself, and in 1897 he started the [Yellow] Pocahontas tribe."[14] But to see the identification with Indian culture as more a matter of choice than a matter of blood lines hardly lessens its significance. While carnival masking for all groups proclaims a generalized "right to be other" (as Bakhtin asserts), the Mardi Gras Indians adopt a very specific sense of otherness. Most other carnival celebrants might dress as pirates or crows or cowboys in any given year to escape from their everyday identities, but the Indians are always Indians. Furthermore, the Indian image calls attention to the initial genocide upon which American "civilization" rests. It challenges the core dualism of American racism that defines people as either white or black. To perpetuate collective consciousness about Indians in this context is to perpetuate memories about runaway slaves seeking shelter. Other revelers may use carnival masking to escape the repressions of their everyday existence, but the Indian tribes' disguise brings out into the open dimensions of repression that the dominant culture generally tries to render invisible. Of course, this kind of inversion runs the risk of being captured by the very forms it seeks to satirize. Native American viewers might not appreciate the Mardi Gras Indian appropriation of demeaning stereotypes; too many groups in American history have used the image of the Indian for their own purposes, and what comprises symbolic emancipation for one group might consequently oppress another. But images in negotiation with power are often ambiguous, complicated, and implicated in the crimes they seek to address.

In both content and form of presentation, the Mardi Gras Indian narratives and imagery revolve around self-affirmation and solidarity. Members of Indian tribes might be construction workers, dock hands, bakers, or porters oppressed by both their race and their class in everyday life, but in their rehearsals and performances as Indians they become part of a community of resistance and self-affirmation. They treat life as precious, celebrating its joys and pleasures, even while mourning the dead. Their song lyrics, costumes, speech, and dances all reinforce the same values—grace, strength, elegance, precision, happiness, composure, and dignity.[15] But the key to their collective story rests in more than specific words and images; it comes from the aesthetics of their performance. The Mardi Gras Indian narrative is eloquent and compelling because the forms used to convey it correspond to its basic message, and because the daily lived experience of its adherents reinforces its core values.

In its aesthetics, the Mardi Gras Indian narrative resonates with the culture and philosophy of African music. Of course, they are Afro-

Americans and make distinctly Afro-American music, but the African-isms within Mardi Gras Indian music raise important ideological and artistic issues. Ethnomusicologist John Miller Chernoff identifies the definitive feature of the African musical sensibility as a "functional integration" of music and culture. In African communities, audience handclapping is seen as a vital part of a musical performance, not merely a response by the spectators. Similarly, during African rituals, music is joined with dance, drama, and visual representation to form a fused art made up of interdependent elements. These musical performances blend with lived experiences, accompanying day-to-day events rather than providing a break from them as a self-conscious form of leisure or enlightenment. Finally, music-making in Africa is a functional group activity—a means for organizing and communicating tradition by giving different social groups rights and privileges connected to specific songs.[16]

The Mardi Gras Indian ritual draws upon these African sensibilities in significant ways. The neighborhood residents who attend weekly practice sessions and who follow the tribes into the streets as their "second line" function as active participants in the performance, not just as passive spectators. Second liners beat on bottles with sticks, shake tambourines attached to long poles, and dance to rhythmic chants in an interactive call and response with the singers and dancers in the tribe. Years ago, the second line had an additional function—to protect the costumes and persons of the Indians when the parade entered hostile neighborhoods.[17] In addition, the tribes function as more than musical aggregations. While they do offer opportunities for leisure, recreation, and creative expression, they also serve as mutual-aid societies providing burial insurance, bail money, or other forms of assistance.[18] Most important, the Indians use artistic expression as a means of reinforcing desired behaviors within their community. As Chernoff says about African music,

> the practice of art is an explicitly moral activity because African art
> functions dynamically to create a context of values where criticism is
> translated into social action. The meaning of the music is
> externalized through an event in which participation parallels the
> musician's artistic purpose: an artist's coolness lends security to
> intimacy, and the rhythms of an ensemble become the movement of
> an event when people dance.[19]

In New Orleans, as in Africa, this translation of criticism to action takes place through a fusion of music, dress, speech, and dance.

Fewer than twenty songs make up the basic corpus of Mardi Gras Indian music, although each song has many variants. New songs have become popular and old songs have disappeared, but year in and year out, on Mardi Gras Day and in rehearsals throughout the year, the Indians rework familiar words and melodies.[20] All the tribes sing all of the songs, changing the words to insert the distinctive histories and features of their own group. Musical traditions from around the globe appear in Mardi Gras Indian music. Songs like "Handa Wanda" and "Get Out the Way" involve an interaction between leader and chorus by means of antiphony, or "call and response," a form which originated in West Africa, but which has become a basic feature of Afro-American and Euro-American popular music. In "Don't Like That Song," the leader and chorus exchange groups of phrases in the manner of Anglo-American Protestant hymns. "Indian Red," the song used to end all rehearsals and to begin the Mardi Gras Day procession, contains Caribbean phrases and styles.[21]

The structural forms of Mardi Gras Indian songs relate directly to their functions. The limited corpus of songs ensures a great deal of repetition, but it also places a premium on subtlety and improvisation. As Chernoff points out about African music

> People can hear the music for years and always find it fresh and
> lively because of the extent to which an African musical performance
> is integrated into its specific social situation. In traditional African
> music-making situations, the music is basically familiar, and people
> can follow with informed interest the efforts of the musicians to add
> an additional dimension of excitement or depth to a performance.
> Relatively minor variations stand out clearly and assume increased
> importance in making the occasion successful.[22]

These musical principles reflect philosophical and moral stances. Unlike the Euro-American musical tradition which places a premium on individual authorship of finite texts, the African tradition manifest in Mardi Gras Indian music values dialogue and conversation between artists and audiences to adapt old texts to new situations. The "audience" participates in the creation of this music by singing responses to the leader, by handclapping, and by dancing or chanting in a way that acknowledges the creativity of the musicians. As Chernoff exlains, "The music works more by encouraging social interaction and participation at each performance than by affirming a fixed set of sanctioned concepts or beliefs."[23]

But it is not merely an abstract philosophy that emerges from the Indian music; the musical forms employed by the tribes reflect concrete social relations. Thus the "call and response" between the leader and the tribe in "Handa Wanda" represents the symbiotic relationship between the individual and the group. The chiefs have certain concrete responsibilities — in life and in songs — and when appropriate they take the lead both musically and socially. But each individual plays an important role in the tribe, replete with occasions to show off individual skills and attributes for the benefit of the entire group. Similarly, the form of "Indian Red" mirrors the social organization of Indian tribes. Only the chief can sing lead on this song, but his responsibility is to call forth the other members of the tribe by naming their roles — spy boy, flag boy, trail chief, etc. In most tribes, each "rank" has three people in it, and appropriately enough, "Indian Red" employs a triple meter.[24] The song "Big Chief Wants Plenty of Fire Water" tells a story about a chief who likes to drink, but the Indian tribes and the audiences know that it is used to take up a collection to buy wine for the Indians.[25] Obviously reflective of Anglo and mass-media stereotypes about Indians and alcohol, this song is one of the places where the metaphor employed undermines the culture of anti-racism intended by the Mardi Gras Indian ritual. Yet the act that accompanies it — hospitality and treating within the community — affirms self-worth and solidarity at the same time.

Like their music, the Mardi Gras Indians' costumes and insignia serve both expressive and functional purposes. Most generally, their beads, feathers, designs, and colors celebrate the bounty of life. Plumes and feathers extend outward magnificently, laying claim to dominion over all the space around them, just as bright colors and rhinestones command spectators' fields of vision. This sartorial display draws upon both the Euro-American sensibility of carnival as a time of pleasure before the deprivations of Lent, as well as on the celebration of life's pleasures ritualized in Afro-American funerals in New Orleans. But it is impossible to understand the full meaning of the Indian suits from their appearances alone. To the Indians, these costumes have meaning only as coded reflections of a complex social process.

Designing and sewing Indian suits is a year-round endeavor; as soon as one carnival ends, the Indians begin to prepare for the next. No one wears the same suit two years in a row; indeed no one wears the same *color* suit two years in a row. Each member of the tribe selects his own colors and designs his own suit, although tribes generally adopt at least one theme color that appears in all of the costumes.[26] Although specialized craftspersons may be asked to assist others with drawing or other particular tasks, Indians are responsible for all their own beading and sewing. The sense of craft is so strong among them that using sewing machines risks unqualified disapproval. Individual expression is encouraged and prized, but most of the sewing takes place in collective work sessions involving the sharing of skills, advice, and opinions.[27] Like music rehearsals, these sewing sessions bring the group closer together and provide an opportunity for passing along skills, attitudes,and traditions.

The costumes and insignia also serve as part of the tribe's communications system. Flags display the names of treasured symbols of each group, but they are also used by the flag boys to signal directions along the line of march, to warn of the approach of other tribes, and even to encourage changes in rhythms for the chants, songs, and dances.[28] The Indians also send a message to the community via the costume of their chief, whose prestige rests largely on the beauty of his suit. One of the stock songs of the Indians boasts "My big chief got a golden crown." The entire tribe takes pride in the chief's appearance as well as responsibility for his protection. Many tribes have body guards in plain clothes accompanying the line of march, and most have a "wild man" whose sole job is to clear the path for the chief and to make sure that no one attacks his costume.[29]

The same calculated playfulness that informs Mardi Gras Indian music and dress makes itself felt in its language as well. Les Blank captures the logic of this speech beautifully in his 1978 documentary film *Always for Pleasure*, in which he has an informant reel off a dazzling set of rhymes in "Indian talk." When asked how he knows what to say, the man replies, "It's no script, no set language; you say what you feel."[30] Of course, most viewers of Blank's film (like most readers of this book) could say what they feel all day and never come up with "Wild Tchoupitoula, uptown ruler, blood shiff ahoona, won't kneel, won't bow, don't know how." Such words come "spontaneously" only to those whose preparation is so thorough that the language has become completely internalized. But the seeming inaccessibility of "Indian talk" plays an important role within the subculture, drawing lines between insiders and outsiders, and cultivating an active sense of ambiguity capable of serving many purposes.

For years, ethnomusicologists have attempted to decode the language of the Mardi Gras Indians. Some phrases contain a direct meaning when chanted or sung during parades. For example, "Two Way Pockaway" conveys a warning to get out of the way, while "on tendais" means approval of the previous phrase.[31] Folklorist Alan Lomax believed that the phrase "Two Way Pockaway" came from Louisiana dialect French *t'ouwais bas q'ouwais*, which he surmised came either from *tu n'as pas couilles* (you don't have testicles) or from *tuez bas qu'ou est* (kill who is over there). Lomax believed that "on tendais" also came from the French *entendez* (understand) or *attendez* (wait up or listen).[32] Similarly, the song "Indian Red" has been traced by Andrew Pearse to a carnival song from Trinidad, "Indurubi," which he felt came from the Spanish *Indo Rubi* (Indian Red). In New Orleans, "Indian Red" is generally preceded by the chant "Ma Day Cootie Fiyo." Jason Berry, Jonathan Foose, and Tad Jones point out that *matar* in Spanish means "to kill," while *qui tu est fijo* can mean "who is immobile to you," giving "Ma Day Cootie Fiyo" the possible meaning of "kill who is in your way."[33]

But to search for a static and literal meaning for each Mardi Gras Indian phrase is to gravely misread their playful and deliberately ambiguous language. Word play provides an important facet of many expressions of Indian identity. As one former chief explained, "The idea of singing a Indian song is rhyming something, thinking fast to rhyme it."[34] When tribes meet on the streets, part of their competition involves "talking" by the chiefs who rhyme praise for themselves and insults for their enemies in the manner of the popular Afro-American folk game "playing the dozens."[35]

Just as the Mardi Gras Indian music features variation and improvisation on traditional forms, tribal speech reflects a similarly creative dynamism. For example, The Golden Blades tribe used to be known as Creole Wild West, but changed their name because of a verbal interchange between one of their singers and someone from their "second line." In 1935, during a rehearsal at a bar near Third and Rocheblave streets, this tribe member started singing about his big chief's "diamond crown." When a woman in the crowd responded "Give it to the boys from Third and Rocheblave," the singer picked up on her phrase but soon changed "Third and Rocheblave" to "give it to the gang from the Golden Blades."[36] Similarly, the 1930s chant by the Wild Squatoolas, "Somebody got to sew, sew, sew," became transformed in the 1960s by the Wild Magnolias to "Everybody's got soul, soul, soul."[37]

The imprecision of "Indian talk" might not engender confidence in the idea of language as a central feature of the Mardi Gras Indian ritual. After all, if the origins of words remain obscure, and if the words themselves change over time, how can we be sure that speakers know the significance of what they are saying? It is likely that the tribes and their followers are not always exactly aware of the denotative meaning of every word they use. But in another sense, the use of this language in collective rituals conveys a greater meaning than can be found in the individual words themselves. Another African example might help illumine the consciousness behind this approach to language. Chernoff interviewed a famous Ghanaian musician known as "The Entertainer" about the meaning of his songs,

> When I asked him what the songs he sang were about, he said that he did not really understand some of them, that he would have to go ask the old men who had given him the proverbs which he had set to music. People from various walks of life told me that The Entertainer's songs were in "deep Dagbani," which they could not "hear." They did not have to understand the songs to be moved, but nevertheless, they valued the songs' expression of their deepest traditional sentiments. What was important to them was that the songs had a depth which they enjoyed trying to interpret even while they acknowledged that the songs were often beyond them. In effect, the music does and does not rely on a specific traditional meaning.[38]

Just as African audiences value the traditions conveyed by The Entertainer, Mardi Gras Indians and their audiences profit from the cultural legacies of the past, even while adapting them to the present. Mardi Indian traditions are not a matter of establishing precise origins or maintaining authentic folk forms; rather, they seek to unite the present with the past in a dynamic, yet continuous process. Words and names often play key roles in building that unity. When new tribes form, they often connect themselves to the past by using the name of a disbanded group. Yet they only do so if they can locate the disbanded tribe's chief and secure his permission.[39]

Song lyrics also connect contemporary heroism to traditional figures. Thus the Wild Tchoupitoulas' "Brother John," pays tribute to John "Scarface" Williams (a rhythm-and-blues singer and Mardi Gras Indian who died from a knifing shortly after carnival in 1972) by comparing him to "Cora" who "died on the battlefield." An earlier song by Willie Turbinton of the Wild Magnolias (based on a chant by the Magnolias' chief Bo Dollis), told the story of a rebellious slave named Corey. In the 1920s jazz musician Danny Barker recorded a song "Corrine Died on the Battlefield," a song which Paul Longpre of the Golden Blades claims told the story of a woman named Cora Anne who masked as queen of the Battlefield Hunters, but who died of gunshot wounds incurred when she got caught in a crossfire between the Hunters and the Wild Squatoolas.[40] Cora thus refers to at least four people living more than a hundred years apart, three of them male and one female. The story touches on the histories of at least five tribes and appeared in four separate songs. There is no one authentic Corey; the purpose of all this borrowing is precisely to fashion a collective narrative embracing a wide range of actual events and individuals. No one lyricist or story-teller can control the narrative about Corey; it filters through the community, undergoing significant changes, yet retaining important continuities.

Language, costumes, and music combine to shape the fused art of Mardi Gras Indian pageantry, but it is largely through dancing that each of these separate forms becomes part of a larger totality. Indians who chant "two way pockaway" ("get out of the way") will dance differently from those chanting "handa wanda" ("we're not looking for trouble"). Dancing offers an opportunity to display the beauty of one's costume; conversely, costume design anticipates the movements of street dancing. Musical selections not only have their own lyrics, melodies, and rhythms, but they also have specific dance steps that accentuate their other meanings.

In recent years, dancing has taken on even greater importance among the Mardi Gras Indian tribes as a symbolic form of combat. At one time the tribes carried real hatchets and spears and used the aggressive festivity of carnival as a cover for gang warfare. After a day of drinking and marching they would meet to settle grudges and rivalries on the "battlefield"—an empty lot at the intersection of Claiborne and Poydras streets. But when urban renewal destroyed the basis for neighborhood competitions, and when police vigilance made violent acts on carnival day more difficult, a new spirit began to emerge. Aesthetic rivalries took the place of street fighting, and dancing became a key way of demonstrating one's superiority over others. When Indians challenge each other in the streets, they draw an imaginary line between them and compete by dancing as close as possible to it without crossing. Their dance enacts a mock fight replete with attacks on territory and each other's bodies. The dancers capable of giving the appearance of fighting without resorting to actual combat win the highest esteem from their tribe and from other spectators.[41]

The transformation of actual violence into symbolic aesthetic competition has many precedents and parallels in Afro-American communities all across the nation, but it has a special history in New Orleans. Art Neville, a rhythm-and-blues musician who has played with the Hawketts, the Meters, and the Neville Brothers (and whose "Uncle Jolly" formed the Wild Tchoupitoulas tribe in 1972), remembers music as a viable alternative to gang fighting in the public housing project where he grew up in the 1940s and 1950s. "We used to do the doo-wop thing," Neville recalls, referring to the close harmonies and scat singing favored by his friends and relatives at that time. "There were gangs from different neighborhoods and some would fight. I was with a gang that did the singing, so I didn't have nothing to worry about."[42]

Yet dancing means much more to the Indian tribes than the mere displacement of aggressive tendencies. Dancing is a communications system in its own right. In parade situations, certain steps by the spy boys and flag boys alert the rest of the tribe to the presence of hostility ahead.[43] Second liners and tribe members create the rhythms for chants and songs with their dancing, every bit as much as the beating of tambourines and sticks conveys a beat for the dancers. Willie Turbinton of the Wild Magnolias remembers that it was the dancing of the Indians that attracted him to them in the first place. When he was eleven years old Turbinton saw his first Indian tribe and remembers, "It just always intrigued me. There were certain steps and certain moves they'd make that were synonymous with the kind of rhythm they played."[44] Turbinton liked the Indian costumes and language, and he was fascinated by the rituals that gave each member of the tribe a particular significance. But he felt drawn into the spectacle most strongly by the ways that the rhythms made him want to dance. "It was the kind of groove that you couldn't resist," he recalls. "The pulse affected you. You find yourself patting your foot, and if you're shy, you just feel it inside yourself."[45]

The centrality of dancing to the Mardi Gras Indian ritual reveals yet another layer of African cultural retentions among New Orleans blacks. Chernoff's research on African music discovered villagers who identified pieces of music by the dances that accompanied them, and he found over and over again that musicians expected their audiences and dancers to demonstrate active involvement with the music by providing a beat for the musicians to follow. Unlike the concert and dance traditions of Euro-American popular music, the audience in Africa is part of the performance through their dancing, handclapping, and singing. In addition, dancing in African cultures is a form of public worship, a visual demonstration of belief, just as the dance itself is a visual expression of the music.[46] Like their African counterparts (and forebears), Mardi Gras Indians in New Orleans manifest their values about art and life through performance of a "danced faith."[47] Certainly, Chernoff's analysis of public dancing by African village chiefs applies equally to the chiefs of Mardi Gras Indian tribes:

> In his dance, the chief combines aesthetic command and moral command, and the satisfying beauty of his dance is a visible display of his closeness to his ancestors and his fitness for authority. The chief asserts the community through a dance in which gracefulness implies the tranquility of mature strength, elegance implies the bounty of life, precision implies dedication of purpose, happiness implies the accessibility of compassion, composure implies the discretion of power, and dignity implies destiny.[48]

Much of the power of the Mardi Gras Indian ritual stems from its force as a counter-narrative challenging the hegemony of New Orleans' social elite. During Mardi Gras, New Orleans "high society" celebrates its blood lines and mythologizes itself as the heir to a powerful tradition of mysticism and magic. The elite mask themselves in expensive costumes and ride motorized floats along the city's main thoroughfares, throwing beaded necklaces and souvenir doubloons to crowds of spectators. The Indians subvert this spectacle by declaring a powerful lineage of their own, one which challenges the legitimacy of Anglo-European domination. Their costumes are made, not bought. They avoid the main thoroughfares and walk through black neighborhoods. They define the crowds along their route as participants, not just as spectators. Their fusion of music, costumes, speech, and dance undermines the atomized European view of each of those activities as distinct and autonomous endeavors, while it foregrounds an African sensibility about the interconnectedness of art and the interconnectedness of human beings.

Yet the degree to which this counter-narrative actually threatens the hegemony of the dominant culture is open to dispute. One can well imagine how easily those in power might dismiss black workers in outlandish costumes drinking and dancing in the streets on Mardi Gras Day. Certainly within the black community, the ambiguities and multi-layered symbolism of the Indian ritual might well obscure the historical and social power realities behind its genesis, as the traditional internal rivalries it has provoked have demonstrated. The dominance of males and the peripheral role allotted to females within the Indian ritual reinforces the sexist hierarchies of the dominant culture. Furthermore, even if one were to claim that the Indian ritual served an oppositional purpose within black New Orleans, there would be no guarantee that this particular counter-narrative could transcend specific experiences of race, region, and class to speak to people with different values and histories. The forms and styles fashioned by the Indians seem so rooted in the specific history and culture of New Orleans that it is difficult to imagine how their practice could be representative of counter-narratives generated under different conditions.

Indeed, even the cultural critics most sympathetic to the emancipatory potential of popular narratives express reservations about them that are relevant to an evaluation of the ultimate significance of the practices of the Mardi Gras Indians. Limon warns that ostensibly oppositional behaviors sometimes simply reflect unequal opportunities and resources. Thus, rather than parodying or undermining dominant narratives, these behaviors might instead be imitating them, albeit with inadequate resources. Limon emphasizes that traditional folklore best retains a critical edge in the modern world when it represents self-generated and relatively autonomous cultural practices that contrast radically with the "largely imposed character of mass media culture."[49] In a similar vein, Fox points to the ways in which modern society undermines the kinds of communities and cultures traditionally oriented toward the creation and preservation of folklore. Fox notes that folk practices often draw their critical content from an essentially conservative function—preserving group cohesion and conformity in traditional societies under attack by modernization. He points out that such societies are increasingly rare and increasingly anomalous in the modern world, and that they constitute an inadequate basis for cultural and political contestation.[50] Jameson contends that truly "popular" art has all but disappeared under the assault of commercial mass culture, surviving only in isolated pockets removed from the main channels of communication and commerce.[51]

The concerns raised by Limon, Fox, and Jameson offer useful cautions about analyzing the Mardi Gras Indian ritual as an example of counter-narrative. Like all subordinated groups, the Indians lack access to significant power and resources, and their organizations do serve purposes of mutual aid and self-affirmation denied them in other spheres. Their ritual may have started in relative isolation from the "largely imposed character of mass media culture," but their present-day and future audiences have been saturated with competing images and sounds from other cultures through the mass media. They seem to exemplify Jameson's contention that truly "popular" art exists only in specialized and marginalized circumstances, far removed from the centers of mainstream commerce and culture.

Yet the same forms of commercial culture that destroy the organic basis for traditional folklore enable people to escape the prejudices and parochialisms of their own communities. The same forces that relegate ethnic, linguistic, and subcultural minorities to the margins of contemporary culture, also transmit the oppositional sensibilities of marginal groups to a mass audience. The same feelings that motivate people to fashion autonomous signs and symbols within folkloric traditions impel them to put the stamp of their own experience on the ideas and images circulated within commercial culture. Most important, the internal properties of the electronic mass media favor precisely the kinds of dynamic cultural creation basic to the entire Mardi Gras Indian activity. Commercial culture destroys the sense of "origins" and "authenticity" prized by Euro-American music and folklore, but its biases toward repetition, nonlinear reasoning, and immediacy make it a viable conduit for oppositional narratives like those created by the Mardi Gras Indians. Nothing illustrates this tendency more convincingly than the way in which New Orleans musicians have inserted Mardi Gras Indian music into American and international popular music.

As early as the 1920s, jazz musicians from New Orleans recorded Mardi Gras Indian songs. Danny Barker and his Creole Cats did "My Indian Red" and "Chocko Mo Fendo Hando" on the King Zulu label, while Louis Dumaine and his Jazzola Eight performed "To Wa Bac a Wa" for Vic Records.[52] In 1954, Sugar Boy Crawford inserted Indian music into mainstream popular culture when his song "Jock-A-Mo" became a big regional hit. Although not an Indian himself, Crawford created "Jock-A-Mo" by combining two songs he remembered hearing them sing when he was growing up near the "battlefield" on Claiborne and Poydras streets.[53] Dave Bartholomew's 1957 "Can't Take It No More" begins with chanting evocative of Indian call and response.[54] In 1965, the Dixie Cups, a female trio from New Orleans, reached the national top-twenty list with "Iko Iko"—which like "Jock-A-Mo" originated with the Mardi Gras Indians. In a story that illustrates how commercial and folk cultures can intersect, Barbara Hawkins of the Dixie Cups relates how "Iko Iko" became a record:

> We were clowning around the studio while the musicians were on break, it was just the three of us using drumsticks on ashtrays and glasses singing "Iko Iko." We didn't realize that [producers] Jerry and Mike (Leiber and Stoller) were in the control room with the tape rolling. They came out and said that's great, they had never heard it before, all they added was a calypso box. We had never planned on recording it.[55]

Hawkins described the song as "the type of thing the Indians have always used, inventing new words as they march along."[56] In the late 1970s, Hawkins herself came full circle with the Indians, marching as Queen of the Wild Magnolias on Mardi Gras Day.

Other Indian songs which have been recorded successfully include versions of "Iko Iko" by Doctor John and by the Neville Brothers, "Handa Wanda" by the Wild Magnolias, and compilations of carnival songs by the Wild Tchoupitoulas and the Wild Magnolias.[57] In addition, songs about parts of the Mardi Gras Indian ritual have been recorded by Professor Longhair, Huey Smith and the Clowns, and Earl King. Some of the influence of the Indians on New Orleans pop music has been indirect. Cyril Neville of the Neville Brothers attributes his skill on percussion instruments to the lessons he learned from the tambourine playing of his "Uncle Jolly" (George Landry) who founded the Wild Tchoupitoulas tribe in 1972.[58] Those lessons involved the kind of interactions with African music characteristic of the Mardi Gras Indian aesthetic. As Neville explains:

> The drum comes to me as a symbol of what I, or we, used to be. I can't speak on the drums, but I try to convey my feelings. . . . I think about Africa when I play. To me, right now, my Africa is the drums 'cause when I feel like going back to Africa, I play my drums."[59]

Evidently, Cyril Neville learned his lessons well; when the Neville Brothers played on the bill in Chicago with the Nigerian JuJu band, King Sunny Ade and His African Beats, a reporter for the *Chicago Sun Times* noted, "Many of the African players were enchanted with the funk and soul of the Neville Brothers, most notably the West African persuasions of percussionist Cyril Neville."[60]

But to trace only the direct links between the Indians and popular artists and songs underestimates their true influence on New Orleans, American, and world popular music. An amazing variety of recorded music from New Orleans resonates with the values, aesthetics, and musical traditions of the Indians. Their jubilant celebration of the bounty of life informs Shirley and Lee's 1956 "Let the Good Times Roll," Aaron Neville's 1966 "Tell It Like It Is," and The Meters' 1972 "They All Axed for You." Indian-style call and response dominated Huey Smith and the Clowns' 1958 "Don't You Just Know It," while "second line" rhythms permeated The Meters 1970 "Handclapping Song."

The great New Orleans rhythm and blues pianist Professor Longhair replicated Mardi Gras Indian music in his polyrhythmic compositions, demonstrating a philosophical commitment to the unity among percussion, dance, and melody by refusing to play grand pianos and insisting on uprights so that he could kick the base boards rhythmically at appropriate moments. Alfred Roberts, who played conga drums behind Professor Longhair, once described what the two of them tried to do musically in words that serve as a capsule introduction to African musical sensibilities:

> I try and answer whatever he's doin' and try and lay out a basic
> pattern that he could listen to and build off. Cause this is what he
> made me think of the role he wanted me to play. If the drummer is

playing a certain rhythm with his foot, and Fess [Professor Longhair] got somethin' happenin' with his hands, syncopatin,' it's best for you to play in a space where nothin' is happenin' and kind of blend in with the drummer and the bass player. It's just backwards and forwards your hands and your brain, your eyes, your ears, and it's just flowin' like that into a rhythm.[61]

Just as Alfred Roberts and Professor Longhair reproduced African musical forms in New Orleans, musicians from all over the world knowingly and unknowingly absorbed Mardi Gras Indian music into the basic vocabulary of rock and roll. New Orleans drummer Earl Palmer laid a solid "parade beat" beneath the rhythm-and-blues hits of Little Richard and Sam Cooke, while the melody and chord progressions from the parade song "Second Line" predate their appearance in Bill Haley and His Comets' "Rock Around the Clock."[62] New Orleans rhythm-and-blues artist Ernie K-Doe exaggerated only slightly when he said in 1979, "I'm not sure, but I'm almost positive, that all music came from New Orleans."[63]

In 1986, rock singer Cyndi Lauper delayed the release of her "True Colors" album in order to include "Iko Iko" on it. Lauper had been listening to playbacks of her rendition of Marvin Gaye's 1960s anti-war, anti-racist "What's Going On," and she began to be reminded of another song. Eventually, she realized that the rhythms she had been using in "What's Going On" fit perfectly into "Iko Iko," which came to Lauper through listening to the Neville Brothers, Doctor John, and the Dixie Cups.[64] On the surface, her connection might seem absurd. The profound political lyrics of "What's Going On" bear little resemblance to the nonsense rhymes of "Iko Iko." The life experience of a white woman rock star from New York seems to have little in common with the historical struggle against racial and class domination waged by the Mardi Gras Indians. Yet Lauper's intuition led her to the right place. "What's Going On" and "Iko Iko" *are* both about fighting racism and exploitation. The magnificent plumes and bright colors of the Mardi Gras Indians express in their way what the multi-colored hair and self-parodying costumes of Cyndi Lauper represent in another way. The proto-feminist blend of adolescent female voices and adult sexual desires in the Dixie Cups' "Iko Iko" serves as a legitimate progenitor to Lauper's own breakthrough hit in 1985, "Girls Just Want to Have Fun."

That Lauper came to "Iko Iko" through the apparatuses of commercial culture raises intriguing questions about the supposedly diminishing power of popular narratives. It illustrates how marginalized cultures can insinuate their oppositional values into the texts of popular culture and create allies among people with similar though not identical experiences. It is no more ridiculous for Cyndi Lauper to appropriate "Iko Iko," than it was for nineteenth-century, working-class blacks to use the Wild West Show, Mardi Gras, and gang-fighting as a basis for an oppositional subculture. As part of the history of rock and roll, as part of the historic opposition to hierarchy and exploitation in America, "Iko Iko" offered a logical source of inspiration and celebration for Lauper. The critics may be right when they talk about the decline of traditional narratives, the marginalization of "popular" art, and the "largely imposed character of mass media culture." But people fight with the resources at their disposal, and frequently their pain leads them to quite innovative means of struggle. They do not all have the same story, and they often fail to understand the stories of others. They often suffer terrible oppression and anguish as they search for a narrative capable of making sense out of their existence. But story-telling survives, even when the story-tellers develop coded and secret ways of communicating with one another, inside and outside of commercial culture. For all of his pessimism, even Walter Benjamin understood this. In the same essay in which he fretted about the demise of story-telling, Benjamin offered a phrase which he meant figuratively, but which has a literal meaning as well. "Indeed," Benjamin observed, "each sphere of life has, as it were, produced its own tribe of storytellers."[65]

History and the Future

11

Buscando America (Looking for America): Collective Memory in an Age of Amnesia

> *"Tomorrow people, where is your past?"*
> Ziggy Marley

In his elegantly crafted *All That Is Solid Melts into Air*, Marshall Berman identifies Goethe's *Faust* as a narrative emblematic of modernity. Suffocated by the parochialisms and prejudices of his little village, Faust arms himself with instrumental knowledge and becomes a builder. But a builder of the new is also a destroyer of the old, and when the adult Faust returns to the village of his youth, he finds an exquisite beauty in the world he has labored so hard to destroy. For Berman, the dilemma facing Faust confronts us all. In a world devoted to progress and change, the past becomes ever more precious the more it disappears. Human beings act to change and "improve" the world, but as a result, many feel the sting of disconnection from the past, seeing the villages of our childhoods turn into what Berman calls "little worlds emptied out."[1]

Within much of American commercial culture after World War II, the "little world emptied out" became the industrial city. During the war production boom and the vast migrations that accompanied it, Americans formed a new pluralist culture in urban industrial centers. Mass strikes and political mobilizations expressed popular desires for material advancement in the postwar era, while new cultural and social formations reshaped race, class, ethnicity, and gender in lasting ways. The possibilities generated within wartime industrial cities have had enduring consequences, influencing everything from suburban growth to race relations, from foreign policy to gender identity.[2]

But for some the dream died almost as soon as it began. As a white man living within a black community, Johnny Otis thrived on the energy and imagination of wartime Los Angeles. He thought that the social changes he witnessed there signaled the birth of a new pluralism in America, the realization of long suppressed hopes and dreams. He found his previous cynicism about America giving way to a hopeful optimism. "I saw the whole community lifting," he recalls, "I thought we were going to realize the American dream. We'd say 'It's a bitch, there's still a lot of racism, but it's going to be OK because our kids will realize a fresh new democratic America!'"[3] But this optimism did not last, as Otis saw returning white soldiers claim jobs held during the war by female and black workers, federal urban renewal and home loan policies subsidizing white flight from central cities to the suburbs, military spending and corporate investment overseas redirecting funds that might have been use to bolster the American industrial infrastructure or to invest in the nation's social capital through expenditures on education, health, and housing. Otis watched his hopes crumble. "Things were grim, and I realized my original appraisal was accurate and that my enthusiasm and my happiness were not well-founded—that the majority did not give a shit about black folk and in fact despised them."[4] The curtailment of the emerging pluralistic and democratic urban culture that held Otis's allegiance did real harm to Afro-American communities, but it also devastated a variety of urban, ethnic working-class cultures and subcultures on behalf of the suburb-centered consumer mentality of the 1950s. Urban renewal enabled large corporations to build new downtown corporate headquarters at bargain rates. Federally subsidized loans for segregated suburban housing brought millions of dollars in mortgages to financial institutions, while federal highway projects dispersed populations for the enrichment of building firms, not to mention their indirect subsidy to the automobile and gasoline industries. All of these policies had a devastating impact on the pluralistic democratic culture that emerged in American cities during World War II.

Throughout the 1950s and 1960s individuals like Johnny Otis fought to retain the legacies of 1940s urban industrial life. In terrains as diverse as civil-rights activism and popular music they won many important victories, wresting concessions from their enemies and keeping alive an active opposition between corporate culture and democratic culture. But by the late 1970s, corporate culture had won decisive victories: Cutbacks in government spending on social programs reversed previous commitments to education, housing, and health. Plant shutdowns and capital flight undermined the common ground that had given both the poor and the middle class a meaningful stake in society, while tax policies fueled a spending spree by the rich. Some of the distance between blacks and whites, between rich and poor, which had started to close in the 1960s re-opened in the 1970s and 1980s.

During the postwar era, commercial popular culture has functioned largely to fashion a symbolic order conducive to the interests of corporate America. The same investors who redirect capital away from urban industrial areas control the form and content of the commercial mass media. They determine the monopoly structure of commercial network television as well as its identity as an advertising mechanism. They skew the content of mass communications toward the wealthy by making advertising demographics the prime determinant of what appears on radio or television. They ensure that our society devotes superior resources to advertising than to education, and that its central discursive media "naturalize" private commodity consumption while presenting social commitments as unnatural intrusions on private lives. Their marketing research reinforces existing prejudices and retards innovation by silencing images and ideas not already acceptable to broad segments of the population. They suppress knowledge about cultural and historical differences to unite the audience as a homogeneous buying public; then they create and exaggerate petty divisions—based on brand loyalty, fashion, style—to divide the audience into market segments.

Media scholar Ben Bagdikian demonstrates how the commercial imperatives of corporate America undermine local knowledge and a sense of history. His studies of print and electronic journalism reveal a pernicious relationship between the monopolistic tendencies of commercial enterprises and the free flow of information required for informed political judgments. For example, urban renewal not only dispersed central-city populations to the suburbs, it also destroyed the densities favorable to "impulse" buying of newspapers. Fewer street sales made newspapers more dependent upon advertising revenues which in turn mandated less space devoted to news. In addition, the newly dispersed reading audience cost more to reach (by deliveries) and had a more fragmented sense of locality. To appeal to the broadest possible suburban audience, newspapers geared their content toward more general features rather than specific local stories, and they followed the demographic tyrannies that made the appeal of fewer wealthier readers more desirable to newspapers (and their advertisers) than a larger but less wealthy clientele. Bagdikian attributes the drastic demise in the number of daily newspapers since World War II to these changes in format and content, and he shows how television merely extends this process by dispersing its news to an even larger and more diffuse audience.[5]

Commercial mass media fragment and dilute entertainment in much the same way that they do news. In the early 1980s, the Federal Communications Commission restricted the three commercial television networks from initiating programming during the early evening hours on the grounds that this time period should be devoted to local programming needed to ensure diversity and community responsibility. But the reach and scope of television draw such exorbitant support from advertisers that local producers cannot possibly compete with the slick appeal and advanced technologies of national syndicators and distributors. Local stations make the most money when they show programs that bring the highest advertising ratings and that cost the least to obtain. Rather than suffer the expenses of local production or the uncertainty of audience response, they prefer to buy syndicated shows from national producers. Consequently, during the "local access" hours all across the nation, viewers see exactly the same syndicated comedies and game shows which reinforce a mediated national consciousness rather than any kind of local knowledge or memory.

Yet the mercenary aims of media conglomerates and the commercial and ideological imperatives of corporate culture have not quite succeeded in erasing desires for connection to the urban past. As Stuart Hall quips, "hegemonizing is hard work": obliterating suppressed memories and desires requires constant vigilance, especially when the dislocations and fragmentations of the media nurture a longing for reconnection. To be sure, representations of both the past and the industrial city often appear on television and film as warnings against sociability and public space. These portrayals of the

city as so ominous and social difference so threatening invite a retreat into a consumer world bounded by cul-de-sacs and subdivisions. Nonetheless, ideological predilections often conflict with commercial opportunities; cultural portrayals laced with traces of the
urban industrial past can make money, both as novelties within and
as alternatives to a commodity-consumer society. The very forms
most responsible for the erosion of historical and local knowledge
can sometimes be the sources of reconnection in the hands of inge-
nious artists and audiences. By these processes they remember their
own actual pasts, but they also use the powers of electronic mass media to transcend time and space, connecting themselves to the pasts
of others, pasts that bear moral and political lessons. Instead of serving as an instrument of division, commercial culture in these instances
serves as a way for bridging barriers of time, class, race, region, ethnicity, gender, and even nationality. This "return of the repressed"
within the media creates one of its conditions of possibility.

A few examples from popular music and television may help illustrate the persistence and ingenuity of popular memory within the
mass media. In 1982 British rock singer Kevin Rowland recorded an
album titled *Celtic Soul Brother*, exploring his musical and cultural
roots. He wrote a series of songs for himself and his band—Dexy's
Midnight Runners—that foregrounded acoustic instruments and folk
melodies. Raised in working-class Coventry by Irish parents, Rowland mapped his own musical past as a dialogue between the rock-
and-roll music that he heard on the radio and the Irish folk music
that he heard at home. One of the songs on the album, "Come On
Eileen," became a hit single in England and in the U.S., and *Celtic
Soul Brother* became one of the best-selling albums of 1983.

One song on *Celtic Soul Brother* did not seem to fit in an album
from 1982–1983. "Jackie Wilson Said" paid tribute to the American
rhythm-and-blues singer Jackie Wilson, who since 1975 had been in
a coma and who was all but forgotten by the recording industry until
his death in 1984. Kevin Rowland's "folk" memories did not include
Jackie Wilson directly, but the story of how a song about the American singer became included on *Celtic Soul Brother* reveals sedimented networks and associations beneath the surfaces of the seemingly
disconnected world of commodified musical production.

Kevin Rowland sang "Jackie Wilson said it was 'reet petite' . . . " because in 1971 Rowland's fellow Irishman Van Morrison wrote and re-

corded the original "Jackie Wilson Said." Morrison grew up in Belfast enamored of American popular music, and in a moment of reflection about his own musical roots he penned a tribute to Jackie Wilson. This affinity between Irish and Afro-Americans should not be surprising. Wilson himself recorded a magnificent version of the Irish ballad "Danny Boy" in 1965, and Irish-American rock singer Michael McDonald claims that his childhood exposure to Irish ballads enabled him to make a "natural progression" to the music of Ray Charles and Marvin Gaye. "I was attracted to black music for the same reason that I loved those old Irish ballads," McDonald asserts. "Both were social statements of sorts and both were indigenous to their respective cultures: Ireland, where my father had grown up, and towns like St. Louis along the Mississippi River, where I was growing up."[6] But Morrison's memory of Jackie Wilson saying "Reet Petite" held meaning beyond the general families of resemblance tying Afro-American to Irish music.

Jackie Wilson's "Reet Petite" was his first hit as a solo artist in 1957. The song was written for him by aspiring writer and producer Berry Gordy, Jr., who would go on to success as the founding and guiding force behind Motown Records. But in 1957 Gordy was just a former assembly-line worker and failed music-store owner trying to break into the business. He drew the expression "Reet Petite" from the "bop" language of jazz musicians in the 1940s whose music, dress, and speech held an enduring fascination for Gordy. When Jackie Wilson found a mass audience (including Van Morrison) for "Reet Petite," he brought to them a piece of a subculture that was already ten years out of date. "Bop" talkers of the 1940s cultivated an in-group mentality to distance themselves from the homogenizing power of popular culture. They favored a music built on blues chord progressions and abstract improvisations to break with the simple formulas of Tin Pan Alley. They peppered their speech with internal rhymes about exotic clothes. The bop talkers wearing clothes with a draped shape and a reat pleat or a stuffed cuff might catch the eye of a slick chick. The bop talkers and zoot suiters of the 1940s manifested one of the first instances of "prestige from below" in postwar Western societies. Previously, fashion, dress, and speech popular among the middle class started with the wealthy and trickled down. In the postwar period, "bop" talk, zoot suits, and rock music originating in black and Chicano working-class communities filtered up to set the pace for middle-class groups, especially youth.

The complicated genealogy that ties Kevin Rowland to oppositional subcultures of the 1940s via "Jackie Wilson Said" reflects more than the serendipitous confusion of mass mediated culture and art. Because in his own way, Rowland found what he was looking for. Like him, the "bop" talkers and zoot suiters who coined the phrase "reet petite" sought to assert their historical identity and flaunt their social marginality while at the same time staking a claim for participation in global popular culture. Not only did Rowland find an appropriate role model in Van Morrison, but Morrison's discovery of Wilson (and Wilson's use of Gordy, and Gordy's appropriation of the 1940s "bop" talkers) united all of them in an oppositional quest, a search for inclusion in the mainstream of popular music without losing sight of the differences mandated by ethnic and racial history. When he adopted Irish acoustic instruments and melodies, Kevin Rowland aired some roots that he knew about consciously and clearly. But when he chose to record "Jackie Wilson Said," he also connected with some roots that he may have sensed only obliquely and second-hand.

The presence of sedimented networks and associations within rock-and-roll music illumine a career-turn in the life of another musician, the American rock guitarist Billy Peek. Late one night in 1975 Rod Stewart and his band, including Ron Wood, sat in a Colorado motel room watching Chuck Berry performing on "Rock Concert" on television. Stewart found his attention drawn to Berry's lead guitarist, Billy Peek. Stewart wanted to start a new band at the time and Ron Wood suggested that Peek had the talent and the sound that Stewart wanted. It took Stewart and his manager several months to locate Peek, but they set up an audition by the end of the year.

Billy Peek had grown up in the 1940s and 1950s in a white, working-class St. Louis neighborhood known as "The Grove." Peek's father worked in a nearby tobacco warehouse, and his mother was employed by a meatpacking firm; eventually they opened up a neighborhood bar featuring live country-and-western music, the Peek-A-Boo Inn. Although he heard only country music at home, when he was thirteen a friend introduced Peek to Chuck Berry's "Maybelline" on a neighborhood juke box. From that moment on, Peek vowed to make his living playing rock and roll. He practiced for hours in his room, trying to emulate the sounds he heard on records and the radio. As a teen-ager, he went to black night clubs to hear performances by local musicians including Ike Turner, Albert King, and Chuck Berry. He began to play for school dances and was featured on a local television program. One night while playing a string of Chuck Berry songs at a local club, he noticed Berry sitting in the audience. Fearful of offending his idol, Peek steered clear of any more of Berry's compositions that evening, but at the end of the show Berry came up, congratulated him on his playing, and invited him to perform at Berry's club, Berry Park. Their subsequent long-term association culminated in Peek's appearance with Berry on "Rock Concert" in 1975.

Peek auditioned for Stewart a few months later. At the session, Stewart stayed in the control booth with head phones on, and he asked Peek to listen to one track and to play whatever came to mind. The song, which had been giving the rest of the band difficulty, turned out to be "The Wild Side of Life," originally a Hank Thompson country song from 1952. Peek remembered the song as a favorite of his father's, one that he had heard around the house incessantly when he was growing up. In addition, years of playing with Chuck Berry had schooled him in playing a hard-driving St. Louis boogie-woogie riff "that told a story and told it in overdrive."[7] What Peek produced at the audition was his cultural history translated into music, a fusion of white, working-class country music and Afro-American rhythm and blues, but also the organic musical language of the industrial city in which he was raised. Peek knew he had gotten the job when he saw Stewart jump in the air and practically hit the ceiling of the control booth yelling, "That's it! That's it!"

With Billy Peek's guitar helping to set the pace, the Rod Stewart band became one of the best-selling musical aggregations in the world over the next five years. Peek's guitar solos on "Better Off Dead," "Blondes Have More Fun," "Ball Trap," "Hot Legs," and "Wild Side of Life" anchored the band in a traditional rock-and-roll style that provided an effective contrast to Stewart's pop vocalizing. But Peek secured his place in that band through more than technique alone; his entire life history had prepared him for that role. Other musicians could play the same notes, but Peek "had the feel" of the music, a feel he acquired through hard experience in the 1950s.

When Stewart's band dissolved in 1980, Peek returned to St. Louis where he became a local favorite at clubs and dances. His skills at Chuck Berry songs and his connection to the shared pasts of many of his listeners drew Peek into repeated conversations about the origins of St. Louis rock and roll. Eventually he worked those conversations into a song that recalled his desire to learn the blues at East Side night clubs. The song, "Can a White Boy Sing the Blues?" led to a blues album which attracted some attention in the U.S. and England, and which led to Peek's emergence in the late 1980s as a performer on the midwestern blues circuit and as a recording artist with records like "The Hammer" played on blues radio stations.[8]

The sedimented layers of cultural history underlying the music of Kevin Rowland and Billy Peek testify to the dialogic nature of popular music, and they also offer evidence about the capacity of popular culture to serve as a conduit for connection to meaningful possibilities in the urban industrial past. Yet such uses of memory are not always progressive. In the late 1980s, radio stations across the country have adopted another strategy in relation to the past—adult-oriented "oldies" programming, sometimes referred to without a trace of irony as "Big Chill" programming (in "honor" of the popularity of that film's soundtrack). "Oldies" programming in the late 1950s filled an oppositional role; it maintained collective memory and resisted the manipulations of an industry trying to purge itself of its black and white working-class resonances. But in the 1980s, such programming stems from demographic tyranny (the large number of listeners with high disposable incomes who developed their musical tastes in the 1960s) and cultural conservatism (an alternative to new music). At a time when the most creative music—rap and Latin dance mix—come from the pluralities of the postindustrial city, this particular nostalgia for the urban industrial past can be quite racist and regressive, a way of precluding rather than promoting new possibilities. Yet the artists responsible for rap and hip hop musics are masters at appropriating the tools used against them to inject themselves into venues from which they have been excluded. Recent rap artists have colonized the "oldies" format for their own purposes as Run-DMC collaborated with Aerosmith's Steve Tyler to do a rap remake of that group's "Walk This Way," while the Fat Boys teamed up with Chubby Checker to do a rap version of his hit, "The Twist." In a further twist, James Brown laid claim to having originated rap with his "I'm Real" recorded with

Full Force. These collaborative works secure new commercial spaces for the artists involved, defy the record industry's established codes about the inviolability of genres, and reveal an organic cultural memory at the same time: Run-DMC did listen to Aerosmith, the Fat Boys do know about Chubby Checker, and James Brown does hear traces of his old records in every rap and hip hop selection.

If popular music has been a vehicle for artists and audiences to reconnect with the disappearing textures of urban life, commercial network television has done its best to present city life in a negative light. Between 1958 and 1970, American commercial network television largely "abandoned" the city, placing most of its situation comedies in suburbs or rural areas while mainly locating action adventure shows on the western plains or in exotic postindustrial sunbelt or resort settings.[9] But after 1970, American television "remembered" the city and once again adopted it as a location for comedy and drama. Humor no longer remained confined to places like "Mayberry" (*The Andy Griffith Show*) and "Springfield" (*Father Knows Best*) but cropped up in working-class Queens (*All in the Family*), Watts (*Sanford and Son*), and Chicago's south side (*Good Times*). Even middle-class comedies celebrated formerly unprestigious urban locales—Minneapolis (*The Mary Tyler Moore Show*), Indianapolis (*One Day at a Time*) and Cincinnati (*WKRP*). Action adventure shows rediscovered the city as well, but largely to reveal it as a dangerous and threatening place (*Kojak, Starsky and Hutch, SWAT*, and *Streets of San Francisco*). Even if its portrayals made no direct reference to the past, the recovery of forgotten images amounted to a recasting of collective memory about a social formation that had been rendered obsolete by previous television programs.

None of the new urban television programs of the 1970s evoked the historical knowledge or progressive sentiments found in the music of Kevin Rowland or Billy Peek, but these shows did display an interest in the city and a continuum of attitudes about it. Even though set in the present, they inevitably had to work with or against the grain of popular understanding of the historical legacy of the industrial city. The situation comedies tended to take place indoors, revalidating the home (and its consumer purchases) as the center of the psychic world. But these comedies also made a break with the homogeneous nuclear family of 1960s television comedies by emphasizing differences with neighbors (Julio on *Sanford and Son*, Lionel on *All in the Family*), or by remapping the family onto the workplace (*The Bob Newhart Show, The Mary Tyler Moore Show*).[10] The middle-class city dwellers enjoyed the variety of urban experiences even without necessarily being in show business as had been true of previous such shows (*I Love Lucy, The Danny Thomas Show, The Dick Van Dyke Show*), while the mismatched neighbors of the shows about poorer people still managed to maintain some sociability and mutuality despite their differences. Even an action adventure show like *Rockford Files* could finally show the city as an arena of mutuality and affectionate humor among an extended family and work network. What tied these shows to the urban past was not just their use of older dwellings (*All in the Family, Chico and the Man, Good Times*) or urban institutions (radio stations, office buildings, junkyards), but also their liberal politics. Some viewers might side with conservative foils Archie Bunker, Ted Knight, or Les Nessman, but the inscribed preferred readings of these shows encouraged reconnection with urban liberalism. More conservative readings were encouraged by the action adventure shows where paternalistic, male police officers took command over diverse underlings to make them effective in containing the vicious criminals capable at any moment of reducing the city to barbarism. Rather than celebrating the diversity of the city, these shows tended to pose difference as a problem to be solved by authority and discipline. Veteran police officers in *Mod Squad, Starsky and Hutch, Police Woman*, and *Streets of San Francisco* constrain their multi-racial and multi-gendered (and vaguely counter-cultural) subordinates from any real rebellion by convincing them that they are needed in a struggle to control the vicious and threatening "differences" of the city.

The tension between corporate and democratic readings of the urban legacy extend into the 1980s, most notably in the differences between *Hill Street Blues* and *Miami Vice*. Both programs depict an uphill battle by police officers against urban corruption, yet both emphasize the city (or at least its police force) as an arena where people from different backgrounds learn to work together for the common good. Yet their sensibilities head in opposite directions. *Hill Street Blues* emphasizes the decay of the urban industrial city. The defective wiring and plumbing of the station house mirrors the dark terrors and social pollution of the adjacent neighborhood. Like the 1970s action adventure shows, diversity within the police force provides a challenge to management, while diversity outside poses savagery as the alternative to effective hierarchical leadership. Although the show has multiple story lines and no narrator, each episode ends with a summary from the white male managerial hero, Captain Furillo. Alone among the characters, he sees the big picture; he is sensitive enough to work with other races and genders without a hint of prejudice, but seasoned enough to realize that the rules don't work, that the system has failed, and that people like him are asked to do too much. Furillo's liberalism has a residue of self-pity in it; the decline of the industrial city has left him in charge of a lesser entity than he really deserves.

By contrast, *Miami Vice* exposes the corruption of postindustrial society, rooting its critique in the residual morality of the industrial past. For all the avant-garde music video interludes in their show, the fashionable postmodern clothes, and the fancy cars, the officers in *Miami Vice* seem closer to the democratic culture of the industrial city than their counterparts in *Hill Street Blues*. Citizens become victims in *Miami Vice* because wealthy and powerful people control too much and act too viciously. The poor are more likely to be victims than perpetrators here, and while not necessarily better than anyone else, neither are they necessarily any worse. In fact, their dialects, dress, and music add a dignified texture to the urban mosaic, providing a backdrop for drama as well as for crime. The officers in *Miami Vice* routinely fail to hold back evil pressing in on their city, but they insist on trying without resorting to cynicism. Their problems are social rather than individual; the demise of the urban community is a historical rather than a personal problem, one caused by the evils of the kind of city that has supplanted it—a city of indecent gaps between rich and poor, and one with little to offer its remaining middle class.

Televised portrayals of the city inevitably convey the vitality and ingenuity of urban popular music; yet they present city life as far more violent and far less viable than it actually us. But the fact that they have to present it all, that the city remains an important icon for both conservative and liberal politics indicates its enduring fascination. More important than the inscribed biases or resolution of any particular television show are the possibilities still embedded within an urban context. As Marshall Berman writes,

The contemporary desire for a city that is openly troubled but intensely alive is a desire to open up old but distinctively modern wounds once more. It is a desire to live openly with the split and unreconciled character of our lives, and to draw energy from our inner struggles, wherever they may lead us in the end.[11]

This desire to open up wounds seems strangely out of place. In a society given over to suburban subdivisions, where franchised fast-food restaurants guard against surprises, and where cities rebuild their unique and distinctive historical districts by hiring the same developers to build the same kinds of malls all over the country, the fascination with risk may seem like either masochism or madness. To critics like Jean Baudrillard it represents the final triumph of electronic media, an acceptance of total disorientation and fragmentation in a world of totally artificial experience. Baudrillard sees a world composed of signs without referents, of cultural symbols unhinged from any organic social experience.[12] But as Berman makes clear, the mixture of sensations and images in a world excite us not so much because they are fundamentally new, but because they remind us of something familiar but threatened by forgetting.

In some cases, remembering our own pasts links us to people quite different from ourselves. When musician Michael Tempo of the Los Angeles group the Bonedaddys talks about the African influences in his music, he tells people, "I play music indigenous to the natives of Western Kentucky. I could find African records when I grew up in Paducah. That was as much a part of my culture as the country music coming over the radio and through the kitchen window."[13] But one reason why Tempo could absorb the African music that he heard was because African musicians like Nigeria's King Sunny Ade grew up listening to American country-and-western, steel-guitar players like Ralph Mooney and singers like Jim Reeves.[14] Jerry Harrison of the Talking Heads describes his explorations into African music by referring to the Africanisms already present in American rhythm and blues and vice versa. Harrison explains,

I really consider there to be a clear link between African music and R&B and rock'n'roll, and it had not been elucidated clearly before. There are definite connections between Fela and James Brown. That's why we could learn about African music because we had heard about that, and read about that, and we loved James Brown, and we went and looked at it. Once we saw how great Fela was, we started

269

looking at some of the other stuff. It wasn't because we were interested in Pygmy music or something like that. It came up from things that had already developed. It was as if we worked back from our culture, and then we realized things that people had said about these connections.

Harrison and the Talking Heads found their way to Africa the same way that Kevin Rowland found his way to the zoot suiters, the same way that Billy Peek found Rod Stewart—through commercial culture as it reflected and resonated with historical traces relevant to their lives. Commercial culture enabled these musicians, and their audiences, to understand more about their own memory and experience by connecting with the memories and experiences of others.

* * * * *

As much as any single individual, Johnny Otis has devoted his life to appreciating what Albert Murray calls the "incontestably mulatto nature of American culture."[15] He speaks bitterly about what he calls the "predatory capitalism" that enables the culture industry "to grab people from almost the cradle and to cater to the most juvenile tastes."[16] What angers Otis most is not so much what popular culture has produced, but, rather, what it has suppressed. "That's been the big question in my life, " he says, "I've got to figure that one out. Instead of thanking God for the African presence, cause they've been a great gift to this country . . . and they constantly attempted to share this gift. But they were always rebuffed and always used and abused, not accepted."[17] Johnny Otis has always struggled to call attention to that precious resource for America, to use his own life as an example of the kind of culture that could be built on imagination and desire as well as on tradition—the kind of culture that began to emerge in those postwar industrial cities. That quest links Johnny Otis to other Americans, to Herman Melville and Mark Twain and Willa Cather and Scott Joplin, who reveled in America's exuberant pluralities. It links him as well to representatives of other marginalized and suppressed groups—gays and lesbians, Native Americans, Chicanos, Asian Americans, women, workers, and the myriad other voices that find their realities at best distorted and at worst erased from popular culture. But they continue to create, they continue to speak their minds, they continue to learn from each other.

These quests open up wounds, and they take place under conditions of communications distorted by commerce, racism, state power, and sexism. But they persist, even against the grain of economic and cultural matrices, because they keep alive cherished possibilities. In defiance of concentrated economic and political power unprecedented in world history, they continue to look for an America that is a realization of its own best hopes—a chorus of many voices and a land of a thousand dances.

Notes

Notes

CHAPTER 1.

1. Richard Terdiman, "Deconstructing Memory: On Representing the Past and Theorizing Culture in France Since the Revolution," *Diacritics* (Winter), 1985, 14, 19.

2. I am indebted to Bruce Lincoln for pointing out to me that itinerant actors, lecturers, medicine salesmen, and circus performers lacked direct ties of kinship, propinquity, business, or history with their audiences, thus gaining special privileges to perform, but losing certain protections from the consequences of their performances.

3. Michael Bristol, *Carnival and Theater* (New York: Methuen, 1985), 113.

4. For a discussion of the concept of "privacy in public" see John F. Kasson's social history of Coney Island, *Amusing the Million* (New York: Hill and Wang, 1978).

5. See Kathy Peiss, *Cheap Amusements* (Philadelphia: Temple University Press, 1986).

6. Of course, temporary liberation from sexual repression often mandated a reproblematization of sexuality as well in, for example, the melodrama.

7. I. C. Jarvie, *Thinking about Society: Theory and Practice* (Norwell, MA: Kluwer Academic Press, 1986), 372.

8. Stuart Hall, "Notes on Deconstructing 'the Popular,' " in Raphael Samuel, ed., *People's History and Socialist Theory* (London: Routledge and Kegan Paul, 1981), 227.

9. Here I wish to avoid the debates about "popular" vs. "mass" culture, in which popular describes voluntary bottom-up creation and mass refers to top-down, mass-marketed commercial culture. These polarities obscure the important grass-roots creation that takes place within "mass culture," as well as the manipulated "mass" aspects of "popular culture."

10. Stuart Hall, "Notes on Deconstructing 'the Popular,' " 228.

11. Pierre Bourdieu, "The Aristocracy of Culture," *Media, Culture, and Society* n. 2 (1980), 237.

12. Tania Modleski, "The Rhythms of Reception: Daytime Television and Women's Work," in E. Ann Kaplan, ed., *Regarding Television* (Los Angeles: University Publications of America, 1983), 67–75.

13. Fredric Jameson, "Reification and Utopia in Mass Culture," *Social Text* v. 1, 1979.

14. See George Lipsitz, *Class and Culture in Cold War America: A Rainbow at Midnight* (South Hadley, MA: Bergin and Garvey, 1982), 187-88.

15. Kathleen Hall Jamieson, *Eloquence in an Electronic Age* (New York: Oxford University Press, 1988), 81.

16. Quoted by Willard Gingerich, "Heidegger and the Aztecs: The Poetics of Knowing in Pre-Hispanic Nahuatl Poetry," in Brian Swann and Arnold Krupat, *Recovering the Word* (Berkeley: University of California Press, 1987), 100–101.

17. Jane Feuer, "Narrative Form in American Network Television," in Colin McCabe, ed., *High Theory/Low Culture* (New York: St. Martin's, 1986), 112. Laura Mulvey, "Melodrama in and out of the Home," in Colin McCabe, ed., *High Theory/Low Culture*, 96.

18. Pierre Bourdieu, "The Aristocracy of Culture," 239.

19. Stuart Hall,"The Economy of Prestige," Minneapolis, Minnesota, April 9, 1988, author's notes.

20. See Richard Terdiman, "Deconstructing Memory."

21. Fredric Jameson, "Reification and Utopia in Mass Culture."

22. See Hayden White, *The Content of the Form* (Baltimore and London: Johns Hopkins University Press, 1987), 157.

23. Neil Postman, *Amusing Ourselves to Death* (New York: Penguin, 1985), 127.

24. Allan Bloom, *The Closing of the American Mind* (New York: Simon and Schuster, 1987).

25. Maria Damon, " 'Unmeaning Jargon'/Uncanonized Beatitude: Bob Kaufman, Poet," *The South Atlantic Quarterly* 87:4 (Fall) 1988, 708–9.

CHAPTER 2

1. Willa Cather, *My Antonia* (New York: Random House, 1918), 254.

2. Quoted in Neil Postman, *Amusing Ourselves to Death* (New York: Penguin, 1985), 137.

3. Russell Jacoby, *Social Amnesia* (Boston: Beacon Press, 1975), 3–4.

4. Lawrence Grossberg, "Another Boring Day in Paradise: Rock and Roll and the Empowerment of Everyday Life," *Popular Music* 5, 1985.

5. John Berger, "In Opposition to History, In Defiance of Time," *Village Voice*, October 8–14, 1984, 89–90.

6. Warren I. Susman, *Culture as History* (New York: Pantheon, 1984), 25–26.

7. Quoted in *On Campus* (November) 1987, v. 7, n. 3, 2.

8. Quoted in *On Campus*. Cheney's contradictory attitude about "history" is revealed most fully in her 1988 "Report to the President, the Congress, and the American People," where she laments students' lack of historical aptitude yet asserts that the value of the humanities lies in its "timeless" truths. Scholars who attempt to locate those "timeless" truths within historical time draw Cheney's derision for "politicizing" the curriculum. See *The Chronicle of Higher Education*, September 21, 1988, v. 35, n. 4.

9. Allan Bloom, *The Closing of the American Mind* (New York: Simon and Schuster, 1987), 58.

10. Quoted in *On Campus* (November), 1987, v. 7, n. 3, 2.

11. E. D. Hirsch, Jr., *Cultural Literacy* (Boston: Houghton-Mifflin, 1987), 107.

12. Quoted in *On Campus*.

13. Lynne Cheney, "Report to the President, the Congress, and the American People," esp. A18–A19.

14. Allan Bloom, *The Closing of the American Mind*, 37.

15. E. D. Hirsch, Jr., *Cultural Literacy*, 84, 107.

16. Diane Ravitch and Chester Finn, "What Do Our 17 Year Olds Know?" *Chronicle of Higher Education* October 7, 1987, B4. *What Do Our 17 Year Olds Know?* (New York: Harper and Row, 1987) especially pp. 205–14.

17. Hayden White, *Tropics of Discourse: Essays in Cultural Criticism* (Baltimore: Johns Hopkins University Press, 1978), 39.

18. Hayden White, *Tropics of Discourse*, 32.

19. See Dominick La Capra, *History and Criticism* (Ithaca, New York: Cornell University Press, 1985), 106.

20. Michel Foucault, "Two Lectures," p. 108, quoted in Thomas Dumm, *Democracy and Punishment* (Madison: University of Wisconsin Press, 1987), 151.

21. For example, Sande Cohen, *Historical Culture* (Berkeley and Los Angeles: University of California Press, 1986).

22. Quoted in Richard Terdiman, "Deconstructing Memory: On Representing the Past and Theorizing Culture in France Since the Revolution," *Diacritics* (Winter), 1985.

23. Hayden White, *The Content of the Form* (Baltimore and London: Johns Hopkins University Press, 1987), 149.

24. Dana Polan, *Power and Paranoia* (New York: Columbia University Press, 1986), 10.

25. *New York Times*, July 18, 1980, p. A8; July 21, 1981, p. 1; January 22, 1985, p. A17. I am indebted to Ron Takaki for calling this to my attention.

26. *New York Times*, January 22, 1985, p. A17.

27. Gerri Hirshey, *Nowhere to Run* (New York: Times Books, 1984), 266–67). I thank Adam Levy for calling this quote to my attention.

28. Dave Marsh, *Glory Days* (New York: Pantheon, 1986), 35–36.

29. Eudora Welty, "The House of Willa Cather," in Bernice Slote and Virginia Faulkner, ed., *The Art of Willa Cather* (Lincoln: University of Nebraska Press, 1974), 20.

CHAPTER 3

1. David Marc, *Comic Visions* (Boston: Unwin Hyman, 1989) 51.

2. Stuart Ewen condemns these shows for their hostility to immigrant life and their insistence on imposing a consumerist frame upon it in his *Captains of Consciousness: Advertising and the Social Roots of the Consumer Culture* (New York: McGraw Hill, 1976), 208–10. Marty Jezer takes a more favorable view in *The Dark Ages*, (Boston: South End, 1982), 191–94.

3. Erik Barnouw, *The Sponsor* (New York: Oxford University Press, 1979).

4. For a discussion of the "infinitely renewable present" see Daniel Boorstin, *The Americans: The Democratic Experience*, (New York: Vintage, 1973), 392–97.

5. Of course, class, ethnicity, and race remained important, but their relationship to individual identity changed radically at this time. Elsewhere I have argued that the bureaucratization of trade unions and xenophobic anti-communism also contributed to declining identification with ethnicity and class, see my *Class and Culture in Cold War America: A Rainbow at Midnight*, (South Hadley, MA: Bergin and Garvey, 1982).

6. Robert Allen, *Speaking of Soap Operas* (Chapel Hill: University of North Carolina Press, 1985), 126, 164. Richard de Cordova, "The Transition from Radio to Television," unpublished paper presented at the Society for Cinema Studies meetings, New York, New York, June 12, 1985.

7. Note the discussions in this chapter on *The Goldbergs* and *Amos 'n' Andy*, and the evolution of *I Remember Mama* as presented in the next chapter.

8. See Albert U. Romasco, *The Poverty of Abundance* (New York: Oxford University Press, 1965) and Barton Bernstein, "The Conservative Achievements of New Deal Reform," in Barton Bernstein, ed., *Towards a New Past* (New York: Vintage, 1968).

9. Henry Berger, "Social Protest in St. Louis," unpublished paper presented at a Missouri Committee for the Humanities Forum, St. Louis, Missouri. March 12, 1982.

10. George Lipsitz, *Class and Culture in Cold War America*.

11. Ibid.

12. Ibid.

13. *TV Facts* (New York: Facts on File, 1980), 141.

14. Neilsen ratings epitomize television's view of the family as separate market segments to be addressed independently.

15. William Boddy, "The Studios Move into Prime Time: Hollywood and the Television Industry in the 1950s," *Cinema Journal* 12 (4), 1986, 23–37. Jeanne Allen, "The Social Matrix of Television: Invention in the United States," in E. Ann Kaplan, ed., *Regarding Television* (Los Angeles: University Publications of America, 1983), 109–19.

16. George Lipsitz, *Class and Culture in Cold War America*. 120–21.

17. Geoffrey Moore and Phillip Klein, *The Quality of Consumer Installment Credit* (Washington, D.C.: National Bureau of Economic Research, 1967). Marty Jezer, *The Dark Ages* (Boston: South End, 1982).

18. Susan Hartmann, *The Home Front and Beyond* (Boston: Twayne, 1982), 165–68. John Mollenkopf, *The Contested City* (Princeton: Princeton University Press, 1983), 111.

19. "The Lush New Suburban Market," *Fortune* (November) 1953, 128.

20. Michael Stone, "Housing: The Economic Crisis," in Chester Hartman, ed., *America's Housing Crisis: What is to be Done?* (London and New York: Routledge and Kegan Paul, 1983), 122.

21. Quoted in Marty Jezer, *The Dark Ages*, 127.

22. Ernest Dichter, *The Strategy of Desire* (Garden City, NY: Doubleday, 1960), 210.

23. Ernest Dichter, *The Strategy of Desire*, 209.

24. "The Rock and Roll Kid," *Hey, Jeannie*. Academy of Television Arts Collection, University of California, Los Angeles.

25. "The In-laws," *The Goldbergs (Molly)*, Academy of Television Arts Collection, University of California, Los Angeles.

26. "The In-laws," *The Goldbergs (Molly)*.

27. "Moving Day," *The Goldbergs (Molly)* Academy of Television Arts Collection, University of California, Los Angeles.

28. "R228," *Life of Riley*, Academy of Television Arts Collection, University of California, Los Angeles.

29. "R228," *Life of Riley*. "Bad Companions," *The Goldbergs (Molly)*, Academy of Television Arts Collection, University of California, Los Angeles.

30. "Mama and the Carpenter," *Mama*, Academy of Television Arts Collection, University of California, Los Angeles.

31. "Andy the Godfather," *Amos 'n' Andy*, Academy of Television Arts Collection, University of California, Los Angeles. "The Rock and Roll Kid," *Hey, Jeannie*, Academy of Television Arts Collection, University of California, Los Angeles.

32. "Der Fledermaus," *The Goldbergs (Molly)*, Academy of Television Arts Collection, University of California, Los Angeles.

33. Elizabeth Meehan and Bradford Ropes, "Mama's Birthday," Theater Arts Collection. University Research Library. University of California, Los Angeles.

34. Susan Hartmann, *The Home Front and Beyond* (Boston: Twayne, 1982), 168.

35. Elizabeth Meehan and Bradford Ropes, "Mama's Birthday."

36. Elizabeth Meehan and Bradford Ropes, "Mama's Birthday."

37. Charles E. Swanson and Robert L. Jones, "Television Ownership and Its Correlates," *Journal of Applied Psychology* v. 35, 1951, 352–57.

38. Martha Wolfenstein, "The Emergence of Fun Morality," *Journal of Social Issues* v. 7, n. 4. 1951, 15–25.

39. *TV Guide*, May 7, 1954, p. 11.

40. *Ladies Home Journal*, September, 1956. pp. 130– 31. *TV Guide*, August 7, 1953, 7.

41. *TV Guide*, November 2, 1953, 17.

42. Susan Hartmann, *The Home Front and Beyond*, 164–65.

43. Joel Kovel, "Rationalization and the Family," *Telos* (37),13–14.

44. Kovel, "Rationalization and the Family."

45. Nancy Chodorow, *Reproduction of Mothering* (Berkeley: University of California Press, 1978), 189.

46. Nancy Chodorow, *Reproduction of Mothering*, 181. Joel Kovel, "Rationalization and the Family," 14.

47. Quoted in Horace Newcomb, *TV: The Critical View* (New York: Oxford University Press, 1978).

48. "R228," *The Life of Riley*.

49. *TV Guide*, October 1, 1955, 14.

50. Stanley Aronowitz, *Working Class Hero* (New York: Pilgrim, 1983).

51. *TV Guide*, December 29, 1956, 17.

52. "Jeannie the Cabdriver," *Hey, Jeannie*. Academy of Television Arts Collection, University of California, Los Angeles.

53. "The Rent Strike," *The Goldbergs*, Museum of Broadcasting, New York, New York. "The Power Line," *Life With Luigi*, Script 10. Norman Tokar Papers, Special Collections Room, Doheny Library. University of Southern California. Los Angeles.

54. "Mama and the Carpenter," *Mama*, Academy of Television Arts Collection, University of California, Los Angeles.

55. "Bad Companions," *The Goldbergs (Molly)*.

56. I want to thank Ruth Wood of the English Department of the University of Minnesota for calling my attention to these symbols in *The Honeymooners*.

57. "R228," *The Life of Riley*.

58. Ibid.

59. "Is There a Doctor in the House," "Boogie Comes Homes," "Moving Day," *The Goldbergs (Molly)*, Academy of Television Arts Collection, University of California, Los Angeles.

60. Yet the *Mama* show still sought credibility with its audience by relying on the Bay Ridge, Brooklyn chapter of the Sons of Norway order for advice on authentic Nor-

wegian folk customs and stories. Remarks by Dick Van Patten and Ralph Nelson, Museum of Broadcasting, New York, New York. December 17, 1985.

61. "The Loud Speaker," *The Honeymooners*, Academy of Television Arts Collection, University of California, Los Angeles.

62. Erik Barnouw, *The Sponsor* (New York: Oxford University Press, 1979), 106.

63. Erik Barnouw, *Tube of Plenty* (New York: Oxford University Press, 1982), 126. Marty Jezer, *The Dark Ages* (Boston: South End, 1982), 193–94. Stefan Kanfer, *A Journal of the Plague Years* (New York: Atheneum, 1973), 154. *New Republic* January 21, 1952, 8. February 18, 1952, 22.

64. See Nathan Irvin Huggins, *Harlem Renaissance* (New York: Oxford University Press, 1978).

65. Thomas Cripps, "The Amos 'n' Andy Controversy," in John O'Connor, ed., *American History and American Television* (New York: Ungar, 1983), 33–54. J. Fred Macdonald, *Blacks and White TV* (Chicago: Nelson Hall, 1983), 27–28. *Newsweek*, July 9, 1951, 56.

66. *Los Angeles Times* Calendar Section, February 29, 1984, 1.

67. "Kingfish Has a Baby," *Amos 'n' Andy*, Theater Arts Collection, University Research Library, University of California, Los Angeles.

68. Ibid.

69. Julius Lester, *All Is Well* (New York: Morrow, 1976), 14.

70. For an application of Bakhtin's work to television, see Horace Newcomb, "On the Dialogic Aspects of Mass Communication," *Critical Studies in Mass Communication* v. 1, n. 1. (1984), 34–50.

71. Stuart Hall, "Culture, Media, and the 'Ideological' Effect," in James Curran, Michael Gurevitch, and Janet Woollacott, eds., *Mass Communication and Society* (Beverly Hills: Sage, 1979).

72. Jürgen Habermas, *Legitimation Crisis* (Boston: Beacon Press, 1975).

73. "The Rock and Roll Kid," *Hey, Jeannie*. "The Insurance Policy," *Life With Luigi*, Script 2. "The In-laws," *The Goldbergs (Molly)*.

74. Stuart Hall, "Culture, Media, and the 'Ideological' Effect."

75. Gertrude Berg, *Molly and Me* (New York: McGraw Hill, 1961), 167.

76. Jürgen Habermas, *Legitimation Crisis*, 71–75.

77. Jürgen Habermas, *Legitimation Crisis*, 71.

78. Marc Daniels, Presentation at the Directors Guild of America, Los Angeles, California. July 11, 1984.

79. Joel Kovel, "Rationalization and the Family," *Telos* (37), 1978, 19.

80. Protection of the family represents an old theme for conservatives, and it has been a traditional device for creating dramatic tension. But never before have these two traditions been as thoroughly unified as dramatic and political themes, and never before have they dominated conservative thought as they have in the last decade.

81. Fredric Jameson, *The Political Unconscious* (Ithaca: Cornell University Press, 1981), 101.

CHAPTER 4

1. Elizabeth Meehan and Bradford Ropes, "Mama's Birthday," Theater Arts Collection. University Research Library. University of California, Los Angeles.

2. Rick Mitz, *The Great TV Sitcom Book*, (New York: Perigree, 1983), 458.

3. Rosemary Rice, Dick Van Patten, and Robin Morgan, *I Remember Mama* Symposium, Museum of Broadcasting, New York City, December 17, 1985, author's notes. Ralph Nelson, private conversation with author, December 17, 1985, repeated during interview with author on January 11, 1986, Monteceito, California.

4. *Interview with Ralph Nelson*, Monteceito, California, January 11, 1986

5. Rosemary Rice, *I Remember Mama* Symposium.

6. Robin Morgan, *I Remember Mama*.

7. Kathryn Forbes, *Mama's Bank Account* (New York: Harcourt, 1943).

8. *Current Biography*, 1945, 102. John Van Druten, *I Remember Mama* (New York: Dramatists Play Service Incorporated, 1944).

9. *New York Times*, May 17, 1966.

10. Stefan Kanfer, *A Journal of the Plague Years*, (New York: Atheneum, 1973), 154.

11. Andrea Walsh, *Women's Film and Female Experience* (New York: Praeger, 1984), 104.

12. Quoted in Andrea Walsh, *Women's Film and Female Experience*, 106–7.

13. DeWitt Bodeen screenplay, "I Remember Mama," Fred Guiol Collection, California State University at Fullerton, #4–87.

14. De Witt Bodeen screenplay, "I Remember Mama."

15. Ralph Nelson Papers, University of California, Los Angeles. Box 78. Scripts #1, 13, 20, 6. "T.R.'s New Home" and "Mama's Bad Day," Academy of Television Arts Collection, University of California, Los Angeles.

16. Ralph Nelson Papers, Special Collection 875, University Research Library, University of California at Los Angeles. Box 78. Scripts # 9, 2. Frank Gabrielson Papers, Sudbury, Massachusetts, "Mama and the Magic Lantern," "The Pet Show," "Nels and the Girl with the Lively Eyes."

17. "Tricycles Last," T86 1142, Museum of Broadcasting, New York.

18. "Nels and the Train Set," T86 0092, Museum of Broadcasting, New York.

19. "The Hansens Rise in the World," T86 1128, Museum of Broadcasting, New York.

20. Ralph Nelson Papers, Special Collection 875, Box 45, University Research Library, University of California, Los Angeles.

21. Ralph Nelson Papers, Special Collection 875, Box 44. Memo from Doris Quinlan to Carol Irwin, Frank Gabrielson, and Ralph Nelson, December 8, 1954.

22. CBS Press Release, 1949, Ralph Nelson Papers, Special Collection 875, Box 44, University Research Library, University of California, Los Angeles.

23. "T.R.'s New Home," *Mama*.

24. Ernest Dichter, *The Strategy of Desire* (Garden City, NY: Doubleday, 1960), 209.

25. Tania Modleski, "Femininity as Mas(s)querade: A Feminist Approach to Mass Culture," in Colin McCabe, ed., *High Theory/Low Culture* (New York: St. Martin's, 1986), 42.

26. Script #13, Ralph Nelson Papers, Special Collection 875, Box 78, University Research Library, University of California, Los Angeles.

27. Script #2, Ralph Nelson Papers, Special Collection 875, Box 78.

28. Script #15, Ralph Nelson Papers, Special Collection 875, Box 78.

29. *Interview with Hale Lamont Havers*, Sudbury, Massachusetts, May 15, 1987.

30. Murray Schumach, "Writing for Video," *New York Times*, February 18, 1951, x9.

31. *Interview with Ralph Nelson*, Monteceito, California, January 11, 1986.

32. *Interview with Ralph Nelson*.

CHAPTER 5

1. M. M. Bakhtin, *Speech Genres & Other Late Essays* (Austin: University of Texas Press, 1986), 170.

2. Richard Terdiman, "Deconstructing Memory: On Representing the Past and Theorizing Culture in France Since the Revolution," *Diacritics* (Winter), 1985, 23.

3. Lawrence Grossberg, "Another Boring Day in Paradise: Rock and Roll and the Empowerment of Everyday Life," *Popular Music* 5 (1985).

4. E. Ann Kaplan, *Rocking Around the Clock* (New York and London: Methuen, 1987, 145–46), 29.

5. See Richard Terdiman, "Deconstructing Memory," 20. Also see chapter 2.

6. Hayden White, *The Content of the Form* (Baltimore and London: Johns Hopkins University Press, 1987), 156.

7. Robert Hilburn, "Public Enemy's Chuck D: Puttin' on the Rap," *Los Angeles Times* calendar section, February 7, 1988, 63.

8. "David Bowie," *Musician* (May) 1983.

9. Dave Marsh, *Glory Days* (New York: Pantheon, 1986), 36.

10. Simon Frith, *Sound Effects* (New York: Pantheon, 1981), 163.

11. Simon Frith, *Sound Effects*, 158.

12. Simon Frith, *Sound Effects*, 16–17.

13. Simon Frith, *Sound Effects*, 272.

14. Lawrence Grossberg, "Another Boring Day in Paradise."

15. E. Ann Kaplan, *Rocking Around the Clock* (New York and London: Methuen, 1987), 30, 44.

16. Simon Frith, *Sound Effects*, 88.

17. Lawrence Grossberg, "Another Boring Day in Paradise."

18. E. Ann Kaplan, *Rocking Around the Clock*, 31.

19. Stuart Hall, "Notes on Deconstructing 'the Popular,' " in Raphael Samuel, ed., *People's History and Socialist Theory* (London: Routledge, Kegan Paul, 1981), 228.

20. Lawrence Grossberg, "Another Boring Day in Paradise," 229.

21. Simon Frith *Sound Effects*, 75.

22. E. Ann Kaplan, *Rocking Around the Clock*, 31.

23. Robert Pattison, *The Triumph of Vulgarity* (New York: Oxford, 1987), 39.

24. *Living Blues* n. 45/46, 1982.

25. *Wave Length* (January), 1982, 27.

26. Arnold Shaw, *The Rockin' 50s* (New York: Dutton, 1974), 89–92.

27. Jerry Hopkins, *Elvis* (New York: Warner, 1972), 37. *Time*, February 11, 1946.

28. Arnold Shaw, *The Rockin' 50s*, 89–92. George Lipsitz, *Class and Culture in Cold War America: A Rainbow at Midnight* (South Hadley, MA: Bergin and Garvey, 1982), 204–21. John Goldrosen, *The Buddy Holly Story* (New York: Music Sales, 1979).

29. Steve Chapple and Reebee Garofalo, *Rock'n'Roll Is Here to Pay* (Chicago: Nelson Hall, 1978), 29.

30. Arnold Shaw, *The Rockin' 50s*, 247–56. Anthony Heilbut, *The Gospel Sound* (New York: Simon and Schuster, 1971), 297.

31. George Lipsitz, *Class and Culture in Cold War America*, 206–7.

32. See William H. Whyte, *The Organization Man* (New York: Simon and Schuster, 1957), and Herman L. Wouk, *The Caine Mutiny* (New York: Doubleday, 1954).

33. The phrase "prestige from below" is from a talk by Stuart Hall at the Economy of Prestige Conference, University of Minnesota, April 9, 1988, Minneapolis, Minne-·sota.

34. Octavio Paz, *Labyrinth of Solitude* (New York: Grove, 1962), ch. 1. George Lipsitz, *Class and Culture in Cold War America*, 25–28.

35. Dizzy (John Birks) Gillespie, *To Be or Not to Bop* (New York: Doubleday, 1979).

36. Arnold Shaw, *The Rockin' 50s*, 190–93. John Goldrosen, *The Buddy Holly Story* (New York: Music Sales, 1979), 37.

37. Steve Chapple and Reebee Garofalo, *Rock'n'Roll Is Here To Pay*, 41. John Goldrosen, *The Buddy Holly Story* 97.

38. Arnold Shaw, *The Rockin' 50s* 79.

39. "Interview with Chuck Berry," *Jet Lag* (September) 1980, 10.

40. Steve Chapple and Reebee Garofalo, *Rock'n'Roll Is Here to Pay*, 46–47.

41. Steve Chapple and Reebee Garofalo, *Rock'n'Roll Is Here to Pay*, 60–64.

42. Simon Frith, *Sound Effects*, 83, 84.

43. Ted Drozdowski, "Irma Thomas: Radio or Not, She's Still Queen," *Musician* n. 119 (September) 1988, 11.

44. Steve Chapple and Reebee Garofalo, *Rock'n'Roll Is Here to Pay*, 69.

45. *Wave Length* (May) 1982, 21–28, (August) 1982, 12–15. *New Orleans Times-Picayune*, May 3, 1981, 41. Charles Neville was in New York at this time.

46. *Interview with Billy Peek*, August 5, 1982. *Wave Length* (August) 1982, 14.

47. Charlie Gillett, *The Sound of the City* (New York: Dutton, 1970). Steve Chapple and Reebee Garofalo, *Rock'n'Roll Is Here to Pay*, 246–48.

CHAPTER 6

1. Octavio Paz, *The Labyrinth of Solitude* (New York: Grove Press, 1961), 13.

2. Walter Benjamin, *Illuminations* (New York: Harcourt, Brace, and World, 1968), 255.

3. Marshall Berman, *All That Is Solid Melts into Air* (New York: Simon and Schuster, 1982).

4. Paz, *The Labyrinth of Solitude*, 13.

5. The term *bricolage* is from Claude Lévi-Strauss, who uses it to propose a universal description of innate human characteristics, but it is used here simply as a description of cultural amalgamation processes.

6. Berman, *All That Is Solid*, 1982, 15.

7. Antonio Gramsci, *Selections from the Prison Notebooks*, eds., Quintin Hoare and Geoffrey Nowell Smith (New York: International Publishers, l971).

8. Eshref Shevky and Marilyn Williams, *The Social Areas of Los Angeles*. (Berkeley: University of California Press, 1949). Ricardo Romo, *East Los Angeles*. (Austin: University of Texas Press, 1983). Romo also reveals some long-standing ethnic interaction between blacks and Chicanos.

9. *Home Owners Loan Corporation City Survey Files*, Los Angeles 1939. National Archives, Washington, D.C., p. 7.

10. *Home Owners Loan Corporation City Survey Files*, Area D-53.

11. Gilbert G. Gonzales, "Factors Relating to Property Ownership of Chicanos in Lincoln Heights, Los Angeles," *Aztlan*, 2, Fall 1981. pp. 111–14.

Notes to Chapter 6

12. George Lipsitz, "Against the Wind: The Class Composition of Rock and Roll Music," *Knowledge and Society*, v. 5. 1984.

13. Lindsey Haley, "Pachuco Boogie," *Low Rider*, June 1985, 34. *Los Angeles Times* Calendar Section, October 12, 1980, 6. Roberto Caballero-Robledo, "The Return of Pachuco Boogie," *Nuestro*, November 1979, 14–17.

14. Mauricio Mazon, *Zoot Suit Riots*. (Austin: University of Texas Press, 1984). George Lipsitz, *Class and Culture in Cold War America*, 26–28.

15. *Los Angeles Times*, October 12, 1980; *Nuestro*, November 17, 1979.

16. Marshall Berman, *All That Is Solid Melts into Air*, 15.

17. Ruben Guevara, "The View from the Sixth Street Bridge: The History of Chicano Rock," in Dave Marsh, ed., *Rock'n'Roll Confidential Report*. (New York: Pantheon. 1985), 118. Marjorie Miller, "Cholos Return to Their Roots and Find They Bloom," *Los Angeles Times*, September 9, 1984, part I, 3.

18. Ray Topping, "Chuck Higgins Pachuko Hop," liner notes, Ace Records. Ch 81, 1983.

19. Robert Palmer, *Baby That Was Rock and Roll* (New York: Harvest/HBJ, 1978), 19.

20. Robert Palmer, *Baby That Was Rock and Roll*, 16.

21. *Interview with Johnny Otis*, Altadena, California. December 14, 1986.

22. *Interview with Johnny Otis*.

23. *Interview with Johnny Otis*.

24. *Interview with Johnny Otis*. Steven Loza, "The Musical Life of the Mexican-Chicano People in Los Angeles, 1945–1985," Ph.D. Dissertation, University of California, Los Angeles. 1985, 124.

25. *Interview with Johnny Otis*.

26. *Interview with Johnny Otis*.

27. *Interview with Johnny Otis*. Ruben Guevara, "The View from the Sixth Street Bridge," 118.

28. *Interview with Johnny Otis*.

29. Johnny Otis, *Listen to the Lambs*. (New York: W. W. Norton, 1968). *Los Angeles Times* Calendar Section, April 3, 1985. Joe Sasfy, "Johnny Otis' Fifth Decade," *Washington Post*, June 24, 1985. Section B. 7.

30. Jim Dawson and Bob Keane, "Ritchie Valens—His Life Story," Rhino Records insert. 1981, 10.

31. Beverly Mendheim, *Ritchie Valens: The First Latino Rocker* (Tempe, AZ: Bilingual Press, 1987), 18, 21.

32. Beverly Mendheim, *Ritchie Valens: The First Latino Rocker*, 23.

33. Beverly Mendheim, *Ritchie Valens: The First Latino Rocker*, 34.

34. Jim Dawson, "Valens, the Forgotten Story," *Los Angeles Times*, February 3, 1980, 100. Jim Dawson and Bob Keane, "Ritchie Valens—His Life Story," Rhino Records insert. 1981, 5.

35. Jim Dawson and Bob Keane, "Ritchie Valens—His Life Story," 3–5. Jim Dawson, "Valens, the Forgotten Story," 100.

36. Don Snowden, "The Sound of East L.A., 1964," *Los Angeles* Times Calendar Section. October 28, 1984, 6.

37. Ethlie Ann Vare, "Cannibal and the Headhunters," *Goldmine*, November 1983, 26, 53. Don Snowden, "The Sounds of East L.A., 1964," *Los Angeles Times* Calendar Section, October 28, 1984, 7.

38. Ethlie Ann Vare, "Cannibal and the Headhunters," 26.

39. Ibid. 53.

40. Don Snowden, "The Sound of East L.A., 1964," 6–7.

41. For a detailed explanation of the urban crisis of the 1960s and 1970s see John Mollenkopf, *The Contested City* (Princeton: Princeton University Press, 1983).

42. Luis Rodriguez, "La Veintineuve," in L.A. Latino Writers Workshop, 201—*Latino Experience in Literature and Art*, n.d. 9.

43. Ruben Guevara, "The View From the Sixth Street Bridge," 120. 44. Ruben Guevara, "The View From the Sixth Street Bridge," 120. *Los Angeles Times* Calendar Section, November 9, 1980, 69. El Larry, "Los Lobos," *Low Rider*, Mar–Apr. 1984, 34.

45. Joel Whitburn, *The Billboard Book of Top 40 Hits*. (New York: Billboard, 1984).

46. Melvin Oliver and James Johnson, Jr., "Inter-Ethnic Conflict in an Urban Ghetto," *Research in Social Movements: Conflict and Change*, v. 6, JAI Sage, 57–94.

47. Ruben Guevara, "The View from the Sixth Street Bridge."

48. Michael M. J. Fischer, "Ethnicity and the Post-Modern Arts of Memory," in James Clifford and George Marcus, ed,. *Writing Culture* (Berkeley: University of California Press, l986), 194–233.

49. *Los Angeles Times*, December 28, 1982.

50. El Larry, "Los Lobos," *Low Rider* (March–April) l984, 34.

51. Rob Tannenbaum, "Los Lobos," *Musician* 77 (March) 1985, 19.

52. Antonio Gramsci, *Selections from the Prison Notebooks*, eds., Quintin Hoare and Geoffrey Nowell Smith (New York: International Publishers, 1971), 9–10.

53. Ibid. 9-10.

54. Brenda Bright, "The Meaning of Roles and the Role of Showing: Houston Low Riders," unpublished, l984. Luis F. B. Plascencia, "Low Riding in the Southwest: Cultural Symbols in the Mexican Community," paper for the Center for Mexican-American Studies: University of Texas, Austin, 1984. Don Snowden, "The Sounds of East Los Angeles," *Los Angeles Times*, October 28, 1984.

55. Don Snowden, "The Sound of East Los Angeles," *Los Angeles Times*, October 28, 1984. Lindsey Haley-Alemon, "Zyanya," *Low Rider* (March–April) 1984, 24–25.

56. *Los Angeles Times*, October 12, 1980.

57. Victor Valle, "Chicano Art: An Emerging Generation," *Los Angeles Times*, August 7, 1983.

58. Mary Helen Ponce, "Los Piojos," in *201—Latino Experience in Literature and Art* (Los Angeles: Los Angeles Latino Writers Workshop, n.d.).

59. *Los Angeles Times*, October 8, 1980; November 9, 1980.

60. *Los Angelinos—The Eastside Renaissance*, (Zyanya Records), liner notes.

61. *Los Angeles Times*, October 12, 1980.

62. Rob Tannenbaum, "Los Lobos," 19.

63. Robert Hilburn, "Willie Packs 'Em In, Down on the Farm," *Los Angeles Times* Calendar Section, July 13, 1986, 63.

64. Judy Raphael, "Ragin' Cajun: Jo-El Sonnier's Last Stand," *L.A. Weekly*, August 8–15, 1985, 57.

65. Jean-François Lyotard, *The Postmodern Condition* (Minneapolis: University of Minnesota Press, 1984), 71–82.

66. Jürgen Habermas, *Legitimation Crisis* (Boston: Beacon Press, 1975).

67. Berman, *All That Is Solid*, 15.

CHAPTER 7

1. Roy Rosenzweig, *Eight Hours for What We Will* (Cambridge: Cambridge University Press, 1985). Kathy Peiss, *Cheap Amusements: Working Women and Leisure in Turn-of-the-Century New York* (Philadelphia: Temple University Press, 1985).

2. Dana Polan, *Power and Paranoia* (New York: Columbia University Press, 1986). Peter Biskind, *Seeing Is Believing: How Hollywood Taught Us to Stop Worrying and Love the Fifties* (New York: Pantheon, 1983). Michael Ryan and Douglas Kellner, *Camera Politica* (Bloomington: University of Indiana Press, 1988).

3. William Simon, "Liberty Valance Lives," *Southwest Media Review*. n. 3. 1985.

4. Charles Bitsch, "Interview with Nicholas Ray," in Jim Hillier, ed., *Cahiers du Cinema: The 1950s: Neo-Realism, Hollywood, New Wave* (Cambridge: Harvard University Press. 1985), 120.

5. William Grier and Price Cobbs, *Black Rage*. (New York: Basic, 1986), 72–73.

CHAPTER 8

1. Laura Mulvey, "Melodrama in and out of the Home," in Colin McCabe, ed., *High Theory/Low Culture* (New York: St. Martin's, 1986), 90.

2. Luc Moullet, "Sam Fuller: In Marlowe's Footsteps," in Jim Hillier, ed., *Cahiers du Cinema: The 1950s: Neo-Realism, Hollywood, New Wave* (Cambridge: Harvard University Press, 1985), 149. J. Hoberman, "American Abstract Sensationalism," *Art Forum* (February) 1981, 42. Frank McConnell, "Pickup on South Street and the Metamorphosis of the Thriller," *Film Heritage* v. 8, n. 3 (Spring) 1973, 9.

3. "Samuel Fuller Rises from Oblivion," *Drama-Logue* v. 11, n. 31, July 31–August 6, 1980, 1.

4. Phil Hardy, *Samuel Fuller* (London: Studio Vista Ltd, 1970), 372.

5. McConnell, "Pickup," 10.

6. Moullet, "Sam Fuller," 149.

7. Hoberman, "American Abstract Sensationalism," *Art Forum*, 45–46.

8. Hoberman, "American Abstract Sensationalism," 42.

9. Max Kozloff, "A Way of Seeing and the Act of Touching: Helen Leavitt's Photographs of the Forties," in David Featherstone, ed., *Observations*, 1984, 72.

10. John Raeburn, " 'Culture Morphology' and Cultural History in Berenice Abbott's *Changing New York*," in Jack Salzman, ed., *Prospects* v. 9 (New York: Cambridge University Press, 1984), 256, 263.

11. Raeburn, " 'Culture Morphology,' " 258.

12. See Warren I. Susman, *Culture as History* (New York: Pantheon, 1984) and David P. Peeler, *Hope Among Us Yet* (Athens and London: University of Georgia Press, 1987).

13. See, for example, Edgar Ulmer's *Detour* (1945) or Elia Kazan's *Boomerang* (1947) for representative films, or read fiction from the 1940s ranging from Mickey Spillane to Chester Himes.

14. McConnell, "Pickup," 15.

15. Tom Milne, "Sam Fuller," *Sight and Sound*, n. 49, 1980, 257. Quoted from *Monthly Film Bulletin*, July 1980, 168.

16. Richard Thompson, "Interview with Samuel Fuller," *Film Comment*, v. 13, n. 1 (Jan–Feb), 1977, 25.

17. Alan Hunter, "Sam Fuller," *Films and Filming*, n. 350 (November), 1983, 99–100.

18. Tom Ryan, "Samuel Fuller: Survivor," *Cinema Papers* n. 30 (Dec.–Jan.), 1980–1981, 424.

19. Ginger Varney, "The Fundamental Sam Fuller," *L.A. Weekly*, August 1–7, 1980, 7.

20. Nicholas Garnham, *Samuel Fuller* (London: BFI, 1971), 117.

21. Luc Moullet, "Samuel Fuller," 149.

22. Dave Kehr, "Cinema in 79: The Year's Top Ten Movies," *Chicago Reader*, January 4, 1980, 22.

23. Peter Bogdanovich, "Interview With Edgar G. Ulmer," *Film Culture*, n. 58–60 (1970), 206.

24. *New York Times*, December 25, 1936, 19.

25. Peter Bogdanovich, "Interview With Edgar Ulmer," *Film Culture* n. 58–60 (1970), 222.

26. Dana Polan, *Power and Paranoia* (New York: Columbia University Press, 1986), 194.

27. Tania Modleski, "Film Theory's Detour," *Screen* 23 (5), November–December, 1982, 74–75.

28. See interview with Shirley Castle Ulmer, *San Francisco Chronicle*, November 21, 1982, 33.

29. Todd McCarthy and Charles Flynn, *Kings of the B's* (New York: E. P. Dutton, 1975), 409.

CHAPTER 9

1. Leslie Marmon Silko, *Ceremony* (New York: American Library, 1977) 2.

2. Zora Neale Hurston, *Their Eyes Were Watching God* (Champaign, Illinois: University of Illinois, 1979), 1.

3. Barbara Johnson, "Metaphor, Metonymy and Voice in *Their Eyes Were Watching God*," in Henry Louis Gates, ed., *Black Literature and Literary Theory* (New York and London: Methuen, 1984), 218.

4. Donald F. Bouchard, ed., Sherry Simon, tr., Michel Foucault, *Language, Counter-Memory, Practice: Selected Essays and Interviews* (Ithaca: Cornell University Press, 1980), 139, 144, 150.

5. Jean-François Lyotard, *The Postmodern Condition* (Minneapolis: University of Minnesota Press, 1984).

6. Warren I. Susman, *Culture as History* (New York: Pantheon, 1984), 8.

7. Warren I. Susman, *Culture as History*, 12.

8. Hayden White, *Tropics of Discourse* (Baltimore: Johns Hopkins University Press, 1978), esp. chapter 1.

9. Will Wright, *Sixguns and Society* (Berkeley: University of California Press, 1975), 187.

10. Roland Barthes, *Mythologies* (New York: Hill and Wang, 1972), 129.

11. Toni Morrison, *Song of Solomon* (New York: New American Library, 1977), 53.

12. Eudora Welty, *Losing Battles* (New York: Random House, 1970), 298.

13. Ibid. 432.

14. Ibid. 432.

15. Leslie Marmon Silko, *Ceremony* (New York: New American Library, 1977), 19.

16. Ibid. 99.
17. Ibid. 199.
18. Ibid. 257.
19. Ibid. 132.
20. Barbara T. Christian, *From the Inside Out: Afro-American Women's Literary Tradition and the State* (Minneapolis: Center for Humanistic Studies, 1987), 4.
21. Ibid. 16.
22. John Okada, *No-No Boy* (Seattle: University of Washington Press, 1976), 159.
23. Rudolfo Anaya, *Bless Me Ultima* (Berkeley: Tonatiuh International, 1986), 115.
24. Ibid. 113.
25. Barbara T. Christian, *From the Inside Out*, 4.
26. Marshall Berman, *All That Is Solid Melts into Air*, 15.
27. Quoted in Elizabeth Long, *The American Dream and the Popular Novel* (London: Routledge, Kegan Paul, 1986),191.
28. James Clifford, "On Ethnographic Allegory," in James Clifford and George Marcus, ed., *Writing Culture* (Berkeley: University of California Press, 1986), 121.
29. Julia Kristeva, "Women's Time," in Toril Moi, ed., *The Kristeva Reader* (New York: Columbia University Press, 1986), 193–94.
30. Ibid. 207.

CHAPTER 10

1. Laura Mulvey, "Myth, Narrative, and Historical Experience," *History Workshop* (Spring) 1987.
2. Walter Benjamin, *Illuminations* (New York: Shocken Books, 1969), 83.
3. See Paul Buhle, *Popular Culture in America* (Minneapolis: University of Minnesota Press, 1987).
4. José E. Limon, "Western Marxism and Folklore," *Journal of American Folklore*, v. 96, n. 379, 1983, 49.
5. Fredric Jameson, "Reification and Utopia in Mass Culture," *Social Text*, v. 1, n. 1, 1979.
6. William Fox, "Folklore and Fakelore: Some Sociological Considerations," *Journal of the Folklore Institute*, v. 17, n. 2–3, May–December, 1980, 249.
7. David Elliott Draper, "The Mardi Gras Indians: The Ethnomusicology of Black Associations in New Orleans," (Ph.D. dissertation, Tulane University, 1973), 7, 27, 38, 40.
8. Draper, "The Mardi Gras Indians," 35, 54.
9. Les Blank, *Always for Pleasure*, Flower Films, 1978.
10. See Jason Berry, "Controversy Swirls Around Mardi Gras Indian Origins," *New Orleans Times-Picayune*, February 17, 1984. sec. 1, 6.
11. Jason Berry, Jonathan Foose, and Tad Jones, *Up from the Cradle of Jazz* (Athens and London: University of Georgia Press,1986) 210, 218.
12. Helen Joy Mayhew, "New Orleans Black Musical Culture: Tradition and the Individual Talent" (M.A. Thesis, University of Exeter, 1986), 187–88.
13. Jason Berry, Jonathan Foose, and Tad Jones, *Up from the Cradle of Jazz*, 210.
14. Jason Berry, "Pomp and Circumstance of the Mardi Gras Indians," *Dynamic Years*. n. 16. March 1981.

15. Draper, "The Mardi Gras Indians," 42. John Miller Chernoff identifies grace, strength, elegance, precision, happiness, composure,and dignity as key elements in performances by African chiefs on p. 150 of his wonderful book *African Rhythms and African Sensibility* (Chicago and London: University of Chicago Press,1979).

16. Chernoff, *African Rhythm and African Sensibility*, 33–34.

17. Draper, "The Mardi Gras Indians," 54. See also Alan Lomax, *Mr. Jelly Roll* (Berkeley: University of California Press, 1950, 1973), 12.

18. Draper, "The Mardi Gras Indians," 23. See also John Blassingame, *Black New Orleans, 1860–1880* (Chicago and London: University of Chicago Press, 1973).

19. Chernoff, *African Rhythms and African Sensibility*, 143.

20. Draper, "The Mardi Gras Indians," 218, 360.

21. Draper, "The Mardi Gras Indians," 227, 276, 286. Jason Berry, Jonathan Foose, and Tad Jones, *Up from the Cradle of Jazz*, 213.

22. Chernoff, *African Rhythm and African Sensibility*, 61.

23. Chernoff, *African Rhythm and African Sensibility*, 125.

24. Draper, "The Mardi Gras Indians," 362, 363.

25. Finn Wilhelmsen, "Creativity in the Songs of the Mardi Gras Indians of New Orleans, Louisiana," *Louisiana Folklore Miscellany*, v. 3, 1973, 58.

26. Draper, "The Mardi Gras Indians," 130, 166, 167.

27. Draper, "The Mardi Gras Indians," 122, 166, 167.

28. Draper, "The Mardi Gras Indians," 103.

29. Draper, "The Mardi Gras Indians," 51, 53, 54.

30. Les Blank, *Always for Pleasure*, Flower Films, 1978.

31. Draper, "The Mardi Gras Indians," 115. Jason Berry, Jonathan Foose, and Tad Jones, *Up from the Cradle of Jazz*, 221.

32. Jason Berry, Jonathan Foose, Tad Jones, *Up from the Cradle of Jazz*, 218.

33. Ibid. 213.

34. Ibid. 218.

35. Draper, "The Mardi Gras Indians," 117, 118.

36. Jason Berry, Jonathan Foose, Tad Jones, *Up from the Cradle of Jazz*, 218.

37. Ibid.

38. John Miller Chernoff, *African Rhythm and African Sensibility*, 124, 125.

39. Draper, "The Mardi Gras Indians," 69, 70.

40. Jason Berry, Jonathan Foose, Tad Jones, *Up from the Cradle of Jazz*, 224, 235.

41. Ibid. 216. David Elliott Draper, "The Mardi Gras Indians," 36, 38.

42. Don Palmer, "Gumbo Variations," *The Soho News*, August 11, 1981, 23.

43. Draper, "The Mardi Gras Indians," 103.

44. Jason Berry, Jonathan Foose, Tad Jones, *Up from the Cradle of Jazz*, 220.

45. Ibid.

46. John Miller Chernoff, *African Rhythm and African Sensibility*, 50, 144, 150.

47. The phrase "danced faith" is Robert F. Thompson's. See Chernoff, *African Rhythm and African Sensibility*, 144.

48. Chernoff, *African Rhythm and African Sensibility*, 150.

49. José E. Limon, "Western Marxism and Folklore," *Journal of American Folklore*, v. 96, n. 379, 1983, 39.

50. William Fox, "Folklore and Fakelore: Some Sociological Considerations," *Journal of the Folklore Institute*, v. 17, n. 2–3, May–December 1980, 249, 255, 256.

Notes to Chapter 10

51. Fredric Jameson, "Reification and Utopia in Mass Culture," *Social Text*, v. 1, n. 1, 1979, 134, 137, 138.

52. Draper, "The Mardi Gras Indians," 389.

53. Jeff Hannusch, *I Hear You Knockin'* (Ville Platte: Swallow Publications, 1985), 262.

54. Helen Joy Mayhew, "New Orleans Black Musical Culture: Tradition and the Individual Talent" (M.A. thesis, University of Exeter, 1986), 215.

55. Shepard Samuels, "The Dixie Cups," *Wavelength*, May 1982, 18. For a description of Leiber and Stoller's role in disseminating other popular narratives, see George Lipsitz, "Land of a Thousand Dances, Youth, Minorities, and Rock and Roll," in Lary May, ed., *Recasting America* (Chicago and London: University of Chicago Press, 1988).

56. Shepard Samuels, "The Dixie Cups," *Wavelength*. May 1982, 18.

57. See Jeff Hannusch, *I Hear You Knockin'*, 359–73.

58. Jason Berry, "Pomp and Circumstance of the Mardi Gras Indians," *Dynamic Years*, n. 16, March 1981.

59. Jason Berry, Jonathan Foose, and Tad Jones, *Up from the Cradle of Jazz*, 232.

60. Dave Hoekstra, "King Sunny Brightens Sound of Juju Music," *Chicago Sun-Times*, May 10, 1987, 10.

61. Jason Berry, "The Caribbean Connection," *New Orleans*, v. 19, May 1985, 67.

62. See also Hal Singer's song "Cornbread," and Hank Williams's "Move It On Over."

63. Quoted in *Wavelength*, n. 19, May 1982, 3.

64. Jon Bream, "Cyndi Lauper," *Minneapolis Star and Tribune*, December 7, 1986. 1G. A 1982 recording of "Iko Iko" by the Belle Stars appeared in the 1988 film *Rain Man* and subsequently made the best-seller charts in 1989.

65. Walter Benjamin, *Illuminations* (New York: Shocken, 1969) 85.

CHAPTER 11

1. Marshall Berman, *All That Is Solid Melts into Air* (New York: Simon and Schuster, 1982).

2. George Lipsitz, *Class and Culture in Cold War America: A Rainbow at Midnight* (South Hadley, MA: Bergin and Garvey, 1982).

3. *Interview with Johnny Otis*, December 14, 1986, Altadena, California.

4. *Interview with Johnny Otis*.

5. Ben Bagdikian, *The Media Monopoly* (Boston: Beacon Press, 1987).

6. Thomas K. Arnold, "Yes, There Is Life after the Doobie Brothers," *L.A. Times*, March 24, 1988, Sec VI, 1–6.

7. *Interview with Billy Peek*, August 5, 1982, St. Louis, Missouri.

8. *Interview with Billy Peek*, March 19, 1988, St. Louis, Missouri.

9. Action adventure show *Naked City* and dramatic series *East Side, West Side* were exceptions to these trends; they resonated with the sensibilities of an earlier era.

10. See Jane Feuer, "Narrative Form in American Network Television," in Colin McCabe, ed., *High Theory/Low Culture* (New York: St. Martin's, 1986), 106. Ella Taylor, *All in the (Work) Family* (Berkeley: University of California Press, forthcoming).

11. Marshall Berman, *All That Is Solid Melts into Air* (New York: Simon and Schuster, 1982), 171.

290

12. Jean Baudrillard, "The Ecstasy of Communication," in Hal Foster, *The Anti-Aesthetic* (Seattle: Bay Press), 1983.

13. Don Snowden, "Global Music with a Single Heart," *Los Angeles Times* Calendar section, August 7, 1988, 3.

14. "King Sunny Ade," *Musician* (May), 1983.

15. Albert Murray, *The Omni-Americans* (New York: Vintage Books, 1983), 22.

16. *Interview with Johnny Otis*, December 14, 1986, Altadena, California.

17. *Interview with Johnny Otis*.

Index

Index

Index

Index

Index

Index

Index

Index

301

Index

Index

Peek, Billy, 263–65, 266, 270, 283n, 290n
Peeler, David, 286n
Peiss, Kathy, 164, 165, 275n, 286n
Perez, Louis, 150, 156–57
Perkins, Carl, 116, 119, 121, 127
Perry, Joe, 99
Philadelphia (PA), 117, 196
Phillips, Sam, 119
Pickett, Wilson, 114
Pickup on South Street, 181, 182, 183, 185, 186, 187, 188, 189, 190, 191
Picnic, 169–70, 172
Pinski, David, 199
Plascencia, Luis, 285n
Plato, 7
Pledging My Love, 114
Plummer, Christopher, x
Poe, Edgar Allan, 197
Polan, Dana, 31, 99, 164, 165, 201, 277n, 286n, 287n
Police Woman, 267
Pomus, Doc, 127
Ponce, Mary Helen, 155, 285n
Popular culture, vii, 12, 13
Port Arthur (TX), 129
Posey, Sandy, 116
Postman, Neil, 17, 18, 276n
President's Analyst, The, 173–74
Presley, Elvis, xiv, 105, 113, 114, 118, 119, 121, 124, 126, 129, 138
Price, Lloyd, 114, 127
Producers Releasing Corporation, 200
Professor Longhair, 250, 251, 252
Puente, Tito, 127

Queens (NY), 266
Quinlan, Doris, 91, 281n

Radio, 40–41, 87
Raeburn, John, 286n
Rambo, 173–74
Randisi, Jennifer, 220
Rap music, 265–66
Raphael, Judy, 285n
Ravitch, Diane, 23, 24, 25, 26, 277n
Ray, Nicholas, x, 175, 195
Reader's Digest, 82

Reagan, Ronald, xii, 19, 22, 32, 33
Rebel Without a Cause, x, 174–75, 176
Red Hot, 114
Reed, Ishmael, 17
Reet Petite, 121, 262–63
Reeves, Jim, 269
Reinhardt, Max, 195, 204
Reynolds, Marjorie, 53
Reynolds, William Bradford, xii
Rice, Rosemary, 77, 78–79, 94, 281n
Ride the Pink Horse, 165–67, 168, 169
Riley, Billy Lee, 114
Rip It Up, 116
Rivers, Johnny, 114
Rivieras, 113
Roach, Hal (studios), 72
Roberts, Alfred, 251–52
Robertson, Cliff, 78
Robins, The, 144
Rocha, Gil, 144
Rock and Roll Music, 127
Rock Around the Clock, 113
Rockford Files, 267
Rockin' and Reelin', 113
Rodgers, Jimmie, 114, 129
Rodriguez, Luis, 285n
Roe, Tommy, 114
Rogers, Roy, 143
Roll Over Beethoven, 127
Rolling Stones, 113, 127, 128, 130, 146
Romancers, The, 145
Romasco, Albert U., 278n
Romo, Ricardo, 283n
Ropes, Bradford, 279n, 280n
Roosevelt, Franklin Delano, 43
Rosenzweig, Roy, 164–65, 286n
Rowland, Kevin, 261, 263, 265, 266, 270
Rubber Dolly, 114
Ruben and the Jets, 155–56
Run DMC, 265, 266
Run Red Run, 115
Ruthless, 203, 206
Ryan, Michael, 164–65, 286n
Ryan, Tom, 286n

Salas, Brothers, The, 145
Salazar, Ruben, 147, 155
Sally Go Round the Roses, 115

303

Index

Index

Index

George Lipsitz is an associate professor of American studies and history at the University of Minnesota. He received his master's degree from the University of Missouri-St. Louis and his doctorate from the University of Wisconsin-Madison. Lipsitz has been an assistant professor of historical studies at the University of Houston and a visiting professor at Mount Holyoke College and the University of Missouri-St. Louis. He is author of *Class and Culture in Cold War America: A Rainbow at Midnight* (1985) and *A Life in the Struggle: Ivory Perry and the Culture of Opposition* (1989), and a contributor to *Critical Studies in Mass Communication*, the *Journal of American History, Cultural Critique, Cultural Anthropology*, and *Society*.